W9-BBS-922

Kuru Sorcery

KURU SORCERY

DISEASE AND DANGER IN THE NEW GUINEA HIGHLANDS

Shirley Lindenbaum

Routledge
Taylor & Francis Group

LONDON AND NEW YORK

First published 2013 by Paradigm Publishers

Published 2018 by Routledge
711 Third Avenue, New York, NY 10017, USA
2 Park Square, Milton Park, Abingdon, Oxon OX14 4RN

Routledge is an imprint of the Taylor & Francis Group, an informa business

Copyright © 2018 by Taylor & Francis

All rights reserved. No part of this book may be reprinted or reproduced or utilised in any form or by any electronic, mechanical, or other means, now known or hereafter invented, including photocopying and recording, or in any information storage or retrieval system, without permission in writing from the publishers.

Notice:
Product or corporate names may be trademarks or registered trademarks, and are used only for identification and explanation without intent to infringe.

Every effort has been made to secure required permissions for all text, images, maps, and other art reprinted in this volume.

Library of Congress Cataloging-in-Publication Data
Lindenbaum, Shirley.
 Kuru sorcery : disease and danger in the New Guinea highlands / Shirley Lindenbaum.—Second edition.
     pages cm
   Includes bibliographical references and index.
   ISBN 978-1-61205-276-2 (paperback : alk. paper)
    1. Fore (Papua New Guinean people)—Diseases. 2. Fore (Papua New Guinean people)—Medicine. 3. Kuru—Papua New Guinea. I. Title.
   DU47.42.L56L56 2013
   305.899'12—dc23

                                                    2013002223

   ISBN: 9781612052762 (pbk)

CONTENTS

PREFACE

The epidemic of kuru, the neurodegenerative disease that once threatened the survival of the Fore people, has now ended. With Nobel Prizes awarded to Carleton Gajdusek in 1976 for successfully transmitting kuru to chimpanzees (confirming the status of the disease as infectious), and to Stanley Prusiner in 1997 for his discovery of prions (the infectious agent responsible for fatal neurodegenerative disorders in humans and animals), kuru has a permanent place in the history of medicine. Kuru research illustrates the importance of an interdisciplinary approach to the investigation of disease. Since the late 1950's, when the disease was first reported, government officers, anthropologists, medical investigators, and the Fore have shared information.[1] The Fore provided knowledge that often redirected the research.

Kuru attracted increased international attention in the 1980's with the appearance of bovine spongiform encephalopathy (BSE), a disease in cattle in the United Kingdom, and the appearance of variant Creutzfeld-Jakob Disease (vCJD), the human form of so-called "mad cow disease" caused by the ingestion of contaminated beef. BSE and vCJD were novel diseases associated with the prion protein, while kuru had provided the principal experience of an epidemic of human prion disease transmitted predominantly by the oral route. In 1996, based on reports of the remarkable length of incubation in kuru and information that cases were still occurring, the Prion Unit of the London-based Medical Research Council (MRC) began to study kuru in an affiliation with the Papua New Guinea Institute of Medical Research (IMR). The project was designed to document the range of incubation periods

vi

possible in human prion infection; investigate maternal and other potential routes of transmission; characterize genetic susceptibility and resistance factors; and compare clinical and other diagnostic features of kuru patients with other human prion diseases, notably iatrogenic and variant CJD.[2]

Prion infections are associated with long, clinically silent incubations, and until recently the number of asymptomatic individuals with vCJD prion infection in the United Kingdom was unknown. New data now point to around one in 2,000 of those exposed to BSE becoming carriers of vCJD.[3] Whether these presumably BSE prion–infected individuals will remain subclinical carriers for life or develop clinical disease after long incubation, and whether they might unwittingly transmit the disease by blood donation or surgery, are critical questions for public health. The kuru epidemic remains important for understanding the behavioral aspects of prion disease transmission as well as the fundamental mechanisms underlying the asymptomatic carrier state in neurological disease.

For many decades, some investigators have come to the Fore region to study kuru, while others have carried out research in distant laboratories, providing an unusually complete record of an epidemic that has been documented from beginning to end. Anticipating the end, a celebratory conference was held in London in 2007, attended by kuru investigators from around the world along with fifteen Papua New Guineans, twelve of them from the Fore region. The first day of the meeting was devoted to historical aspects of kuru research, which included presentations by the Fore recalling their participation in a project that for some of them began when they were between ten and sixteen years of age.

This edition of *Kuru Sorcery* provides a chronicle of the epidemic from the point of view of those who observed and studied the disease, as well as those who experienced and endured the epidemic. It is, in a way, a journal of the plague years.

The 1979 version of *Kuru Sorcery* presented South Fore society as it was in the early 1960's, when Papua New Guinea was administered by the Commonwealth of Australia as a trust territory under the aegis of the United Nations. Most of the early field research that Robert Glasse and I carried out occurred during the period before Papua New Guinea became an independent nation (1975) and also before the first Local Government Councils were established in the area (1966). The councils were formed so that rural communities could determine their own local enterprises, develop a wider base for regional integration, and eventually become participating units in the national government.

The 1950's and early 1960's were years of rapid social change but also turmoil, as the Fore experienced the peak of the kuru epidemic, which they believed was caused by sorcerers. My aim in the original version was to document the social effects of kuru, and to represent local and biomedical understandings of the disease. The importance of sorcery in Fore thought and practice reflected the social tensions arising from the high kuru mortality. Beliefs about the cause and cure of disease threw light on the Fores' view of themselves, their concepts of knowledge, and the moral obligations they felt toward one another. The social and medical themes came together in what could be called an epidemiology of social relations.

When I returned for several weeks in 1970, signs of a new way of life abounded. Local groups had built their own feeder link to the single road between the North and South Fore. Several hamlets had trade stores that stocked canned foods and household goods. The accelerating demand for cash was such that it now cost more to purchase a chicken in the South Fore than it did in New York. Just as startling, I was awakened on the first morning by a small party of children shouting "Good morning!" as they hurried to the new primary school higher up the mountainside.

I left in September 1970 with no plans to return. My friend Kassam Uvinda, who had a firmer sense of the future, gave me a finely carved arrow that he said would bring me back. In six short return visits between 1991 and 2008, I observed the steady decline in kuru mortality and an increase in Fore self-confidence as the shadow of the epidemic faded slowly away. Following the prohibition on cannibalism in the 1950's, no one born since 1959 has come down with the disease, and it seems now that the last death from kuru occurred in 2009. Like other epidemics in the history of medicine, the kuru epidemic has a familiar dramaturgic form: starting at a moment in time, proceeding on a stage limited in space and duration, following a plot line of increasing and revelatory tension, moving to a crisis of individual and collective character, and then drifting toward closure.[4]

This updated version of the book retains the old text, placed between a new preface, two new end chapters, and an epilogue. The temptation to revise the original version was easy to resist. Keeping it reveals how much the Fore and the fields of anthropology and medicine have changed. In the later research, sorcery accusations and suspicions remained important even as the epidemic declined. In quieter deliberations, however, a small number of the Fore had begun to consider whether the disease was perhaps a form of sickness, not caused by sorcerers. Transformations in the Fore political economy were apparent, gauged also by the way the Fore perceived and told their own history following Independence. Issues of modernity and development—market relations, ceremonial exchange, and Christianity—were of central concern, and the full story of the epidemic could now be told. Theories of disease causation remained central, but the AIDS epidemic had directed anthropologists to look at new forms of sociality and the place of the emotions in cultural life.

The overarching history of the kuru epidemic still serves as a prism through which to view the changes taking place among the Fore, even as anthropological questions and my own interests became more entangled with ideas in the history of science. A close reading of the bibliography will show the shift in both anthropology and medicine during these years.

Many people have contributed to the story of kuru. My greatest debt is to the Fore who shared with me their thoughts and feelings, and drew me into their networks of kinship. In the earlier version, I thanked by name many friends who were no longer living. That list is now too long, but I want their children to know that I remember them all with fondness and admiration. For those of us who witnessed the peak years of the epidemic, our memories are suffused with feelings of sorrow and loss.

I have changed the names of most people in order to protect their privacy, but not those of my research assistants, without whose help and companionship this book would not have been written: Inamba Kivita, Patali Anuma, Kassam Uvinda, Nantale Kaguya, and Agame Abao. Singko Patali was the last to join the team, replacing his father, Patali Anuma, and then an older brother, Kauya Patali, who had both died. The advent of the Internet has recently made it possible for anthropologists to communicate with friends and research assistants in Papua New Guinea, a magical narrowing of the distance between us. Patterson Kassam and Henry Pako, whom I have known for many years, have enriched my understanding of Fore culture. Enoch Kale provided important information about the Gimi, as did Katayo Sagata in his emails about the Kanite.

There are many others to whom I am indebted. In the 1960's, Robert Glasse and I appreciated the hospitality offered by Mert Brightwell, Andrew Gray, Wendy and Michael Alpers, Jon and Judy Hancock, and Richard Hornabrook. I thank John Womersley for identifying botanical specimens. In 1970, I had the company of John Lindenbaum, who suggested medical diagnoses for some Fore disease categories. In later visits, Michael Alpers, the director of the Institute of Medical Research from 1977 to 2007, provided strategic institutional support, as did Peter Siba in 2008. Deborah Lehmann and Michael Alpers provided friendship and good care when I visited Goroka. To Mike and Debby Brandt, I owe my special thanks. Warm and generous hosts at the Open Bible Mission, the Brandts' long acquaintance with the Fore broadened my appreciation of local history.

I am grateful to friends and colleagues who made enlightened contributions to the new chapters: David Boyd, John Collinge, Kate Crehan, Gavan Daws, Dawn Glass, Ken Inglis, Simon Mead, Anthony Pickles, Jane Schneider, and Jerome Whitfield. How to thank Michael Delugg, who rescued, refined, and gave new life to the old and new photos? I am grateful also to Robert Edgerton and Lew Langness, the editors of *Explorations in World Ethnography*, for first encouraging me to write about kuru, and to Dean Birkenkamp for his enthusiastic support for this new edition.

I have received financial support from the Department of Genetics, Adelaide University, and from the Department of Public Health and the Institute of Human Biology in Papua New Guinea. The City University of New York provided travel funds during the 1990's. I thank all these institutions for their generous support.

NOTES

1. Medicine was represented by a range of subfields that included genetics, cell biology, virology, infectious disease, neurology, neuropathology, and epidemiology.

2. Collinge 2008:3691.

3. Simon Mead, personal communication, July 19, 2012.

4. I adopt this imaginative conceit from Charles Rosenberg 1992:279. Lindenbaum 2001:367–374 discusses the dramaturgic form in more detail.

KURU SORCERY

INTRODUCTION

1

In the lower montane forests of the Eastern Highlands of Papua New Guinea, a population of some 14,000 slash-and-burn horticulturalists known as the Fore (pronounced FOR-AY) tend gardens of sweet potato, taro, yam, corn, and other vegetables. They also grow sugarcane and bananas, keep pigs, and, in the sparsely populated regions near their southern boundaries, still hunt for birds, mammals, reptiles, and cassowaries. Unlike the open country to the north around Kainantu or Goroka, where long-established grasslands prevail, this part of the Eastern Highlands consists of mixed rainforest broken by small clearings and grasslands of no great age. The forest includes oak, beech, Ficus, bamboo, nut-bearing Castanopsis, feathery Albitzia, red-flowered hibiscus, and many other species used for food, medicines, and stimulants, as well as salt, fibers, and building materials.[1] Pandanus grows at higher altitudes. The ground is covered with a wealth of edible shrubs, delicate tree ferns, fungi, and creepers. Red, white, and salmon-colored impatiens sparkle in the shafts of sunlight beside forest paths, and ferns, orchids, and rhododendron grow as epiphytes in the canopy overhead. The forest rings with the sound of birds feeding on tall fruit trees.

The Fore-speaking population lies in the wedge created by the Kratke Mountains to the north, and the Lamari and Yani Rivers to the east and west. Although the terrain ranges in altitude from the mountains at 9,000 feet to southern valleys at 2,000, gardens and hamlets are scattered across the zone between 7,500 and 3,500 feet, where the population has access to

Traditional Fore hamlet near the edge of the forest. Photo by Dr. E. R. Sorenson, "The Edge of the Forest," Smithsonian Institution Press, 1976.

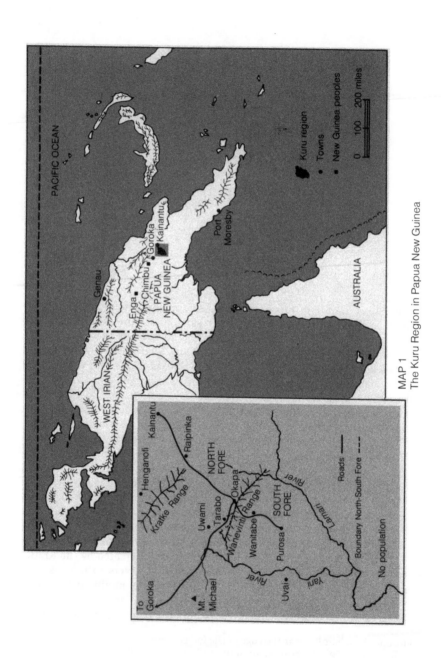

MAP 1
The Kuru Region in Papua New Guinea

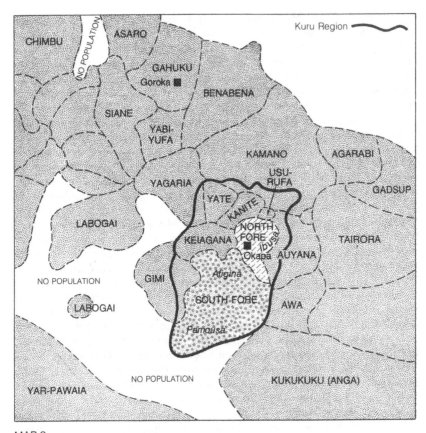

MAP 2
The Fore and Their Neighbors

SOURCE: Adapted from E. Richard Sorenson, *The Edge of the Forest*
(Washington, DC: Smithsonian Inst., q2976), p. 20 © Smithsonian

both montane and lowland environments. Hamlets typically consist of seventy to 120 people, living in twelve to twenty houses, and their adjacent gardens. Surrounded on three sides by populations speaking Gimi, Keiagana, Kanite, Kamano, Auyana, Awa and Kukukuku (also known as Anga), the Fore are reluctantly penetrating the uninhabited region to the south. Stories of illness and hardship characterize their view of existence in these frontier communities.

The Fore represent the most southerly extension of the East New Guinea Highland linguistic stock,[2] but they have much greater genetic heterogeneity than most linguistic groups in the Eastern Highlands. The

Fore, with a remarkably flexible kinship system, do not constitute an isolated breeding population. Genetic studies show their close association with populations in two directions. To the northwest, they are most closely associated with the Kamano, Gimi, and Keiagana, and to the southeast with the Awa, Auyana, and Tairora.[3] Kukukuku populations across the Lamari Valley and the Yar-Pawaian groups beyond the uninhabited zone appear to belong to different linguistic, genetic, and cultural communities.

The Fore are afflicted with a rare disease. Since record-keeping began in 1957, three years after the Australian administration established a patrol post at Okapa, some 2,500 people in this region have died from kuru, a subacute degenerative disorder of the central nervous system. Approximately 80 percent of all kuru deaths have occurred among Fore-speaking people, with the remaining 20 percent striking neighboring populations. In the early years of investigation, over 200 patients died annually, which at that time approached 1 percent per annum of the affected population.[4] In recent years, kuru rates have steadily declined, and in 1977 only 31 persons died of the disease. Following several decades in which kuru was the major cause of death among the Fore, the disease is rapidly disappearing.

My main focus is on the 8,000 South Fore. Identified by Australian government officials in the 1950's as a single census division within the Okapa Subdistrict, South Fore is separated from North by a low mountain range (Wanevinti) that hinders but does not preclude contact between the two populations. Marriage partners, trade goods, food, refugees, illnesses, and ideas move between North and South, but South Fore social life is focused on the lands sloping southward from the mountain barrier. There two dialect groups (Atigina and Pamousa) with a high frequency of cognate words are recognizable. The two southern dialects have more in common than either has with Ibusa, the dialect of the North Fore.[6] It is among the South Fore that the incidence of kuru has been highest. Between 1957 and 1968, over 1,100 kuru deaths occurred in a South Fore population of 8,000, and most cases reported for 1976 and 1977 come from this region. Since kuru is predominantly a disease of adult women—the childbearers, pig tenders, and gardeners—its effects on Fore society have been particularly deranging. When the incidence of kuru reached a peak, in the 1960's, the South Fore believed their society was coming to an end. And indeed, with their high female mortality and low birth rates, in the early 1960's their numbers were truly declining. South Fore were aware that the disease was striking them hardest.

This book discusses the Fore response to kuru in the 1960's, when the epidemic was at its height. In Chapter 2, I trace the interest of Western scientists in the disease, from the time they learned about it in the early 1950's to the present. Chapter 3 surveys Fore medical disorders, and shows that apart from kuru, their health status resembles that of kuru-free populations in the Eastern Highlands of New Guinea. Chapter 4, an analysis

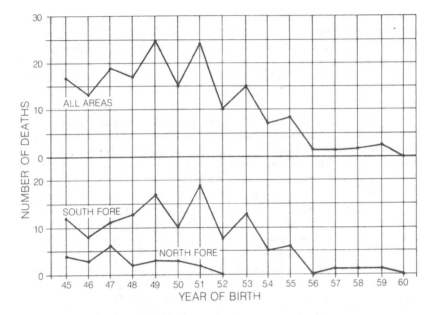

FIGURE 1
Number of Persons Dying of Kuru (since 1963) for each year of birth from 1945
SOURCE: Adapted from Hornabrook and Moir 1970

of South Fore kinship, indicates that Fore establish ties by demonstrating commitment to a relationship. Kinship is as often based on common interest and support as it is on heredity.

In Chapters 5 and 6, I present Fore views of the cause of disease, and suggest that Fore beliefs are appropriate to a particular way of life and period of time—that is, to communities of partially intensive swidden horticulturalists in the 1960's. In the three decades since the Australian administration at Port Moresby sent the first patrol through Fore territory, both their mode of existence and Fore beliefs about it have undergone rapid change, allowing us an opportunity to observe the ways that philosophical systems depend on context. A new way of life gave rise to greater manipulation of the environment, and to differences in rank requiring the coercion of others in order to maintain an elevated position. New diseases also took their toll. As these changes occurred, ghosts of the dead and spirits of the forest receded, displaced by growing numbers of sorcerers.

The early 1960's were crisis years for the Fore. They hunted for sorcerers and consulted curers (Chapter 7), and finally they called great public meetings (Chapter 8). There, they denounced the performance of sorcery that was decimating their women and creating a wasteland. Sorcerers were said to be the agents of all that was wrong with the human condition. They were seen as the negative of all that is fine, good, and moral, as instruments of impoverishment and decline, and as a burden on the community (Chapter 9). Notions of sorcery, witchcraft, and pollution emerge as ideologies of containment, by which wielders of power attempt to degrade their opponents, coerce social inferiors, and allocate resources. Sorcerers, witches, and polluters therefore have universal attributes. They appear in different manifestations and with varying powers of retaliation in New Guinea and elsewhere. The direction from which they project their feared energies is a clue to an asymmetrical interchange, either between individuals or between regions (Chapter 10). Chapter 11 considers the intricate historical and ecological contexts in which populations respond to the threat of extinction. The new chapters, 12 and 13, describe many recent changes, both material and spiritual, and how these shifts in daily life provide a parallel reading of local medical beliefs and practice.

In the search for the cause of kuru, Western science unraveled a biological mystery; the solution has applications for neurological afflictions that range far beyond the borders of New Guinea. The Fore analysis of the problem revealed more about victimization, and told us more about ourselves. While their medical observations were frequently accurate, they were embedded in social codes, and in messages about the nature of existence. In their statements about the cause of disease, the Fore also considered those conditions under which a threatened society might ultimately endure.

KURU AND SORCERY

2

As he passed through the hamlets at Amusi during an Australian government patrol in the South Fore region, Patrol Officer McArthur made a significant notation. "Nearing one of the dwellings," he wrote in August 1953, "I observed a small girl sitting down beside a fire. She was shivering violently and her head was jerking spasmodically from side to side. I was told that she was a victim of sorcery and would continue thus, shivering and unable to eat, until death claimed her within a few weeks."[1] Although the disease had been mentioned in earlier government reports,[2] this was the first official description of kuru, a fatal neurological disorder very common among Fore, and present to a lesser degree among neighboring groups, but unknown elsewhere in the world. The discussion that follows presents kuru as a disease entity as perceived by Western observers, and follows the evolution of medical thought over more than two decades. Western scientists now consider kuru to be a slow virus infection spread by the ingestion of human flesh. This view contrasts with that of the Fore, who remain convinced that the illness results from the malevolent activities of Fore sorcerers.

CLINICAL FEATURES OF KURU

A Fore word meaning trembling or fear, kuru is marked primarily by symptoms of cerebellar dysfunction—loss of balance, incoordination (ataxia), and tremor. An initial shivering tremor usually progresses to complete motor incapacity and death in about a year. Women, the prime victims

9

N

• Kagu
Kianosa •   • Ibusa
Uwami •   NORTH
               FORE
        • Awande
           • Pusarasa
           ■ Okapa
        • Yasubi
• Amusi   Yagusa
Tamogavisa•   • Okasa
   Igitaru• • Amora Keiagasa
   Kume•   ■ Wanitabe   • Kasokana
      • Yagareba
Mentilesa •   Wanda • Abomotasa
Intamatasa•   Kamila
      Waisa
      • Takai   Ilesa •
   Umasa • Ketabe
      • Purosa   • Awarosa
Uvai •   Ivaki •   Agakamatasa
   • Orissa   • Mougai
            Amusa   • Agamusa
   Kasalai SOUTH
Paiti •   FORE

CENSUS DIVISIONS ‒ ‒ ‒

Scale 0 1 2 3 4 5 miles

MAP 3
Fore Settlements

of the disease, may withdraw from the community at the shock of recognizing the first symptoms—pain in the head and limbs, and a slight unsteadiness of gait. They resume their usual gardening activities a few weeks later, struggling to control their involuntary body movements until forced by gross physical incoordination to remain at home, sedentarily awaiting death.

The clinical progress of kuru is remarkably uniform. It has been divided into three stages by Dr. Carleton Gajdusek, who has made extensive clinical studies of the disease:

> The first, or ambulant, stage is usually self-diagnosed before others in the community are aware that the patient is ill. There is subjective [self-perceived] unsteadiness of stance and gait and often of the voice, hands and eyes as well. Postural instability with tremor and titubation [body tremor while walking] and ataxia of gait are the first signs. Dysarthria [slurring of speech] starts early and speech progressively deteriorates as the disease advances. Eye movements are ataxic. . . . A convergent

A woman in the primary stage of kuru, steadied by her husband.

strabismus [crossed eyes] often appears early in the disease and persists. Tremors are at first no different from those of slight hypersensitivity to cold; the patient shivers inordinately. Incoordination affects the lower extremities before progressing to involve the upper extremities. Patients arising to a standing posture often stamp their feet as though angry at them. In attempting to maintain balance when standing, the toes grip and claw the ground more than usual. Very early in the disease the inability to stand on one foot for many seconds is a helpful diagnostic clue. . . . In the latter part of this first stage, the patient usually takes a stick to walk about the village unaided by others.

The second, or sedentary, stage is reached when the patient can no longer walk without complete support. Tremors and ataxia become more severe and a changing rigidity of the

Pregnant young kuru victim goes to work in her garden supported by stick. She was dead a few months later, less than a year after the first symptoms appeared. Photo by Dr. D. Carleton Gajdusek, 1979.

A middle-aged kuru victim braces herself with both arms to maintain balance while sitting. Photo by Dr. D. Carleton Gajdusek, 1979.

An elderly kuru victim who can no longer walk waits for the other women to return from their gardens. Despite the heat of the sun, she feels chilled.

limbs often develops, associated with widespread [repetitive muscular spasms], or sometimes shock-like muscle jerks and occasionally coarser [irregular, involuntary] movements, especially when the patient is thrown into an exaggerated startle response by postural instability, or by sudden exposure to noise or bright light. Deep tendon reflexes are usually normal. . . . Although muscle activity is poorly maintained there is no . . . real weakness or muscle atrophy. Emotional lability, leading to outbursts of pathological laughter [is] frequent, sometimes even appearing in the first stage of the disease, and smiling and laughter are terminated slowly. . . . Some patients, especially adolescent and young adult males, become depressed, and a rare patient develops a pathological belligerence [in response to] disturbances by family members or others. Mental slowing is apparent, but severe dementia is conspicuously absent. No sensory changes have been noted. . . .

The third, or terminal, stage is reached when the patient is unable to sit up without support, and ataxia, tremor and dysarthria become progressively more severe and incapacitating. Tendon reflexes may become exaggerated. . . . Some cases show characteristic . . . defects of posture and movement. Terminally, urinary and faecal incontinence develop and dysphagia [difficulty swallowing] leads to thirst and starvation . . . and the patient becomes mute and unresponsive. Deep . . . ulcerations [of the skin over bony prominences and] pneumonia appear in this stage and the patient finally succumbs, usually emaciated, but occasionally quickly enough to be still well nourished.[3]

THEORIES OF THE ETIOLOGY OF KURU

At first, kuru was thought by Western observers to be a psychosomatic phenomenon, "directly associated with the threat and fear of what was believed to be a particularly malignant form of sorcery."[4] A provisional medical diagnosis of the first case sent to the Australian government hospital at Kainantu for close observation in 1955 elicited a diagnosis of "acute hysteria in an otherwise healthy woman."[5] In 1957, Drs. Vincent Zigas (working for the Papua New Guinea Department of Health) and Gajdusek (from the United States National Institutes of Health) began an intensive study of the disease, and Gajdusek was soon to write in a note to the anthropologist Ronald Berndt:

We cannot yet claim any clues to its pathogenesis, and infectious and toxic factors which might be responsible for its etiology have thus far eluded us. However—and most unfortunately for us—all the guidance is pointing toward the vast group of chronic-progressive-heredo-familial degenerations of the central nervous system. . . . We have recently had the assistance and advice of Dr. Sinclair, Director of Psychiatry from the Royal Melbourne Hospital, and he agrees with our current opinion that fatal kuru . . . cannot by any stretch of the imagination be identified with hysteria, psychoses or any known . . . psychologically-induced illnesses . . . the evidence for direct central nervous system damage is far too great in the strabismus, and pictures . . . of advanced neurological disease shown by the advanced cases.[6]

Later the same year, 1957, Gajdusek and Zigas published their first medical assessment. They emphasized the high incidence of kuru in certain families and hamlets, its localization to the Fore and adjacent peoples with whom they intermarried, and its predilection for children and adult women.[7]

The boundaries of the kuru region as defined by these investigators in 1957 have changed little since that time, although the region of high incidence has gradually been contracting.[8] The kuru region comprises most of the Okapa Subdistrict of the Eastern Highlands District, a population of over 40,000, belonging to nine language groups and representing about one-fifth of the population of the Eastern Highlands District. The Lamari River to the southeast and a large expanse of uninhabited country to the southwest sharply separate the southernmost Fore villages, which are regularly afflicted with kuru, from the Kukukuku and Yar populations, who have never experienced the disease. Elsewhere, the boundaries of kuru incidence are not sharply defined. To the east, Awa and Auyana peoples rarely contract kuru. North of Fore, kuru has occurred in Usurufa villages and in the adjoining part of Kamano. Some Yate and Yagaria peoples to the northwest have been affected, and to the west kuru is found in those parts of Kanite, Keiagana, and Gimi which border Fore territory.

Because kuru seemed to run in families and was localized to a small interrelated population, a genetic basis for the disease was suspected. In the late 1950's, it was proposed that kuru was a hereditary disorder, determined by a single autosomal gene that was dominant in females but recessive in males.[9] The implications of such a hypothesis were somber. By the mid-1950's, Highland men had been encouraged to participate as migrant laborers under the provisions of the Highlands Labour Scheme, administered from Goroka. Each worker signed a two-year contract. Although the government employed some of these men on public works, the majority were under contract to private copra, cocoa, and rubber plantations in coastal and island regions of Papua New Guinea, where labor was scarce. The laborers received food, clothing, lodging, transport, and medical attention. Half their low wages was deferred and paid in a lump sum at the termination of the contract. Government officials and kuru investigators debated whether it would now be possible to erect an invisible fence around the Fore, to prevent their participation in the Highlands Labour Scheme, and to discourage the exodus of the affected population from the region. Only if such a plan were found feasible and morally acceptable, it was said, could other peoples be protected against the lethal kuru gene. In the meantime, Fore would continue to transmit the disease one to the other until their tragic extinction.

The investigation of kuru in the 1950's was hampered by a lack of information about Fore kinship. As we shall see in Chapter 4, many of the supposedly related kuru victims were not closely related biologically, but were kin in an improvised, non-biological sense. An analysis of the Fore kinship system does not support a purely genetic interpretation of the disease. Moreover, as John Mathews, a physician whose study of kuru began in 1963, noted:

> This purely genetic model, if true, implied that kuru must
> have been of remote evolutionary origin and that it ought to
> have been in epidemiological equilibrium. It was soon apparent
> that kuru was too common and too fatal to be a purely genetic
> disorder unless the hypothetical kuru gene was maintained at
> high frequency by a mechanism of balanced polymorphism.
> There was no evidence to support the latter suggestion.[10]

In other words, an inevitably fatal genetic disorder could not reach the incidence kuru then had among the South Fore without soon killing off the host population, unless the gene for kuru in some other way conferred a selective survival advantage.

Anthropological evidence gathered in 1962 by Robert Glasse and myself from dozens of Fore informants indicated that kuru had spread slowly through Fore villages within living memory, and that its progress through Fore territory followed a specific, traceable route. Entering from a Keiagana village to their northwest around 1920, the disease, according to Fore testimony, proceeded down their eastern border, and then swung westward into central South Fore. From this point, it turned again to the north and also continued to move south. Its appearance in the extreme south was thus relatively late, and many people gave persuasive accounts of their first encounter with the disease.

Owata (not his real name) of Wanitabe was about 55 years of age when he described his experience with kuru:

> When I was a young boy, I didn't know anything about kuru. I
> was initiated [at 9 or 10 years] and I still hadn't seen kuru. It
> wasn't until I was married that I first saw it. That was true of
> many places around here. I visited Purosa and Aga Yagusa, and
> it wasn't there. I heard rumors of it at Kasokaso before it came
> to Wanitabe. My mother died of kuru at Wanitabe. I was married then, but it was before I had any children. She wasn't the

first to die of it here; a few other women died of it before her.

When I heard it arrived at Kamila, I went to Kamila to look at it. Men asked at first, "Is it sickness or what?"[11] Then they said that men worked it [i.e., caused it by sorcery]. We fought against Kamila after this. We were angry with them because all the women were dying of kuru. We asked them where we would get wives from if this continued. . . . Then some men of Wanitabe purchased it [i.e., paid for knowledge of the sorcery technique] from Kamila, and now we get it here too. Now it has spread everywhere. In the past, we fought only with bow and arrow. Then kuru came and killed the women one by one. I can't see of course, since I am blind, but I hear others talking about it, and they say it kills everyone now.

This places the arrival of kuru at Kamila in the late 1920s, and at Wanitabe by about 1930. The first cases at Purosa, six miles south of Wanitabe, are also associated with a sorcery purchase from Kamila at about the same time, in the early 1930's. A week after the death from kuru of a twenty-year-old Purosa youth in 1962, his mother (Inata), his mother's mother (Asa'ina), and her husband (Tano) speak of the first appearance of the disease at Purosa:

Asa'ina (grandmother): Kuru came to Purosa only recently. I had carried all my children and my hair was white before it came here.

Question: Was Inata married?

Inata (mother): Yes, I had given birth to all my five children. . . . my first child, a son, was about ten years old.

Inata (in response to question): We were afraid when we first saw kuru. We asked the men what kind of sickness it was, and they told us it was kuru. . . . When it first arrived, only one woman would get it, then a little later, another. Now, since the *tetegina* [red people, that is, "whites"] have arrived, plenty of people get the disease.

Question: Can you remember the names of the first people here to get kuru?

Tano (husband of Asa'ina, interjecting): These two can't remember. I can. The first woman to get it here was Agiso. She lived in a house on this hill. We were free of it in the past. Then we heard rumors of this trembling thing, this kuru, at Kasokana. From Kasokana it came to Wanikanto where four women got it. Still we didn't have it, we had only heard of it. Then the men of Kamila had four women who died of it, and still we had only heard of it. Then Agiso, who was a Kamila woman, came here to live and she wasn't here long before she died of it. She left her

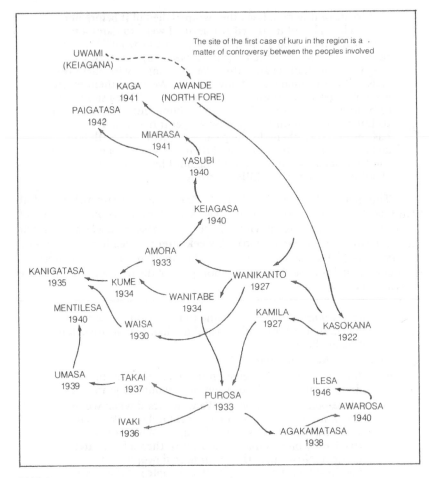

MAP 4
Epidemiological Map of Kuru

SOURCE: Adapted from J. D. Mathews 1971, p. 134.
(unpublished thesis)

husband at Kamila and came to marry a man here at
Purosa. She was a young woman when she died, about
eighteen or twenty years old [her age is conveyed by
comparing her to another girl now living]. The next to die
of it was a woman called Alakanto . . . and we saw that it
had come to us and we wondered who had purchased it
and brought it here. . . . I was married with one child, a

daughter called Tabelo who was about five years old [in-
dicating a child of similar age in the group] when Agiso
died. . . . This was a child of my first wife. I married
Asa'ina later.

From scores of such accounts there emerges a broad chronology of the
spread of kuru, with its arrival in some northwestern and southeastern areas
convincingly dated as late as the 1940's.

Fore accounts had a ring of epidemiological accuracy. They noted the
initial incidence of kuru among women, and describe its subsequent shift to
children of both sexes and to adult men. They also indicated uncertainty in
the diagnosis of early cases. At Umasa, the first case occurred in a woman
who had arrived recently from the North Fore. A young widow, she had been
inherited in marriage by her husband's age-mate, and people at Umasa were
puzzled by her illness. Noting that her tremor resembled the swaying of the
casuarina tree, they supposed that she had a shaking disorder called cassowary disease, by the further analogue that cassowary quills resemble waving
casuarina fronds. They fed the victim pork and casuarina bark, a
homeopathic treatment that gave little relief. When the woman's brothers
came to visit her, they, having already seen the disease, told the people of
Umasa what it was.

Many people first called the disease *negi nagi*, a Fore term meaning
silly or foolish person, because women afflicted with the ailment laughed
immoderately. In those early days, our informants said, they joked and took
sexual levities with the sick women as they do with those who manifest
temporary mental derangement or bizarre behavior. When it became apparent that the victims were uniformly dying, they were forced to conclude
that the matter was more serious than they had thought, and that sorcerers
were at work. Early medical reports also emphasized the sufferers' emotional lability, leading to the unfortunate characterization of kuru in the
Australian press as "the laughing death." Only a minority of the patients
examined in the 1960's were said to smile or laugh inappropriately; it is
possible that the clinical features of the disease have changed.[12]

CANNIBALISM

In 1962 and 1963, Robert Glasse and I presented evidence gathered in two
extended stays among the Fore that kuru had spread through the Fore population in recent times, and that its high incidence in the early 1960's was
related to the cannibal consumption of deceased kuru victims. We also
provided evidence that for the South Fore, the depletion of women was a
recent phenomenon.[13] Our cannibalism hypothesis seemed to fit the
epidemiological evidence. The first Australian government patrols in the
late 1940's reported cannibalism throughout the entire kuru region. By

1951, the Berndts, living on the North Fore borders, noted that government intervention had put a stop to cannibalism in that area, although it was still practiced surreptitiously farther afield. The South Fore confirmed the Berndt's observation. One elderly man from Wanitabe said in 1962 that the exhortations of the first patrol (1947) were disregarded. "We hid and ate people still. Then the *luluais* [government-appointed local leaders]and *tul-tuls* [their appointed assistants] tried to stop us, but we hid from them, too. We only stopped when the big road came through from Okapa to Purosa [1955]." Thus, in the South Fore, the area with the highest incidence of kuru, cannibalism had continued later than in the North.

When a body was considered for human consumption, none of it was discarded except the bitter gall bladder. In the deceased's old sugarcane garden, maternal kin dismembered the corpse with a bamboo knife and stone axe. They first removed hands and feet, then cut open the arms and legs to strip out the muscles. Opening the chest and belly, they avoided rupturing the gall bladder, whose bitter contents would ruin the meat. After severing the head, they fractured the skull to remove the brain. Meat, viscera, and brain were all eaten. Marrow was sucked from cracked bones, and sometimes the pulverized bones themselves were cooked and eaten with green vegetables. In North Fore, but not in the South, the corpse was buried for several days, then exhumed and eaten when the flesh had "ripened" and the maggots could be cooked as a separate delicacy.[14]

Thus, little was wasted, but not all bodies were eaten. Fore did not eat people who died of dysentery or leprosy, or who had had yaws. Kuru victims, however, were viewed favorably, the layer of fat on those who died rapidly heightening the resemblance of human flesh to pork, the most favored protein. Nor were all body parts eaten by everyone. For instance, the buttocks of Fore men were reserved for their wives, while female maternal cousins received the arms and legs. Most significantly, not all Fore were cannibals. Although cannibalism by males occurred more frequently in the North, South Fore men rarely ate human flesh, and those who did (usually old men) said they avoided eating the bodies of women. Young children residing apart from the men in small houses with their mothers, ate what their mothers gave them. Initiated boys moved at about the age of ten to the communal house shared by the adult men of the hamlet, thus abandoning the lower-class world of immaturity, femininity and cannibalism. As will be discussed in greater detail in Chapter 10, men in this protein-scarce society claimed the preferred form of protein (wild boar, domestic pigs), whereas women supplemented their lesser allotment of pork with small game, insects, frogs, and dead humans. Women who assisted a mother in childbirth ate the placenta. Both cannibalism and kuru were thus largely limited to adult women, to children of both sexes, and to a few old men, matching again the epidemiology of kuru in the early 1960's.

As mentioned earlier, body parts were not randomly distributed. The

The cherished indigenous pig.

corpse was due those who received pigs and valuables by rights of kinship and friendship with the deceased (primarily maternal kin), and the gift had to be reciprocated. Pig and human were considered equivalent. The death of a breeding sow in 1962 evoked the following speech of mourning: "This was a human being, not a pig. One old woman among us has died." Pig and human were dismembered and allocated in similar fashion. Among South Fore, a man's brain could be eaten by his sister, and in the North, by his sister as well as his son's wife and maternal aunts and uncles. A woman's brain, perhaps the most significant body matter in transmission of the disease, was said to be given to her son's wife or her brother's wife.

Ethnographic accounts of the consumption of the first kuru victim in a certain location also describe cases four to eight years later among those who had eaten the victim.[15] Moreover, the average risk of kuru in wives of kuru victims' brothers was three to four times as great as that in a control group of women who were not related either genetically or by marriage to kuru victims. Furthermore, the risk of kuru in females related to kuru victims by marriage only (41 percent) was almost as high as the risk in females genetically related to kuru victims (51 percent).[16] This conforms to the stated regulation that brothers' wives receive the victim's brain, and the opportunity of these women to participate in kuru cannibalism along with the victim's mother, sisters, and daughters. The distribution of human flesh for consumption thus crossed genetic lines much as the distribution of kuru did.

THE ADOPTION OF CANNIBALISM

Fore had not been cannibals for long. Within the zone of cannibal peoples to the east and south of Goroka, they may have been among the last to include human flesh in their diet. Cannibalism was adopted by the Kamano and Keiagana-Kanite before it became customary among Fore. North Fore say they were imitating these northern neighbors when they became cannibals around the turn of the century, while among South Fore, cannibalism began as recently as fifty or sixty years ago, or about a decade before the appearance of kuru there. Old people in the South Fore, whose memory of the matter appears unclouded, describe their attraction to human flesh. There was no thought of acquiring the power or personality of the deceased. Nor is it correct to speak of ritual cannibalism, although many medical and journalistic accounts do so.[17] While the finger and jaw bones of some relatives were retained for supernatural communication, Fore attitudes toward the bodies they consumed revolved around their fertilizing, rather than their moral, effect. Dead bodies buried in gardens encouraged the growth of crops. In a similar manner human flesh, like pig meat, helps some humans regenerate. The flesh of the deceased was thought particularly suitable for invalids.

As a Wanitabe man born about 1890 said: "The Ibusas [North Fore] were visiting the Kamano and saw them stealing and eating good men. They heard it was sweet to taste, and tried it themselves. I was about ten years old when we heard these stories." North of Fore, then, aggressive exocannibalism, or the eating of dead enemies, appears to have been the prevailing practice. Among South Fore, however, it was usual to eat kin or people of one's own residential group after they had died (endocannibalism).

A variable enthusiasm for human flesh runs from Goroka through the Fore area, coming to an abrupt halt in the southeast, where the Awa, in contrast to their Fore neighbors, were not cannibals at all. This is a gradient that matches an environmental shift from grassland groups for whom hunting plays but a small part in the diet[18] to the Fore, who have not yet denuded their land of forest and for whom until recently wild game was readily available. By 1962, traditional gifts of wild protein between matrilateral kin were rare in the South Fore; possum and cassowary were being replaced by chicken and canned fish purchased at the local trade store. The last wild boar injury in Wanitabe occurred around 1940, and by 1970 South Fore groups who had supplied feathers for the northward trade began to buy them from the forest-dwelling Kukukuku further south. A less agricultural recent

A hamlet and adjoining gardens recently carved out of the forest. Grass and scrub are overtaking the older, abandoned site above. Photo by Dr. E. R. Sorenson, "The Edge of the Forest," Smithsonian Institution Press, 1976.

past is portrayed in Fore stories of men and their humanoid dogs encountering possum, birds, snakes, and flying foxes. Fore also have an elaborate zoological classsification system, which represents a relict of vanishing hunting habits.[19]

Population increases in the region and the conversion to the sweet potato as a dietary staple thus appear to have led to the progressive removal of forest and animal life, to cultivation methods involving more complete tillage of the soil, and to the keeping of domestic pig herds, which compensate for the loss of wild protein. As the forests protein sources became depleted, Fore men met their needs by claiming prior right in pork, while women adopted human flesh as their supplemental *habus*, a Melanesian pidgin term meaning "meat" or "small game." Fore still refer to the human corpse and the stillborn infant as "the true habus of women." Men at Awarosa, who insisted that cannibalism was a female habit, argued that

Mixed garden of sweet potato, taro, and spring onion.

in this southeastern Fore region there was "plenty of habus in the forest for men." They noted, in addition, that "if we men ate people, we would fall ill with respiratory disorders and our flesh would waste away," a rationale they also gave for their initial rejection of chicken (more will be said about these attitudes in relation to pollution in Chapter 10). Traditional male curers guarded their powers and are said never to have practiced cannibalism.

The case of the non-cannibal, grass-dwelling Awa does not weaken the supposition that human flesh is ingested as a relevant source of dietary protein.[20] Fore at Awarosa report the neighboring Awa as saying they have never been cannibals. "We have no forests of our own," they reportedly told the Fore, "so we give you our sisters in marriage, and in exchange we eat your habus." The Awa sources of protein were pigs given them as brideprice, and subsequent gifts of wild protein received as birth payments each time their sisters gave birth to children. Ronald Berndt also takes seriously Fore statements on the value of human flesh. Noting that in the 1950's pigs were not plentiful, he records a story in which Fore first taste human flesh. "This is sweet," they said. "What is the matter with us, are we mad? Here is good food and we have neglected to eat it."[21]

Epidemiological evidence reported in the mid-1960's indicated that the age and sex distribution of kuru was changing. Young children were less often affected, and the disorder was more often seen in adolescents and young adult men and women, as well as in older women. Moreover, the overall incidence fell in all areas except the Gimi.[22] A purely genetic explanation of kuru no longer seemed plausible.

KURU AS A SLOW VIRUS

After the first clinical descriptions of kuru were published, this unusual disorder attracted considerable international attention. In England, W. J. Hadlow, working on scrapie, a degenerative disease of the central nervous system in sheep, pointed to the remarkable similarities in the clinical and pathological features of kuru and scrapie. Moreover, the disease of sheep was transmissible by inoculation.[23] Unlike most infectious disorders, which have a relatively short incubation period, scrapie did not become manifest until many years after inoculation. Stimulated by the parallel with scrapie, Gajdusek and his coworkers at the National Institutes of Health in Bethesda, Maryland, injected the brains of chimpanzees with brain material from Fore patients who had died of kuru, and in 1966 they reported that after incubation periods of up to fifty months, the chimpanzees had developed a clinical syndrome astonishingly akin to human kuru.[24] Kuru, like scrapie, thus appeared to be a viral disease of extraordinarily long incubation, a "slow virus infection."

This finding lent support to our idea that the disease had reached epidemic proportions among the Fore as a result of the eating of dead kuru victims. That hypothesis had also assumed that kuru would not strike those born after the abandonment of cannibalism, which in South Fore occurred as a result of government and missionary intervention in the middle to late 1950's.[25] The prediction now appears substantiated by the virtual disappearance of kuru among children, and by the earlier decline in childhood cases among North Fore, where government influence suppressed cannibalism years earlier than in the South or in the Gimi, where childhood kuru occurred until 1970.[26] The Gimi, even more remote from government influence than South Fore, continued as cannibals for longer.

Epidemiological data gathered between 1970 and 1977 strengthen the hypothesis that kuru is a disease transmitted by cannibalism and caused by a slow virus with an extremely long period of incubation. There has been a continued decline in the annual incidence of the disease, particularly in females. The greater decline of new cases in females can be explained by the fact that those who ate human flesh as adults were predominantly women, and they have already died of kuru. They leave behind an increasing majority of new cases resulting from *childhood* ingestion of the virus, a condition for which both sexes were equally at risk since cannibal flesh was consumed equally by male and female children. With the passage of time, the sex ratio of new kuru victims should thus approach parity. This has already occurred in North Fore, where government influence eliminated cannibalism earlier, and a similar trend is now appearing in the South.[27] Moreover, while there were two twelve-year-old patients with kuru in 1970, the youngest current case in May 1978 was more than 20 years old. Thus both childhood and adolescent cases have disappeared completely. The only Fore and Gimi currently coming down with kuru are those who participated in cannibal meals prior to 1955.

Recent data also allow us to delineate the behavior of the virus more precisely. Since the youngest victim is now twenty-five, while the youngest patients ever seen have been four years of age,[28] the virus may be estimated to have a minimum incubation period of roughly two years (from the first ingestion of solid meat) and a potential maximum of at least twenty-three years. This upward limit may be raised as data are gathered in the next few years, but the pattern already known depicts an extraordinary infectious illness in which symptoms may appear decades after the causal event.

While the means by which the disease was transmitted thus seems clarified, kuru continues to provoke scientific curiosity. Recent research has focused on the pathogenesis of slow virus infections, on documenting of new epidemiological trends, and on attempts to establish the kuru virus in tissue culture.[29]

The pathogenic agent responsible for the disease has recently been isolated and transmitted to spider, capuchin, squirrel, rhesus, woolly, and marmoset monkeys, as well as to chimpanzees, yet the virus itself has proved elusive. It seems to elicit in its host none of the usual immune responses. Kuru does not produce detectable antibodies. Nor has the virus been depicted under the electron microscope. As the first chronic or sub-acute degenerative disease of humans proven to be a slow virus infection, however, kuru has stimulated the search for virus infections in other sub-acute and chronic human diseases, particularly of the nervous system. Multiple sclerosis is the most common central nervous system disorder believed (though in this case not yet proven) to be caused by a slow virus infection.[30] The evidence for other neurological diseases is more conclusive. For example, it now appears that Creutzfeldt-Jakob disease, one of the presenile dementias (mental deterioration at a relatively young age) that occur sporadically and in familial patterns in humans throughout the world, is also transmissible to chimpanzees and monkeys, and is caused by a virus with properties much like those of the kuru virus.[31] Moreover, the incidence of Creutzfeldt-Jakob disease among Jews of North African and Middle Eastern origin in Israel is thirty times the rate for Jews of European origin. Since only the former customarily eat the eyeballs and brains of sheep, scrapie-infected sheep tissue has been suggested as the source of infection.[32]

Two other rare disorders of the central nervous system—subacute sclerosing panencephalitis (SSPE) and progressive multifocal leukoenceph-alopathy (PML)—have been shown to be due to slow virus infection.[33] The kuru model may also apply to amyotrophic lateral sclerosis, Alzheimer's disease, and other presenile or senile dementias.[34]

Thus, as research proceeds, the concept of a related group of diseases of viral etiology has emerged. These are all virally transmitted diseases of the brain, infections that do not provoke the typical inflammatory response, caused by viruses with very unconventional properties. The kuru agent remains stable on storage at 70°C. for many years and after freeze-drying. It is not totally inactivated when subjected to a temperature of 85°C. for thirty minutes.[35] Fore cooking methods therefore did not destroy the kuru virus. After the brain of a dead person was removed from the skull, the tissue was squeezed to a pulp and steamed in bamboo cylinders at temperatures that would not completely inactivate the virus, since in high altitudes water boils at 90–95°. No serological tests for the virus have been found. There is no evidence of an immune response, and no antibodies have been detected. Nor is there evidence of an antigen related to any of the more than fifty known virus antigens.[36] Yet the kuru–scrapie agents persist in laboratory cultures of infected brain tissue, and they are readily transmissible in extremely low dilutions by intravenous, intramuscular, or subcutaneous injection, and from tissues other than brain (pooled liver, kidney, spleen, and lymph nodes).[37]

Kuru has not yet been transmitted to animals via the gastrointestinal tract. Gajdusek therefore has suggested that a likely route of infection from contaminated brain was through the skin, entering either through cuts and sores or upon being rubbed by unwashed hands into the nose or eyes.[38]

Research continues on the question of susceptibility to the agent, and on refining our knowledge of its properties. Kuru is already an established landmark in neurology and virology. In neurology, it is the first human degenerative disease shown to be caused by a virus. In virology, it is the first human disease shown to be caused by a novel kind of viral agent.[39] The implications of the discovery of the slow virus etiology of kuru for the understanding of other diseases have only begun to be explored. The Fore experience will be remembered for decades to come as investigators use the kuru model in their search for the cause of disease in other populations of the world.

FORE SORCERY

To this day, Fore universally believe that kuru is caused by malicious sorcerers in their midst. Early observers of the Fore population were struck not only by the concern of the people with this strange and dramatic disease, but by their more general focus on sorcery. In the report of August 1953 quoted at the beginning of this chapter, Patrol Officer McArthur wrote: "In this area, I regard sorcery as a powerful foe.... Its results are serious. Even since the last patrol in December 1952, it has caused one tribal fight and two desertions of ground [evacuations of hamlets].... There are ... a large number of sorcerers."

Fore have a powerful reputation as sorcerers among other populations in the region.[40] As far away as Kainantu and Henganofi, forty miles and two to three days' walk from Wanitabe, people believe that methods and ingredients can be obtained from Fore,[41] while their immediate neighbors view Fore with considerable anxiety. Gimi have a particular fear of sorcery emanating from their eastern neighbors,[42] and Kamano confide that they take special care not to throw away scraps of food (which can be used against them in sorcery bundles) while parties of Fore are visiting. Keiagana admit to a similar caution about providing Fore with potential sorcery materials, and when traveling in Fore territory they deposit sweet potato and sugarcane skins in their string bags, to discard on the return home. South Fore at Ilesa, by contrast, pay no heed to their food scraps or feces while visiting the Awa, but resume vigilance as soon as they return to home territory. Not only do neighboring peoples fear Fore, but Fore fear one another.

Patrol Officer Colman's 1955 report describes South Fore hamlets barricaded behind wooden constructions and impenetrable canegrass. Across the entrance corridor to the hamlet lies a small gate. "When all the people are inside after dark," he writes, "this gate is closed and generally a sentry is posted. These precautions stop intending sorcerers from entering the hamlet.... Some of the men's houses have an additional encircling stockade for the same reason." Commenting on sanitation and hygiene, he adds: "The fault in most native areas is a shallow latrine," but Fore anxiety to keep excreta from potential sorcerers results in the construction by South Fore of "a latrine hole that seems bottomless."[43]

In recent years the Fore reputation for sorcery has become widespread. New Guinea and Australian newspapers carry occasional accounts of sorcery-related deaths in the Okapa region,[44] and in 1973 the government's Law Department inquired into allegations of fifty to sixty sorcery-linked deaths a year at Okapa said to be caused by professional killers who were being paid up to five hundred dollars for murder "contracts."[45]

The distribution of kuru lends credence to the belief that Fore sorcery is vastly more powerful than that of their neighbors. While kuru is present

Barricaded hamlet entrance. Photo by Dr. E. R. Sorenson, "The Edge of the Forest," Smithsonian Institution Press, 1976.

in surrounding populations (as mentioned earlier, 20 percent of kuru deaths each year occur among other peoples), the prevalence of the disease is markedly higher among Fore, particularly South Fore. In 1964 it was estimated that Gimi males had only one chance in twenty-five of dying from kuru, while the risk for South Fore males exceeded one in five. For females, the main victims of the disease, the difference was even greater. Eighty-four percent of Gimi women had a chance of surviving the reproductive period without a fatal attack of kuru, but fewer than one in ten South Fore women might do so. The average life expectancy for South Fore women born in the mid-1960's was estimated at little over twenty years.[46] That the South Fore were engaged in dangerous sorcery seemed incontestable.

OTHER
MEDICAL DISORDERS
3

Apart from kuru, the diseases suffered by Fore are similar to those found in many other Highland peoples. Some of these populations show striking fluctuations in size from year to year, as do the Fore, which points to infectious disease as a major determinant of mortality among Highlanders.[1]

During the late 1930's and early 1940's, a number of epidemics swept southward through the Fore region—mumps, measles, whooping cough, and dysentery. Many people died, but the new diseases were not regarded by Fore as new forms of sorcery, although the loss of certain important men lay behind later sorcery accusations between some local groups. The simultaneous incapacitation of large numbers of people is what Fore recall most vividly about these epidemics. Disorganization of labor was at times so great that normal agricultural activities were halted, and the ripening corn and cucumbers are said to have rotted while people lay recovering in their houses. Aware that the dysentery epidemic of 1943 had swept down upon them like a great wind from the north, South Fore at Purosa responded by refusing visitors access to their hamlets, and by persuading fellow residents to remain at home until the epidemic had passed. With clinical perception, Fore noted that the second wave of some diseases, such as mumps, was less serious than the first. In 1959 and 1962, however, influenza epidemics caused many deaths, especially among children under the age of five.

Discounting kuru, the commonest problems afflicting Fore at present are upper-respiratory infections, bronchitis, pneumonia, diarrhea, gastroenteritis, and complications of childbirth. Meningitis and tetanus also occur, as does anemia in association with hookworm, closely spaced pregnancies,

31

marginal nutrition, and occasionally malaria, although malaria is in general confined to the deep valleys near the Lamari River. Tropical ulcers, scabies, and leprosy are present; less common are brain tumors, epilepsy, brain hemorrhages and strokes, kidney disease due to amyloidosis (caused by deposit of a protein called amyloid in body tissue), cardiac failure, cor pulmonale (heart failure secondary to lung disease), and cirrhosis.[2] As we shall see in Chapter 5, many of these diseases are attributed by the Fore to specific forms of sorcery.

As elsewhere, early government patrols eliminated yaws by injecting the population with penicillin. Although the syphilis and yaws bacteria are morphologically indistinguishable, yaws is not transmitted venereally and is a disfiguring but nonlethal childhood disease. It does not involve the heart or nervous system, and is not known to be transmitted from mother to fetus during pregnancy.

Yaws and syphilis appear to result from infection with the same organism, with differing immunity and circumstances of infection being responsible for their contrasting clinical manifestations. In the past, virtually all children in New Guinea were exposed to infection with yaws, thereby acquiring an immunity which protected them as adults from infection with syphilis. The government yaws campaigns of the 1950's, however, appear to have created a generation of young adults lacking the cross-immunity provided by childhood yaws against venereal syphilis.

Surveys in the Eastern Highlands in 1964–65 and again in 1968 turned up no active cases of yaws, although in some areas bowed legs and saddle noses, attributed to old yaws infections, were seen in middle-aged people. No evidence of venereal syphilis was found. By 1970, however, large numbers of patients at Goroka hospital were suffering from the disease. A syphilis epidemic in New Guinea had begun, appearing almost simultaneously in most of the Goroka and Chimbu valleys, its occurrence coinciding almost exactly with the disappearance of yaws from those regions.[3] Venereal disease has now arrived among the Fore. In 1974, there were 55 cases of gonorrhea and two possible cases of syphilis. By 1975, there were 24 additional cases of gonorrhea and seven of syphilis. In 1976, 59 gonorrhea and eight syphilis cases were reported from Fore and Gimi groups.[4]

The syphilis epidemics now occurring in Papua New Guinea, then, appear to result from biological alterations in the immunity of the population, along with profound alterations in modes of life that have created a situation favoring the spread of the disease. The migration of single men and the appearance of female prostitutes in the new towns have played a part. The spread of syphilis in New Guinea, as Hornabrook notes, is reminiscent of similar biological and social dislocations which have occurred during wartime or in other colonial encounters, and which may transform a benign disease into a potentially lethal one.[5]

Two diseases that affect Fore as well as other Highland groups are also

Man with yaws disfigurement helps assemble a brideprice.

of interest to medical anthropologists: endemic goiter and the severe abdominal disorder known as "Pig Bel." In 1967 the Fore suffered an outbreak of enteritis necroticans, called Pig Bel because it is associated with large-scale feasts at which pig meat contaminated by a strain of the Clostridium bacteria is consumed. The symptoms include bloody diarrhea, stomach pain, nausea, and occasional vomiting. The disease progresses, if untreated, to complete gangrene of parts of the small intestine. Among patients admitted to Highland hospitals between January 1961 and November 1964, there was a death rate of 57.7 percent in children under five years of age and 46.2 percent in persons over forty. Although mainly an illness of children, with a peak incidence at age four years, a higher proportion of adults over forty have an antibody to the Clostridial toxin in their blood, a pattern which suggests that childhood exposure produces relative immunity in adulthood.

Children glean meat scraps from inside a pig during a feast. Photo by Dr. E. R. Sorenson, "The Edge of the Forest," Smithsonian Institution Press, 1976.

Bacterial contamination of the pork eaten at large feasts can occur during butchering, when the hands of those dissecting the pigs directly contact pig feces or the pig bowel is perforated. Stray dogs, piglets, chickens, and children wander at will amidst the butchering, with the children nibbling on raw morsels such as ear tips and snouts, and using the inflated bladders as balloons or footballs. Parents wrap entrails and sex organs about their wrists to promote future fertility. After a delay for singing and dancing, the pigs are cooked in earth ovens at temperatures which ensure that large chunks of meat are not thoroughly cooked. It is after cooking that contamination may be most significant. Arguments concerning distribution of the meat may continue for a whole day, while people debate the relative advantages of sending payments to kin, trade partners, or allies. In transit to its destination, a half side of pork may then change hands as many as five times. At this point, another day may elapse before the pork is cut into smaller pieces and a second distribution is held. This may be as much as four days after the pig was butchered. The meat is reheated in a smaller earth oven, so that any prior bacterial spoiling becomes a potent culture with a high infective dose.[6]

It has recently been suggested that Pig Bel occurs among Highlanders because they have low levels of protein-digesting enzymes in their intestines. These low enzyme levels are postulated to be the result of a low protein, high sweet potato diet. A low protein intake may cause decreases in the level of digestive enzymes. In addition, sweet potato, the Fore staple, contains an enzyme inhibitor. The destruction of bowel tissue in Pig Bel is attributed to a toxin secreted by the Clostridia, which is a protein. According to this theory, patients cannot inactivate the toxin because of their decreased level of protein-digesting enzymes. The disease is not present in the Lowlands even though the organism and poor nutrition are both common there, because the diet of coastal people is more varied and does not depend on the sweet potato. According to this theory, Pig Bel is mainly a childhood disease because Highland adults, apart from having acquired an immunity, also have a more adequate protein intake than do growing children.[7]

The Fore region is not markedly afflicted by goiter (enlargement of the thyroid gland), except in villages along the Lamari River, where some goiter has been found. These cases, noted in 1965, represent the southern limit of a narrow "goiter belt" extending northeast beyond the kuru region, through the Auyana and Tairora linguistic groups near the Lamari to Baira (approximately 35 miles northeast of Okapa), where endemic goiter is a serious problem.[8] Since 1965, a high incidence of endemic cretinism associated with goiter has also been reported in the Jimi Valley in the Western Highlands. A medical census there in 1966 discovered that 148 people in a population of 8,000 had hearing and speech abnormalities, with most of those examined being deaf mutes. It was then established that prior to 1953, few children were born with congenital neurological damage, but that the prevalence had increased markedly after 1955. The outbreak of endemic cre-

A small boy plays with a pig bladder before a feast.

tinism in the Jimi Valley thus occurred after contact with Australian patrols. Early government patrols and mission personnel bartered for food and services with a type of rock salt deficient in iodine. Iodine deficiency is a well-established cause of thyroid enlargement. The Jimi stopped consuming the indigenous salt they had previously acquired in trade from the Simbai Valley, where it was laboriously distilled from springs rich in iodine. The epidemic of cretinism was therefore associated with a disturbance in traditional social and economic relationships. Goiter is now treated by intramuscular injection of iodine in oil, and averted by the use of iodized salt.[9]

Fore appear to have avoided a major brush with goiter because early patrols in their area bartered with shells rather than salt. Although salt was later accepted as an exchange commodity, Fore expressed greater interest in such items as paper, tobacco, knives, axes, beads, and for a time, safety pins, which were a fashion in earrings for young girls.

Essential tremor, a benign, heredo-familial disorder of the nervous system, is reported from the Fore region. This syndrome, stemming from an apparent genetic predisposition, affects predominantly women in middle to old age. It has been suggested that the heavy manual labor which is the lot of females in the Highlands may evoke a tremor in those genetically predisposed to it. Essential tremor is less common among the Fore than among neighboring Kamano, Auyana, Gadsup, Tairora, and Agarabe populations.[10]

Fore birth rates show a periodic fluctuation in three- to six-year cycles, as in other parts of New Guinea.[11] This fluctuation may in part reflect the timing of fatal epidemics among infants and young children, with "extra" pregnancies being undertaken to replace children lost to infectious diseases. On the other hand, similar fluctuations in the birthrate could be achieved by the combined effect of restricted intercourse and the partial suppression of fertility which occurs during lactation.[12] These human cycles may also be related to other periodic events, such as a fluctuation in food supplies following periods of excessive rainfall or the ritual exchange of pigs. Pig exchanges not only improve the nutritional status of women, which may directly affect ovulation,[13] but are an occasion for the negotiation of new marriages. During these periodic exchanges men are exhorted to return home to work at creating a new cycle of growth in their gardens and in their wives.

Apart from kuru, then, the Fore population exhibits disease, birth, and death rates similar to those of kuru-free populations in the Eastern Highlands. Periodic fluctuations in the birth rate, death rates, and the prevalence of certain diseases all reflect a complex of biological and social factors. South Fore local groups maintain with one another, as well as with populations to the north, significant genetic and social connections. The flow of genes, diseases, goods, and technical information across the region is facilitated by a South Fore kinship system that gives as much authority to relationships based on elective association as to those based on genetic bonding.

EXTENSIONS OF SELF

4

The high prevalence of sorcerers can be understood within the South Fore setting of a social system largely based on improvised relationships. Fore in one location have ties with kin and friends in a variety of other places. Moreover, their affiliations rarely overlap. Individuals and groups readily change their place of residence and their personal affiliations, and mutual support requires constant demonstration. South Fore political behavior is not the predictable outcome of a territorially based lineage system.[1] Loyalties among co-residents are thus in doubt, and under the stress of social dislocation brought about by kuru, personal relationships lacking historical depth are easily severed.

THE POLITICS OF RESIDENCE

South Fore have a sense of recent settlement in their present location, and of having plenty of land. Gesturing at the forested mountainside, one man observed: "If we had been here longer, I think we would have cut down more trees." With population densities averaging only 54 persons a square mile in the north and 27 in the south, their political problem is not to restrict the access of outsiders to group resources, but rather the opposite: how to maintain group strength in the face of aggressive neighbors. South Fore residential units therefore readily admit newcomers and provide them with fertile land. Subsistence is based on pig-keeping and on the cultivation of a sweet potato staple within a framework of a mixed garden producing taro, yams, sugarcane, beans, pitpit(Saccharum), and other vegetables. The

Yasubi hamlet formed by segmenting groups from two other hamlets; a recent arrival has started to build the unfinished house at left. Photo by Dr. E. R. Sorenson, "The Edge of the Forest," Smithsonian Institution Press, 1976.

gardens are seasonal and require irregular labor input, allowing time for women to collect frogs, rats, mushrooms and wild greens, and for men to hunt for small birds, marsupials and sorcerers.

The Fore agricultural system remains extensive, and fields are frequently relocated. The population is mobile, continually dispersing through the territory. Groups fragment, move, and recombine in new alignments. Most adult men report residing in different places at birth, initiation, marriage, and fatherhood. A sample of the residential movements of Wanitabe men aged forty-five or more shows that three major shifts is the norm, while some Fore change residence five or six times in their lifetime.

While Fore have been gradually encroaching on the uninhabited land at their southern border, fragmentation of a residential unit does not always lead to movement toward this frontier zone, which is regarded as dangerous and unhealthy. Ousted groups may be invited by hosts elsewhere to form a new coalition for defense. A glance at a map shows the most far-flung Fore settlements flanking the Yani River in the extreme southwest, and the Lamari River in the southeast, where Gimi- and Awa-speaking people, respectively, are close neighbors. Although there may be some advantage to gardening close to the rivers, the scattering of these southern settlements along the western and eastern borders appears to resolve a major problem facing colonizers of new territory—the need to traffic in women, food, and goods.

When the Australian administration imposed peace in the 1950's, the press of population toward the south came to a temporary halt. With peace established, the government in 1957 announced its plan to take the first census. At this moment, many people changed residence, wishing to identify themselves with territory from which they had recently been ousted. Most of the residents of Wanitabe counted in the 1957 census returned there from places as distant as Purosa, Awarosa, Mentilesa, Kume, Amora, and Kasokaso. These population movements were in general a retreat from frontier settlements toward the more densely settled regions of the center and north.

Before contact with the Australian administration, Fore had no name for themselves, nor any conception of such large political units as the census divisions known subsequently as the North and South Fore. During an early patrol, a government officer standing in a northern location had asked the question: "Who are the people living down here?" The reply, "Pore kina," meaning "the people downhill" and applying to Fore-speaking people in the lower, warmer regions as well as to the Awa, has since been accepted by Fore to apply to themselves alone.[2] Although they do name large clusters to which they believe they belong (such as Ibusa, Atigina and Pamousa), these *district associations* are misty entities. Owning no property in common and never fighting as a unit, they are population aggregates that cannot be defined in the usual political terms. They seem instead to represent zones of ecological similarity, within which periodic rituals are coordinated, and crop and pig production calibrated to provide a ripple of social activity within a compact period of time. The pig festivals of 1969 and the anti-sorcery meetings described below in Chapter 8 appear to fall within such a regional design, a pattern of intense local social intercourse that in time gives rise to small differences in dialect and custom.

Within these vaguely defined regional clusters, there are social units, or *parishes*, which are distinct political entities. The parish consists of one or several adjacent hamlets, with its members having a corporate interest in a defined territory and sharing one *Ples Masalai* (Pidgin for spirit place or sacred grove). Ideally, the parish unites for defense when threatened by

outsiders and settles internal quarrels peaceably. In the South Fore there are
39 parishes, ranging in population from 41 at Wanda to 525 at Yasubi, with a
mean of 180.[3] Twenty-four parishes number between 100 and 200 members,
and only one has under 50, a consequence of recent fission; three exceed
350. As noted in Chapter 9, sorcery beliefs play a role in regulating the size
of political units. Sorcery accusations erupt periodically within and between cooperating groups, leading to the estrangement and eventual separation of former co-residents and allies.

Within the parish are two subunits: the *parish section* and a smaller
unit again, the Fore *lounei,* which loosely translates as "line." In practice
the section, rather than the parish, was the effective military unit. In the
past, the section negotiated its own military alliances and mobilized when
threatened or attacked. Unlike some other New Guinea peoples, the Fore
readily acquiesced in the Australian-imposed peace of the mid-1950's. Now
the section settles grievances without recourse to arms, and has recognized
Big Men who represent it in public affairs. Like the parish, it is a residential
unit, and consists of one or more hamlets known by a single name.
Wanitabe parish, for example, has 351 residents in three sections, with 170,
139, and 42 members.

The smallest parish subdivision, the line, may be distinguished from
the section on several grounds. It is a genealogical unit, in the sense that one
can assemble a genealogy of a line, though all details may not fit together
perfectly. Members of a line usually reside together as part of a single hamlet, and they form an exogamous unit (i.e., they marry outside the group).
Wanitabe parish has nine exogamous lines, ranging in size from 71 to four,
with a mean of 39. Although members say that the line makes marital
arrangements with other lines such that brides move in one direction and
goods in the other, no permanent or consistent division between wife-givers
and wife-takers can be established. Rather, there is periodic residential dis-
placement of lines, and the roles of wife-giver and wife-receiver are
switched repeatedly. The first marriage between neighboring lines does set
the pattern for the exchange of women for the next few years. Yet individual
men continue to acquire wives outside the line relationship, among
daughters of their mother's brothers residing in other, often distant,
parishes.[4]

Allied lines reside together and are subject to a single incest taboo:
women of both groups are considered by the men to be mothers, sisters, or
daughters. Such allied lines call themselves *ami-kina* ("little people"), although the constituent lines retain their original parish identification.
Ami-kina do not give each other "head pay" (*wergeld*) for deaths incurred
while fighting for a common cause. As a further mark of their single identity, ami-kina join in assembling brideprice and in giving deceased kin to the
mothers's brothers' lines to consume.

A line's name may reflect something of the group's history. Thus,

*A South Fore bride,
accompanied by her
brothers, leaves her
father's residence to
join her husband. She is
wearing the clothing and
wealth she will distribute
among her affines.*

*Visitors arrive at a
Wanitabe marriage
and greet particular
kinsmen among the
hosts.*

within sections of Wanitabe parish, immigrant lines bear the original parish names of Kume, Takai, Purosa, and so on. The immigrants may have resided with many parishes in past decades, but absorption into a host parish does not cancel former ties; enclave lines enjoy dual rights as long as they continue to visit and maintain an interest in their original parish of residence. The concern to preserve their immigrant origin affords a number of social advantages. In times of war, external bonds provided refuge and possible avenues of communication that could be used to terminate fighting. In present times, men can more readily acquire wives from lines associated as wife-givers (the mother's brothers) to the parish of origin.

The parish acceptance of newcomers solves a major problem facing colonizing populations, the shortage of marriageable women. The arrival of a number of exiles among new settlers delivers a loyal opposition (mother's brothers) with whom the establishment can exchange women, goods, and symbols, and provides frontier groups with a quick sense of political identification. Big Men also welcome the attachment of single individuals or married couples as members of their own line, providing them with food and refuge until they reimburse the debt with produce from their own gardens.

The disadvantage of such ready incorporation falls on the newcomers, whose kinship status depends on demonstrated loyalty and the continuous observance of the behavior expected among kin. When South Fore refer to each other as fathers and sisters, or as mother's brothers and sister's sons, they propose a notion of kinship that differs from our own. Kin titles do not necessarily refer to biological kin. Nevertheless, they are important statements of relatedness. When parish members speak of possessing "one blood," and of deriving from a common ancestor, they convey the idea of the unity of those who reside and act together. It is an expression of common identity, enabling recently merged groups to observe an ordered existence. Although the reference to common substance may not be a statement of genetic accuracy, it defines and regulates the mutual aid and reciprocity expected among certain categories of kin. There is, in addition, the implication that kinship is demonstrated, and that somewhere along a line of progressive commitment, individuals "become" the sisters or mother's brothers the relationship proposes.

Fore sorcery beliefs aid in defining group borders. Neighboring parishes or parish segments periodically accuse each other of invisible acts of aggression, thereby announcing and even redefining their own political identities. The mutual enmity that emerges in the course of sorcery accusations contributes to the consolidation of each of the local communities.

Parish unity, however, is a tenuous affair. Members do in fact come to blows, and newcomers are occasionally made the target of criticism. At Wanitabe, parish sections have in the past accepted bribes from outsiders and joined with them to oust a group of immigrants. Moreover, dissidents can always leave and find sanctuary in parishes elsewhere. The great barricades formerly surrounding settlements seem to have been designed, like the Great Wall of China, as much to keep some residents in as to keep others out.[5] By contrast, Western Highland societies like the Enga appear to have no need of such architectural braces for social unity, and there are no villages. Despite their dispersed residential arrangements, agnatic kinship provides a clear definition of group boundaries.[6]

Parish endogamy is an important feature of the South Fore marriage system, and appears to be increasing. Of 552 marriages contracted by Wanitabe parish members before 1955, 165 or 30 percent appear to be endogamous to the parish, while 31 of 42, or 74 percent, of those which took place after 1955 were intraparish marriages. Although there is some uncertainty about the place of residence at the time of marriage for the earlier period, the finding is in line with reports of increasing endogamy in other Eastern Highland societies.[7] It may be that the absence of warfare and the presence of direct access to cash and consumer goods through the sale of coffee and exported labor leads to different arrangements among property-exchanging groups.[8] Small units have less need of refuge among distant neighbors. Nor need they depend solely on affinal trading partners for goods and ideas. Meanwhile, the inflated brideprice, partly caused by kuru, further diminishes the desire to exchange women at a distance.

Endogamy contributes to the development of local units whose members have multiple connections within the parish. It should be noted that this relatedness is both social and genetic, an observation confirmed by Eastern Highlands genetic surveys.[9]

FORE MODES OF AFFILIATION

The high mobility of South Fore groups might be considered a problem for a society in which economic exchanges and other kinds of social intercourse operate through channels provided by genealogical ties. The repeated separation of kin diminishes their capacity for reciprocal support. In practice, as already noted, Fore do not use biological ties to demonstrate extensive consanguinity. Instead, they expand the classes of people they treat as kin. They accomplish this lateral expansion of affiliates with remarkable ease. They readily permit adoption. They have a means of formally creating kinship between previously unrelated persons, and they elevate to kinlike status other categories of social relations such as agemates, namesakes, trading partners, and friends. By recognizing ties based on intimacy and analogy in addition to those derived from biological reckoning, Fore gain the capacity to establish an immediate community and to transact important social affairs in the face of constantly changing parish composition.

LONG-TERM RESIDENCE   South Fore draw distinctions based on residential stability and mobility. They speak of *tuba gina* or *mago gina,* in contrast to *ambi gina* and *aguya gina.* Mago gina means "ground source people," and like tuba gina conveys the idea of permanent or long-term residence. On the other hand, ambi gina ("those who gather") and aguya gina ("those who have been beaten"), or immigrants and refugees, are similarly qualifications of residence rather than status by descent. Group names do not memorialize founders, but derive instead from topographical features or botanical species associated with a locale. Wanitabe, for instance, means Big Water, and Kume is a kind of tree (*Garcinia*). Although original residents (mago gina) have no more land than immigrants (ambi gina), the distinctions hints at a difference in status. The relationship began when the founders supported the newcomers, a debt the latter repaid when their own gardens were ready to harvest. While affairs between the two groups remain peaceable, no mention is made of the late arrivals' slight disadvantage. If relationships sour, however, the aguya gina may be reminded publicly of their early dependence and told to return to their former parish—an insult rather than a command.

ADOPTION   Fore pay no heed to the distinction we make between real and fictional kinship. The statistical frequency of adoption is therefore difficult to estimate. Adoption is, however, common and easily arranged. With the death of many mothers from kuru, and, in the past, of fathers from war injuries, orphaned children find substitute parents in the father's line. In some cases, too, the husband's line takes legal responsibility for the offspring of a woman who has a liaison with another man, or of a widow who remarries into another parish. Such fostering arrangements are found in many societies.

South Fore have additional avenues of adoption. A newly married couple may offer food to the biological parents of a young child. When the child no longer depends on the mother's nurture, it comes to live with the new parents, who now hold jural rights in the infant. Three such cases of adoption occurred recently in one small hamlet of Wanitabe parish. In all three cases, negotiations took place between classificatory agnates, the adopted child was female, and she was acquired by a newly married couple. This is not adoption to solve the emergencies of abandonment or orphaning, or even of infertility, since it occurs during the first months of a new marriage. The custom may encourage quicker conception by both women involved; relieved of nursing, the biological mother is free to become pregnant again, while the adopting woman may benefit from the hormonal stimulation of mothering. This is of consequence in the New Guinea Highlands, where the onset of menstruation, at eighteen years, is later than in any other population reported to date,[10] and the reproductive span of women is thereby constricted.

Adoptions between small groups of classificatory kin may also be seen as gifts of labor and an exhange of wealth that intensifies the relationship between the adults concerned. It gives them an identity of interest in the survival and development of a single child. In addition, the adopting father enters rapidly into affinal exchange networks, without having to await the birth of his own offspring. In one case, the adopting father made the introductory gift of food to the prospective mother of the child he would adopt when she became pregnant with her third child. This occurred shortly after he had given the brideprice to his affines but before his wife had come to live with him, an interval that among Fore ranges from a few months to a year later. When the infant was born, the adopting father took the birth payment of wild game to the seclusion hut. At the gathering to celebrate the emergence from the hut of mother and child, the adopting father again gave food and $12 in Australian money to the woman's father and brothers, anticipating in return a gift of food. In both payments he was assisted by his own brothers, who thereby propelled themselves vicariously into the business world of the exchange of wealth with affines. In addition to this new relationship with matrikin not directly his own, the adopting father gave a small birth payment to his own wife's brothers, as if the child were the product of his marriage, and promised to send them another portion when his wife eventually gave birth. In 1970, his wife came to live with him, and he awaited the imminent arrival of the adopted daughter. When that came to pass, he would tell the *Kiap* (government administrator) to alter the census records, for with this shift in residence, he said, "I will be the true father."

In another instance, in the late 1950's Wanitabe gave a young boy to their northern neighbors, the Kamano, in exchange for food and lodging for Wanitabe members traveling to the township of Kainantu. Children, like women, bind their donors and recipients in an economic, legal, and affective interchange.

KINSHIP BY CONTRACT

A more frequent manipulation of biological kinship occurs with the creation of *kagisa* (literally, "from the mid-day sun") kin. Here, kinship is created between individuals with no known consanguineal tie by an exchange of wealth and the sharing of a formal meal in the *kagine*, or early afternoon. The sun, a male Cosmic Being, sanctions the newly established bond just as the ingestion of substance, food grown on home territory, transforms fellow residents into close kin.[11] In 1970, I was told that I had earlier become the kagisa mother of a child by giving a chicken to her mother in the birth hut. Should I be present when my kagisa daughter marries, I might expect a portion of her brideprice, the equivalent of the gift returned with interest. On the day she leaves her parents' hamlet to join her husband's kin,

I should again give some clothes, a spoon, or a piece of cloth. Goods and affection would continue to flow between us, strengthening that first filament of social investment.

Kagisa kinship, like Fore kinship in general, centers particularly on brothers and sisters, and on young men and their mother's brothers. These are pragmatic additions to the kinship system, since the former exchange pigs, food and valuables, while the latter relationship provides young men with wives.

South Fore consider some kagisa kin to be more important than biological kin. "Biological" sisters may reside after marriage in a distant parish, or be separated from their brothers by fluctuating hostilities between neighboring parish groups. Many kagisa sisters, on the other hand, are created at the place of residence, where the tie can be strengthened daily. For the brother, it means a reliable source of food and affection, and additional women to help raise his pigs. The sister, in return, receives occasional gifts of beads and clothing, and supervisory male protection, ensuring her against gross physical abuse by her husband.

THE KINSHIP OF COMMON EXPERIENCE

AGEMATES   Agemates refer to each other as *nagaiya*, "my umbilical cord." They may be boys or girls born on the same day or secluded at the same time with their mothers in a birth hut until their umbilical cords wither and fall. (No living twins exist in the South Fore. Women kill one of the pair while in the seclusion hut, a fact widely suspected but not witnessed by men.) The term also applies to co-wives of a polygamist, and more broadly to individuals who share some important common experience, such as initiation at the same time, simultaneous employment as a contract laborer on a coffee plantation, or, for girls, marriage on the same day. It is more difficult for girls other than co-wives to maintain the relationship, since it is less likely they will reside near each other after marriage, and co-wives are rare. In 1970, owing to the acute shortage of women, there were only two pairs of co-wives in the entire South Fore. Yet older men could recall that before kuru depleted them of women, the co-wife relationship was well recognized as an inharmonious situation. Moral stories of family life portray the intermittent antagonism of "two women who share one penis."

Men regard nagaiya as a kind of relative, who along with other categories of kin, receive the death payment of their deceased agemates. Nagaiya precede brothers in claiming widows. If the woman chooses to marry a different man altogether, the new husband should compensate the agemate and not her brothers for the loss.[12] The agemate bond, like other forms of kinship, endures after the death of those who formed the relationship. Children of nagaiya refer to each other as siblings, and so-called cousins often prove to be agemates' children or grandchildren.

Men acquire a number of agemates throughout their lives, but in practical terms, changes in residence usually mean they can fully sustain the relationship with only one or two. While six or seven agemates may reside in one parish at the time of their nose-piercing initiation, in the following years they tend to disperse [Agemates are portrayed ideally as a male pair, two flutes whose secret sound expresses the solidarity and precarious dominance that men exert over women.] Fore stories tell of two nagaiya sharing a house and garden, companions in the forest. They are intimates, confidants, facing life's dangers together. Men express fear of attack by sorcerers when their agemates have died, for they no longer have nagaiya committed to protecting them and avenging their death. One story describes a ghost who appears in battle to direct the path of his agemate's avenging arrow. Another tells of an agemate who lies in his dead friend's grave while a third man hides in a nearby stand of sugarcane. As female cannibals arrive to dismember their friend's body, the "buried" agemate springs to life and rapes the first woman while his companion makes thunderous noises in the sugarcane grove, flaying about with the bone of a wild pig. The women flee, defecating as they run, leaving the first woman to be raped again by the noisemaker. The recurrent themes of agemate homilies are mutual support, and an emotional commitment to the relationship, as this final story shows:

> When Amora and Kume were at war with Yagareba and
> Kamila, one man's wife gave birth to a child. Her husband went
> deep into the forest to hunt game to give to her brothers. In his
> absence, the enemy killed his agemate. That night the age-
> mate's ghost appeared in the bush and joined his companion.
> By the light of the fire the hunter saw that the ghost had plug-
> ged his arrow wound with a ball of leaves, which from time to
> time he removed in order to suck at the blood. Afraid, the man
> asked what had happened, and the ghost replied: "I just heard
> from the others that you were alone in the bush. I felt sorry and
> I came to keep you company. I will sleep with you this night."
> Then the two shared some possums from the hunt and slept.
> Next morning, the ghost said to his friend: "Do you remember
> that once we said if men were to kill me I would come and sit
> with you till morning? Well, they have killed me, and I have
> slept with you. Now you must go back home." The ghost de-
> parted, and his friend returned to the hamlet carrying the re-
> maining animals from the hunt. He walked directly into his
> house and picked up his bow. One end he put in the smoulder-
> ing fire, and the other he placed in his nostril. The flame ran
> along the rope of the bow and into his nose. They later found
> him dead, and they buried the two agemates in a single grave.

This affecting story plays on echoes of initiation, on mutual responsibility, and on the intimacy and intensity of the bond.

Two old agemates resting.

Agemates are in essence "two men of one kind." Their behavior indicates that they regard each other as twins, symbolic equivalents. Something suffered by one affects them both. Two or more agemates thus band together when faced with the threat of female sexuality, observing food taboos in unison when the wife of one menstruates or gives birth to a child. The first to experience marital intercourse confides to the others that something has occurred which has polluted them all. "Oh my nagaiya," he says, "I have done a terrible thing." Together they must purify themselves, and the husband gives them a payment to make amends (in the past shells, but nowadays money), which in time their own behavior will force them to return. The agemates also abstain from eating feminine foods such as green leafy vegetables, as part of the purification campaign to restore their recently undermined self-image. Agemates dramatically support a husband whose wife strikes him so sharply as to draw his blood. They rub themselves with the ashes and mud of mourning, treating the assault as a little death. Then they eat one of the woman's pigs in disciplinary compensation. While status may be encroached upon in private, it must be restored in public. Joined in ritual, nagaiya make authoritative statements about the position of men and women in the social hierarchy.

NAMESAKES To a lesser degree *naukwa*, "my one skin," or namesakes, also share a mutual identity. Parents name a child in honor of a person with whom they wish to establish a relationship, a desire fulfilled if the original name-holder acknowledges the bond with a gift. By calling their son *Yus* one family had established a patron-client relationship with the government magistrate or "Judge" (Yus). When his circuit rounds brought him to Wanitabe, the Judge gave the child gifts of soap and clothing, receiving food in return. A generation of children in the South Fore have names reflecting similar efforts at bridge-building. Their names record the government officers, coastal policemen, anthropologists, and medical research workers who have lived and worked for several decades in the region. As with adoption, the tie benefits those who initiate the link as much as the intermediary in whose name the association is made.

People physically resembling each other are also said to have "one skin," a bond the pair acknowledge and sustain by food exchange. The naukwa relationship may be improvised when Fore travel in unfamiliar terrain. Since it is unacceptable, even shameful, to approach a stranger with a request for food, men traveling some distance from home feign kinship. They may greet an unknown woman by expressing astonishment at her likeness to a favorite sister. Flattered by the attention, the woman rewards the "brother" with a yam or sweet potato, and Fore savor accounts of men who have acquired food in this way. They show a merry appreciation of the style and daring involved. It is a play on kinship: if food creates kinship, kinship can create food.

TRADE PARTNERS, ALLIES AND FRIENDS   *Wagoli* ("base" or "root" men) are war allies and trade partners whose territories in the past were considered places of refuge. Wagoli address each other as "my special friend," or "my father figure," or by 1970, in Melanesian Pidgin as *wantok* ("one talk" or compatriot) When one of the two dies, the survivor, along with the dead man's matrilateral kin and agemates, receives a portion of the death payment. Qualitatively, the relationship most closely resembles that of agemates, in its absence of hierarchy and stress on amicability. Wagoli attend each other's rituals, and on more casual visits carry gifts and receive elaborate hospitality and affection from the host, his wife, and their co-resident kin. Sisters of a host wagoli become kagisa sisters of the visitor, and the host's children his "son" and "daughter." The bond thus becomes an avenue for the distant exchange of food and trade goods.

In a sample of 100 South Fore men, every one named at least one parish away from home that he visits as a wagoli, participating in exchanges of food and goods. One man listed five such parishes, and the average was nearly two. These parishes are potential places of permanent residence. Men take up residence with their wagoli when they are in trouble at home. It is said that if a man kills his brother or injures his father,[13] he lives out his temporary banishment with distant wagoli until the anger of his brothers and agemates subsides, a period of about three years or more.

Although men usually visit parishes that are not currently hostile to their home parish and often speak of interparish and interline relationships in group terms ("Mentilesa men are our wagolis"), every man has an array of affiliations which does not always coincide with that of his co-residents. Sometimes a man visits a parish considered enemy territory by his fellow parishioners and perhaps risky even for the visitor, who will collect a payment due him there but refuse to eat for fear of being poisoned.

Wagoli delegate each other to act as substitutes toward their own distant kin. Thus, the mother's brothers at Amusa nominated a Wanitabe wagoli to act as kagisa mother's brother to a young Wanitabe man. The two Wanitabe men exchange food and services, and the youth may in time marry the daughter of this kagisa kinsman. Like agemates, wagoli may marry each other's widows, and those who take refuge or make extended visits need not return to their home parish, but may in time be absorbed by the host group. As a matter of private reckoning, the immigrants retain an ultimate affiliation with the group of origin, but their children grow up unaware that they have no prior tie with members of the current parish.

THE CENTRIFUGAL NETWORK   Individual Fore, then, are at the core of a centrifugal network of relationships which includes, along with biological kin, wagoli, kagisa kin, agemates, and namesakes. Some of these relationships they inherit from their parents, some they establish or activate as the need arises. While all Fore have such webs of attachment, Big Men have more than others and tend to maintain them longer.

South Fore kinship is thus an ephemeral matter. For a variety of purposes, individuals are defined in and out of categories of relationship. "True" kinship derives from co-residence and from continually reciprocated support. Distant claimants who attempt to press their rights with regard to long-abandoned or long-separated relatives may be rebuffed.

Fore are sensitive to the legal and social niceties of waxing and waning kinship. A Wanitabe man who gave his sister in marriage to an agemate rather than to his patrilateral cross-cousin (his father's sister's son) earned that kinsman's resentment; the latter no longer visits his cousin. Another severed ties with his former parish when he was refused his agemates's widow, while a third, having been refused his mother's brother's daughter in marriage, made public his desire that her brothers (his mother's brothers' sons) be refused their share of his own death pay. That is, he disinherited them.

Levity in the use of kin terminology permits emphasis on certain aspects of a relationship rather than others. The affinal term for sister's husband may be substituted by the more intimate term "friend" or "agemate." Young men sometimes call nearby wagoli "little father" and older sisters "mother." As one Wanitabe man comments: "I sometimes call my father's sister's husband 'father,' but at other times I like to call him 'affine,' which is the term my father used for him." Fore are open and affectionate.

Men frequently walk about arm in arm, and people embrace each other verbally as well. When a woman refers to her elder sister by a term usually reserved for a male's elder brother, there is little confusion about the nature of the relationship. But when two men refer to each other as "my special friend" or "my little kinsman," one cannot infer their genealogical relationship, but only that the tie is one of intense affection.

Inventive bonding and various fictions of identity reflect the improvisatory character of a frontier society. In recognizing ties based on mutual experience as well as biology, on fundamental similarities rather than common origin, Fore extend the network of those from whom support may be expected. Despite the expressed ideology that people act in groups, an individual lives at the center of an array of affiliates. Of all kin relationships, however, the most important is that of brother and sister.

THE PRIORITY OF SIBLINGS   Fore repeatedly comment on the priority of care they afforded sisters before the intervention of a Western judicial system that gave greater protection to wives. Cross-sex siblings stand in contrast to husband and wife, who in the Fore view form a necessary but fundamentally incompatible duo. Fore myths of origin gloss over sex, that antisocial force in evolution, and tell instead of an original female Being from whose pregnant belly exploded males and females, plants and rocks, and all the other things in the world. Some stories portray a pair of more modest founders, who create a population of fellow humans from a bamboo container of leaf greens (symbolically female) cooked with a human bone (symbolically male), or from a shower of cooked red pandanus. Like the origin stories of Christianity, or of the Papuan Marind Anim who posit male parthenogenesis, Fore myths avoid the behavioral conundrum introduced by sexual reproduction. At another level, the myths are messages of transubstantiation; food becomes humanity, the very idea of kinship.

Fore focus their attention on the less problematic brother-sister pair. A Fore man speaks of his sister as the archetypal "good woman." Food from the sister's hand, unlike food from the wife's, carries no threat of contamination. Sisters, unlike wives, represent no confusion between dominance and dependence, between food and sex, between the hand and the vagina.[14] Sisters augment rather than deplete a man's wealth. When the sister marries, has children, and dies, her brother receives payments from her husband and sons. Father's sister, an important sibling of the prior generation, is considered a relative of fundamental value, and the nephew receives a large part of the payment distributed at her death.[15] Mother's brother also takes a proprietary interest in his sister's son, protecting him throughout childhood to initiation, when he is paid for the ritual services that transform the boy from youth to adult. If the youth then marries his mother's brother's daughter, in principle the ideal form of marriage, this sibling tie of a prior generation becomes an affinal one, and the reciprocity between the progeny of siblings will serve as the pivotal point in a continuing system of exchange.

As noted earlier, attention is not limited to biological siblings, who often are separated by marriage and group fission. Some sisters become impacted in enemy groups, "so we tell others to take food from them in our stead." Men therefore direct their energies to the network of kagisa sisters, where gifts, affection, and the mutual exchange of favors occur daily. Yet the facile transformation of neighbors into kin reflects more than the solution to a logistical problem. It is part of a fundamental dispersive principle of Fore social organization. Men accept food from biological siblings and matrilateral cross-cousins, but do not consume the brideprice that is given for them. Similarly, brideprice pigs are given to father's brother and his wife, but not to the bride's father and mother. In addition, men will not eat pigs raised by their own wives, and the rules of cannibalism bar parents from eating their own offspring. Fore believe that violation of these rules is repulsive and may also cause illness. The beliefs thus have the effect of discouraging incest, cannibalism of "self," and the private hoarding of wealth, three kinds of failure to cooperate with others.

KINSHIP AS AN EXTENSION OF SELF

Fore society is laterally oriented, a characteristic reflected in kinship terminology that is heavily weighted toward an individual's contemporary generation. Only five generations are recognized: two above and two below the self. (This contrasts with the Huli of the Southern Highlands, for instance, who recall eighteen generations before the present.) As we move away from Ego's generation, the terminological distinctions decrease. While terms denoting sex and age are used for siblings, and there are special terms for cousins, agemates, and special friends, such particularity diminishes in the ascending generation. Here, one term applies not only to father, but to father's brother, father's sisters' husbands, and mother's sisters' husbands. Another similarly applies to mother, to her sisters, and to father's brothers' wives. Each of these parental figures refers to Ego as "son" or "daughter." As indicated above, only father's sister and mother's brother and his wife are singled out for their special relationship to Ego, which rests on the sibling relationship of the prior generation. For all kin more than one generation removed from Ego, the terminology becomes exceedingly spare. All relatives two generations removed, both consanguineal and affinal, are referred to as "grandfather" or "grandmother," with the reciprocal "my grandchild." Generations further removed are simply lumped together as "my extremities."[16] Since the image of the human body is used to make symbolic statements about the body politic, the Fore use of the term "extremities" (or more precisely "my fingers" and "my toes") to refer to the third ascending or descending generation defines the limit of Fore relationships based on genealogy.

While I cannot translate all kin terms into body parts to construct the total person, some important terms clearly represent symbolically appropriate segments of the human body. Mother is referred to as "my own breast,"[17] while father is "my own bone," the two conveying the complementary distinction between flesh and bone, soft and hard body matter, and the original female and male beings alluded to in the myths of origin. Certain classes of affines—the husbands of sisters or female cousins, and the wives of brothers or male cousins—call one another "my little eye," a clue to their parallel place in family structure and to the similarity of their predicament. Agemates and co-wives underscore their twinlike commonality by referring to each other as "my umbilical cord," while the more incidental attachment of namesakes is conveyed by calling them "my skin." The term for grandfather derives from "the head," but by the grandparental generation, the term loses the double index of possession, "my own" (na prefix, nempa suffix). The absence of this specific denotation again confirms the absence of particular identity and of lineality in the system.

This language of body parts occurs both in kin terminology and in the metaphors of daily speech. Men say of their wives, "They do all the work, they are the hands of men"—the word for wife being a compound of man + hand + my. Men also say, "Our sisters are our mouths," and "Father's sister is the main source." The term for father's sister combines father and mouth. Since the word for mouth also means "egg" and "mountain," this is again a reverberation of the origin myth in which the mountainous belly of the primeval woman spewed forth the topographical features and plant species of the South Fore domain. "My little mouth," a term used by two women related as brother's wife and husband's sister, conveys the life-sustaining quality of this sibling-like tie, since one woman gives breastmilk to the other's child while the new mother is recovering from the labors of childbirth.

Kin terminology, like the idioms of speech, is constructed of graftings on the self. The implicit model is one of parts, appendages, incorporations, and subsitutions. The Fore universe is constructed by lateral connections and attachments to Ego. Affiliations are pinned to an individual core, and power derives from the number of attachments one can maintain by constant exchange. The power of Fore Big Men rests not so much on the capacity to mobilize a predictable number of agnatically related kin, as on the ability to inflate the self by sustaining a personal web of affiliates. A wealthy man is literally "cargo he sees man," the linguistic construction implying not that others see his wealth, but that he himself sees that he has plenty of cargo.

In the mid-1950's, the North Fore met Ronald and Catherine Berndt with the friendly greeting, "I eat you," an apt metaphor of incorporation for the endocannibal, where food equals substance equals kinship. Since the very idea of a social relationship rests on the sharing and exchange of food, ambiguity in social relations leads to the concern that shared or exchanged food may be polluted or poisoned. Hesitation in accepting food in certain locations is a diagnostic clue to the tenor of affairs among kin and allies. The rejection of food is a denial of kinship. Moreover, since ingested food becomes human substance, food leftovers contain some element of the person who consumed the main portion. Sorcerers and other persons of ill-will are believed to steal food scraps, hair clippings, feces and other extensions of the victim to perform their murderous acts. Sorcerers may direct their assault against particular enemies or their personal attachments, their sisters (mouths) and wives (hands). To trim the body's appendages is to sufficiently diminish the stature of the opposition.

The Fore kinship system may be characterized as one that is spread laterally and based on optional bonding. This is kinship by election rather than ascription, and the suffix in many kin terms ("my special friend," "my little eye") conveys qualities of intimacy and affection. Yet bonds of sentiment may quickly fade, particularly under severe stress. Fore ties are a pastiche of biology and fiction, of legality and affect, and close relationships are clouded by ambiguous loyalties. Despite the density of links that unite parish members, a submerged hierarchy exists between first settlers and immigrants, fathers and sons, husbands and wives, young and old, and between lines currently giving and receiving women. As later chapters reveal, cries of pollution and sorcery are directed against individuals suspected of trying to reorder the hierarchy.

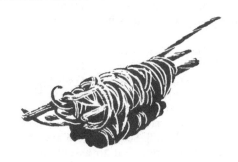

ETIOLOGY AND WORLD VIEW

5

As we saw in the preceding chapter, the South Fore image of the human body, the metaphorical basis for their kinship terminology and their body politic, is one of accretions appended to a core—a structural format of uncertain strength. In South Fore perception, both individuals and groups have porous boundaries. The composition of political groups encourages mutual mistrust at close quarters. Every man has a discrete network of personal affiliates—sisters, mother's brothers, sister's sons, affines, age-mates, namesakes, and wagoli—in other parishes, including parishes that are sometimes on hostile terms with his home parish. The fear of competing loyalties is thus both pervasive and realistic.

Neither the recognition of kinship nor the demands of day-to-day gardening give rise to large-scale political units. Cooperative gardening groups are small (varying between one and seven men, not all of whom have wives, with a mean of four), and the somewhat lonely status rise of individual men depends on the labor of wives and support from the network of affines, kin, and friends they attach to their own interest. This vulnerable assemblage suffers both from the inevitable drift of loyalties and from the illness or death of members of the network, which is attributed to the attack of sorcerers attempting to undermine the social position of particular persons or groups. The Fore concern with sorcery, part of a larger preoccupation with the pathogenesis of disease, conveys a particular world view. Survival and status are endangered by incapacitating illness, crop infestation, insufficient rain, wandering pigs, recalcitrant women, and aggressive men.

Beliefs about the etiology of disease are statements about the nature of existence, explanations of why things happen as they do.

DISEASE CLASSIFICATION

Fore classify illnesses in a systematic way. Within the overall class of illness, there are two significant categories of disease, defined by beliefs about causation. First, there are maladies resulting from the malicious actions of men against men. These diseases are the consequences of acts of sorcery (kio'ena, literally, "it is hidden"). Second, there are diseases attributed not to the machinations of sorcerers, but to assault by various less malign forces—by nature spirits inhabiting spirit places associated with one's parish of residence (in Fore, "that ground hit him"), and by ghosts of the recently dead (in Fore, "beaten by a ghost")—and to punishment for violations of social rules and expectations among co-residents. Calamities ascribed to sorcery involve life-threatening diseases, such as kuru, serious respiratory infections, and liver disorders. They endanger the survival of important members of society, the women who ensure its continuity and the men who protect it. Ailments ascribed to other causes involve minor afflictions and temporary illness among adults, and sickness and death among children.[1]

Spirit-caused ailments result from human intrusion into spirit places or Ples Masalai, the forest reserves associated with every parish. Gardening is permitted at the edge of a spirit place but not within, and certain kinds of timber, vines, animals, and wild foods that may be collected elsewhere should not be touched in one's own Ples Masalai. In some, to speak or even to make a loud noise is considered dangerous. Not all products are absolutely forbidden, however, and limited use is made of these sacred groves. Minor illness in adults, or the birth of a slightly impaired child, indicates the spirit's anger at the removal of a particular item.

Diagnosis is retrospective. A child born deaf or blind is referred to as "spirit child" because the pregnant mother must have touched a certain tree, vine, or other spirit-inhabited object in the forest reserve. Or, a man may wake one morning with a stiff neck, or cut his foot with an axe. Relief is gained by bringing the offended tree a gift of wealth and food. Shells are hung momentarily on the tree's branches, and its trunk is rubbed with pig fat while the victim eats a medicinal meal of pork bespat with Ni (Cyanotis).

Ples Masalai beliefs, then, operate as zoning regulations for the protection of small areas of permanent wilderness. This is of some importance to Fore, who depend on the forest for wild foods, and among whom obligatory exchanges between affines still include game. Moreover, forests act as reserves for the seeds of rainforest species that will regenerate adjacent fallow, and may also serve as barriers against the spread of crop diseases and pests.[2]

The forest is thus shielded from overuse by spiritual sanctions. People with physical impairments are a living reminder of past offenses against this group resource.

Ghost-caused ailments occur if a person removes vegetables, bananas or sugarcane from the gardens of a man recently deceased. To remove the growing plants is to sever the head decorations of the man lying buried in his garden, and if committed during the period of mourning, is an offense. This is the period when death payments should be distributed to the kin and agemates of the deceased, not a time for his property to be plundered. Offenders are said to be punished by the angered ghost. They suffer nausea, weakness, and fainting spells. Similarly, those who have poor relationships with living parents succumb to ghost attack when the parents die.

Ghosts, then, monitor considerate attention toward close kin and the correct modes of property exchange. They also ensure a period of fallow for parish gardens. Curers blow the angered ghost from the victim's body, but an insulted ghost is placated only by the sacrifice of pork and the libation of pig blood poured into the head of the grave.

Infringements of social rules among the living produce the simplest ailments and the most direct remedies. If a man cuts down a tree belonging to another, the offender's son or daughter immediately falls ill. Relief is gained by offering the owner compensatory goods; appeased, the latter provides a reviving meal of pork and medicines for the sick child.

The protected forest of a Ples Masalai surrounded by grasslands resulting from successive gardens on the same site.

These three subcategories of non-sorcery-caused ailments have several things in common. Encroachments against nature spirits, ghosts of the recently dead, or neighbors must all be made good by some kind of indemnity; the spirit and ghost receive symbolic food, the angry person, material payment. The victim is then restored to health. The therapy has a conceptual basis familiar to students of Melanesian societies: the notion of compensation for injury, with its emphasis on equality and a return to the status quo. It recalls indigenous court judgments, where fines are set at amounts equal to estimates of the damage incurred. In addition, the notion of bribery, of persuasiveness accompanied by a gift, resembles the behavior of allies in time of war.

Conditions assigned to neither of the two main categories (sorcery-caused and non-sorcery-caused illness) include deaths from suicide, war fatalities, or extreme old age—where causation is considered self-evident—and mild and temporary conditions such as cold or headache which at some time affect one and all. Dysentery, which caused many deaths in the 1930's and 1940's is similarly not classified as a form of sorcery, since its simultaneous and widespread incidence place it beyond willed, selective malevolence. Thus, all conditions begin as "sickness," but as symptoms persist, increase in severity, and settle upon certain individuals rather than others, the diagnosis is further refined as an attack by spirits, ghosts, or perverted humans. Like its counterpart in the West, Fore medicine is strong on diagnosis and weak on cure.[3]

All the maladies Fore consider significant require a judgment as to cause, which always involves some sort of socially disapproved act, although the ascription of guilt differs for each category. Sorcery results from the deliberate activities of politically hostile outsiders, of enemies in another parish or parish section, who must be exposed by divination or threat. The responsibility for lesser ailments falls within the parish section, the minimal political unit, where the offense is patent and does not require detection. These minor illnesses derive from some wrongdoing by the victim or close kinsperson, and involve the relationship of a person to his or her group's land, to people who have until recently been members of the group, or to present residents. Sorcery allegations thus appear to be statements about political relations with other groups, whereas interpretations of other ailments refer to personal relations, rules of behavior, property rights, and common responsibilities within the group itself. These involve issues common to legal systems everywhere: the proper definition of murder, manslaughter, negligence, and accident.

Fore analyses of the origins of disease can be viewed as assertions about the structure of their society, the dangers to which its composite units are exposed, and the measures that can be taken to protect those units. Lesser dangers originate within the community, greater dangers without.[4] Many sorcery accusations occur between men residing in different parishes.

The accusers' choice of target indicates the state of mutual trust between allies and neighbors. An accusation made within parish borders often signals incipient political fission. Within a parish section, the smallest political unit, it heralds the exclusion of a fellow resident. Normally, members of a parish section are concerned to expand rather than diminish membership, and sorcery allegations within a parish section are rare.

The preceding analysis conveys a masculine view of law and politics. Yet the slippery male universe includes some women who are also difficult to control. The men's conception of sorcery performed by women reveals the nature of the problem. Men believe that female menstrual blood is a potent sorcery item. An angry woman may use it intentionally (see Table 1 below, No. 11) or she may be an unwitting intermediary (No. 12). Female sorcery differs from male sorcery in that it is not amenable to the usual controls. Berndt makes a similar observation about Tugezajana, a form of sorcery used in the region around the North Fore that women reserve for thieves who steal food from their gardens. As with South Fore women, the sorcerous act takes place in the seclusion hut, and uses the menstrual discharge of an enraged female. Bribery and intimidation, the means by which men coerce men, will not dissuade a woman bent on sorcery. The "appeal is made to her as a woman, and there is no other way in which her hand can be forced. Threatening to kill her or work sorcery in return would only increase her anger without freeing the victim."[5] The South Fore sorceress, outside the world of male politics, is also subject to a different set of rules. She is believed to reverse the victim's condition only if she sees and pities him. South Fore men conceive of differences between the sexes in innate capacities and emotional make-up. In their views of female sorcery, South Fore men tacitly acknowledge their inability to manipulate an important biosocial area. This will be discussed further in Chapter 10.

AN INVENTORY OF SORCERY AND DISEASE

The Fore view of disease has its own logic. This is not to say that the inventory of disease states in Table 1 is invariable. Different researchers have elicited varying data from the Fore, which reflect both the personal idiosyncracies of the informants and changing epidemiological and existential concerns over two decades. With the exception of kuru and perhaps leprosy and yaws (all highly visible and distinctive conditions), forms of sorcery do not exactly coincide with the diagnostic categories of Western medicine, as Table 1 illustrates.

DISEASE CAUSATION

Theories of life and death take on great urgency when particular people fall ill. A sample of 473 deaths recorded in the genealogies of Wanitabe parish

TABLE 1
An Inventory of Sorcery and Disease

---

1. YANDA

Symptoms   Loss of flesh. Skin hangs loose on the body. Men must hold the victim down to administer medicine. As death nears, the victim pants for breath and blood flows from nose and mouth. The cause of death was sometimes determined by autopsy, but not since the government outlawed cannibalism.

Sorcery Method   The sorcerer cuts a small length of bamboo, splitting one side to form a flap. He inserts poison and waits by a path. Some sorcerers also add red bird-of-paradise feathers. The victim passes, and the sorcerer pulls the bamboo flap to eject the poison, calling the victim's name. The victim faints.

Suggested Western Diagnosis   Meningitis, hemorrhagic disorder, liver disease.[6]

2. TOKABU

Symptoms   Victim collapses. Inability to eat or talk, or make any noise more than rasping. By the third day, the victim's jaw locks, and his mother, wife, and children begin to mourn him. By the fourth day, alerted to his condition, his friends and distant kin arrive, and by the fifth day he dies.

Sorcery Method   Several attackers creep up on the victim and bite his neck, severing the trachea so he is unable to talk again before death. Wire-like slivers are inserted into his body, starting above the elbow and traveling from there internally to the liver. More slivers are inserted into the thigh, whence they go to the lower internal organs. Slivers finally are inserted in the neck. The attackers retreat and the victim staggers home. In vain, members of his line kill a pig and rub pig grease into his skin. Autopsy reveals holes filled with blood made by the slivers, as well as neck damage.

   Tokabu is a traditional form of vengeance killing, only recently adopted as a retribution for kuru deaths. Men should never travel in the forest alone since companions can frighten off a tokabu killer.[7]

Suggested Western Diagnosis   Tetanus, stroke, viral infection. The cry of "Tokabu!" is frequently heard also from Fore women as lone men creep up on them in their gardens. Tokabu, then, encompasses rape as well as murder and sudden, incapacitating medical conditions.

3. IMUSA

Symptoms   Arms, legs, and body swell. Arms become tight like sticks and cannot bend. Flesh rots quickly. Symptoms are so clear there is no need for autopsy. Liquid bubbles from the mouth after death.

Sorcery Method The sorcerer bundles poison with food scraps and excrement from the victim, along with some sorcerer's stone and sharpened cane slivers, in a tree base and lights it. The poison bundle sings as it burns, causing the victim to cry out in pain. As the tree falls, the victim feels the full force of Imusa.

Until the victim dies, the sorcerer's kin abstain from water, sugarcane, pork, green leafy vegetables, and sexual intercourse. They do not broadcast their success, but quietly kill and eat pigs and resume eating the tabooed foods which are classified as "cooling" and considered an antidote to the "heat" of sorcery. Fore say sorcerers have abandoned Imusa sorcery in favor of kuru.[8]

Suggested Western Diagnosis Liver or kidney disease, heart failure.

4. KAI

Symptoms Similar to Yanda, which it is said to have replaced. With no warning symptoms other than head and body pain, victim collapses without being able to talk to his kin. Victim can be healthy in morning and dead by afternoon, and is often working in hot sunlight when struck down. Arms, legs, and body swell up. Blood runs from nose and mouth.

Sorcery Method Kai is a new form of sorcery. Fore sorcerers are said to have acquired it from the Kamano and Auyana. From North Fore at Okapa and Ofafina, it was transmitted in subsequent purchases to South Fore at Wanitabe. Some South Fore are said to have purchased it from the Gimi.

Suggested Western Diagnosis Cardiac arrhythmia, coronary attack, stroke.

5. KURU

Symptoms Headache, arm and leg pain. Walking becomes unstable, movements uncoordinated. Some double vision. Final immobility, derangement, refusal to eat food. Death within a period of three months to about two and a half years. Body of most kuru victims is full of grease, as with pigs.

Sorcery Method The sorcerer steals food remnants, hair, nail clippings, or excrement from the victim. He makes a bundle with leaves and some sorcerer's stone, places the bundle in muddy ground, and names the victim. As the bundle rots, the victim exhibits symptoms. As with Imusa, the sorcerer's kin abstain from the ingestion of "cooling" foods until the act of sorcery is effected.

Suggested Western Diagnosis Kuru, a slow virus infection.

6. KARENA

Symptoms Stomach is on fire, skin hot, rapid breathing, fever. After the initial illness, victim is more vulnerable to subsequent respiratory illnesses, one of which kills him. Autopsy reveals that enlarged, blackened lungs have risen from the chest to the neck, causing death by choking.

Sorcery Method   The sorcerer cooks medicinal bark with a sorcery stone in a small length of bamboo, and slips this through a fence into his enemy's garden. The victim uses the bamboo to smoke his own tobacco and inhales the poison. Some sorcerers poison the victim's drinking water or sweet potato with the same ingredients.

Suggested Western Diagnosis   Chronic lung disease, including emphysema, tuberculosis.

7. KESENA

Symptoms   Leg pains, swelling, large sores. Some victims die.

Sorcery Method   The sorcerer hides a dry stick with the latex of a fig tree in the middle of a foot path. As the victim passes, the poison shoots into his leg.

Suggested Western Diagnosis   Osteomyelitis, pyogenic arthritis.

8. NANKILI

Symptoms   Severe, sharp chest pains.

Sorcery Method   The sorcerer sharpens the bones of a pig, cassowary, or possum and folds them into leaves. He smokes a pipe and calls the name of the victim. He blows the smoke across the bone needles, which fly into the victim's body. Speciality of the Porakina (the Awa and Fore at Ilesa and Awarosa). The curer sucks out slivers or blows them out with smoke, exhaled across the patient's body.

Suggested Western Diagnosis   Pleurisy.

9. AMEBALAGA KIO

Symptoms   Victim's mouth and nose become covered with sores. He loses his voice. Some victims die.

Sorcery Method   The sorcerer takes a short bamboo and places poison in the hollow with some of the victim's hair, some cold spittle, and red earth. He adds latex of the "Wandami" tree and places the bamboo by a fire to heat and dry.

Suggested Western Diagnosis   Yaws.

10. AGAI'INKINA

Symptoms   Inability to defecate, body swells, the victim dies. Women and "rubbish men" (men of low status) do not suffer from this complaint, only "good" men (men of social worth).

Sorcery Method The sorcerer places poison in a growing banana tree. The victim climbs the tree to cut the fruit, and the poison enters his anus. This form of sorcery came to the South Fore via Kamata and Kamila, originally from the Gimi. A form of sorcery older than kuru.

Suggested Western Diagnosis Bowel obstruction.

11. AGAI-IKIO
(variant of No. 10)

Symptoms The man's belly swells, his neck becomes thin and narrow, eyes sink back, the nose, forehead, and mouth project forward, head shrinks. Victim's head resembles that of a dog. He sleeps close to the fire, becomes dirty with ashes.

Sorcery Method As above.

Suggested Western Diagnosis Bowel obstruction, liver disease?, abdominal cancer.

12. YENTAGIO

Symptoms The victim's stomach swells enormously. Condition affects both men and women, and can cause death.

Sorcery Methods The sorcerer places poison in the women's seclusion hut, thus the name "seclusion hut sorcery." Women are unaware of the poison, and return from the hut after menstruation is over. When intercourse subsequently occurs, the poison passes to the husband.

Suggested Western Diagnosis Liver or kidney disease.

13. KIO'ENA

Symptoms Loss of flesh, fingers wither to the bone, skin loosens. Stomach sinks back to the spine. Men, women and children used to suffer from this in the past.

Sorcery Methods Kio'ena is the generic word for sorcery, and there is some confusion about this type. The sorcerer's behavior resembles that of the Imusa sorcerer. Kio'ena, like Imusa (no. 3), is said to be no longer practiced. Its symptoms differ slightly from those of Imusa.

Suggested Western Diagnosis ?

14. YAKU'KIONEI (KALU'YENA)

Symptoms Skin blotches in white patches. Fingers and toes fall off.

Sorcery Methods Called Yaku'Kionei in North Fore, and Kalu'yena in the South. The supposed cause also differs somewhat in the two regions. In the

North, it is clearly a form of sorcery. The sorcerer places a poison bundle in stones near a fire, beating them while uttering an incantation. In the South, the disease bridges two categories. It is said to be both a kind of sorcery (caused by human opponents), and a disease that results from breaking a taboo by taking from a spirit place the plants *Yeigi* or *Tabuwa* (both have white markings).

Suggested Western Diagnosis   Leprosy.

15. AIYA'KIO (YABA'ILYA'ATAI)

Symptoms   Belly swells, fills with fluid.

Sorcery Methods   This is a new form of sorcery from the Gimi. The sorcerer wraps poison in a leaf bundle and waits for the victim to lift his pipe to his mouth. He unwraps the bundle, and the poison flies into the victim's mouth and eyes. The sorcerer closes the wrapping. Sometimes the poison is transmitted in a handshake.

Suggested Western Diagnosis   Liver or kidney disease.[9]

16. KANINE

Symptoms   Neck swells, victims are short of breath. Epidemic. Death in three days for the entire community, including pigs and dogs.

Sorcery Method   The sorcerer combines kanine (poison from a spirit place) with rats and flies in a bamboo tube through which water flows. The sorcerer inserts this into the water supply, poisoning the entire community. No medicine will counteract the illness, and the only solution is to leave the area. Spirit places that harbor the poison are in hot lowlands at Ilesa. Men of Atigina know the technique, but fear being struck by illness if they enter the spirit place to obtain kanine. So potent is the poison that, in order to avert illness, one should not swallow saliva while speaking of it.

Suggested Western Diagnosis   Possibly viral myocarditis (infection of the heart muscle).

---

shows (see Table 2) that between about 1900 and 1962, Fore attributed more than half of all deaths, 52.7 percent, to sorcery. That is, more than four times as many deaths are assigned to sorcery as to war injury, and only 3.4 percent to old age. Of the deaths attributed to sorcery, kuru accounts for 59 percent, with over eight times more females than males falling victim to the disease.

TABLE 2
Reported Causes of Death in Sample
Wanitabe Genealogies, c. 1900-1962

Cause	Males	Females	Total	Percent
Kuru	16	131	147	31.1
Other sorceries*	66	36	102	21.6
Unknown	41	34	75	15.9
War injuries	42	13	55	11.6
Undiagnosed sickness	16	18	34	7.2
Dysentery	13	14	27	5.7
Old age	9	7	16	3.4
Burns**	6	1	7	1.5
Influenza	2	2	4	.8
Infant malnutrition**	3	1	4	.8
Suicide	—	2	2	.4
Totals	214	259	473	100.0

*Includes predominantly tokabu (No. 2 in Table 1), 5.1%; karena (No. 6), 4.9%; yanda (No. 1) 3.8%; leprosy (No. 14) 7.2%; and yaws (No. 9), .6%.

**Fewer infant females than males are reported to have died of burns and malnutrition. Perhaps the loss of females to kuru led to more protective care of baby girls. It may also be that more infant females died than are recorded in genealogies.

A kuru sorcerer is said to steal some physical particle intimately associated with the victim, such as food scraps, fragments of clothing, hair clippings, or excrement. To this he adds pieces of bark, certain leaves, and a power-imbued karena (sorcery) stone, and binds them in a package with vines and canes. Beating the bundle with a stick, he calls the victim's name and recites a spell: "I break the bones of your arms, I break the bones of your hands, I break the bones of your legs, and finally I make you die."[10] He then places the bundle in muddy ground, and as the bundle rots, the victim's health deteriorates.

The symbolism of the kuru sorcerer's act may be understood on several levels. As a clinical description of the disease, it reflects the victim's progressive motor incoordination, while the location of the bundle in cold, muddy ground suggests the deep chill felt by immobilized kuru patients, who must be covered with blankets even in the hot sun. The rare cases of a (temporary) remission are attributed to the removal of the kuru bundle

Kuru sorcery bundle.

before it disintegrates. The sorcerer has relented, or the victim's kin have discovered the bundle in time.

At another level, the act is an apt description of the peculiar dangers of South Fore social life. Most accusations occur between men residing in different parishes who have a history of rivalry or abrasive encounter. Sorcerers and their victims thus have had some kind of social relationship, and the hostile actor has had an opportunity to steal the particle he needs. Given the presence in all South Fore parishes of recent settlers with personal networks of outside affiliations, it is sometimes suspected that the sorcerer has been assisted by a disloyal insider. Although I heard no direct accusation against a fellow section member, the victim's kin do make general speeches asking those within earshot to retrieve the bundle and relieve the patient of her distress. Late one afternoon an excited man of Yagareba section of Wanitabe parish stood outside his house and unburdened his thoughts:

> I came here as a boy from the North Fore. I remained here and
> grew up to lead you in battle after battle. Now my wife has
> kuru. If someone here has caused it, let him remove the poison
> bundle so that she can recover. My legs pain from the distance
> I have walked searching for cures. During her lifetime, she was

a woman who looked after the needs of many visitors to our
group. She saw that they had food and firewood. Now she has
kuru. If she dies, there will only be rubbish people left here.

This speech, audible only to a small number of hamlet members,
points to the ultimate insecurity of the immigrant. Although the speaker is
a section Big Man, his lack of assurance surfaces in his assumption that the
guilty are within hearing. Delivered to his parish section, the minimal unit
of cooperation, his speech is a plea rather than a threat. It emphasizes the
bonds that should emerge from the services fellow residents perform for one
another.

Having acquired the personal item he needs, the sorcerer collects the
remaining materials from the forest in his own parish, materials deriving
their power from associations with the wild and the spirits (in contrast to
the domestic world of humans and gardens). He then carries out the rest of
his attack by remote control from his own parish ground, confirming a
prediction by Mary Douglas that "an analysis of the symbols of attack
would reveal a close correspondence between the experience of the social
system and the kind of attack most feared."[11] The composition of the kuru
bundle, containing items from both inside and outside the smallest political
unit, accurately reflects the ambiguity Fore experience in their social relationships.

Similar comments can be made about other types of Fore sorcery.
Karena sorcery, for instance (No. 6 in Table 1), causes a variety of respiratory
disorders such as tuberculosis, emphysema, and other debilitating lung
conditions, particularly among the aged. In this case, the sorcerer places
crushed sorcerer's stone in a length of bamboo tube that resembles a man's
pipe. The victim, working in his garden and feeling a desire to smoke,
notices the bamboo tube. He inserts his tobacco in it, and as he inhales, the
poison passes into his body. Karena, which in Fore also means father-in-law
and more loosely "old man," is an appropriate name, since respiratory illness has a reported incidence of 56 percent in New Guinea subjects over age
sixty.[12] Again the sorcery requires proximity between sorcerer and victim.
The theory also implies that smoking may be hazardous to one's lungs.

DISEASE PREVENTION

Men and women attempt to deprive the sorcerer of the materials he needs,
and much day-to-day behavior involves the hiding of hair clippings, nail
parings, feces and food scraps. Fore welcomed the government suggestion
that native populations use toilets, and in the 1950's some of them accompanied a missionary on a journey among the neighboring Awa to teach them
how to construct deep pit latrines. Women, of course, are greatly concerned
with protection against kuru, and when moving from an old house to a new

one, they take pains not to overlook fragments of old clothing. They also scrupulously hide menstrual blood, the emissions from childbirth, and the infant's umbilical cord, in response to the high incidence of postpartum kuru. In 1970, a party of young men leaving Wanitabe for employment in the coastal town of Lae burned their old discarded garments, behavior reflecting the recent increase in kuru incidence among young adult males.

As noted in Chapter 4, the image of the human body is used to make symbolic statements about the body politic. Douglas hás commented that when rituals express anxiety about body orifices, the social counterpart is the group's concern to protect its political and cultural identity. Body parings, body margins, and the matter issuing from them—blood, spittle, feces—are invested with power and danger. Not all societies, however, attribute power and danger to the same body refuse. While Fore males fear menstrual pollution, Kuma males (of the Central Highlands) do not. These contrasting attitudes toward the dangers of female contamination reflect differences in sociopolitical relations between men and women in the Central and Eastern Highlands. Kuma females strive to assert their independence after marriage, protest their lot, and are said to be "ineffectively conditioned to put up with a most unequal social position."[13] In still another variation, when we find societies in which men are believed to pollute women, we should be alert to indications of a more symmetrical political order. This occurs among the matrilineal Wogeo, who inhabit an island thirty miles off the north coast of New Guinea.[14] And although Fore men express anxiety that others might capture their body refuse, they applauded a visiting Chuave's description of how in the 1930's his father stole and ate the hair clippings of Patrol Officer Taylor. In their attitudes toward sorcery and pollution, therefore, Fore are saying that their women are imperfectly subdued, that they fear the aggressive acts of neighbors, and that while their own margins are in danger, the margins of rulers emit positive power.

While protecting the body's boundaries, Fore also police the borders of their social groups. In 1963, following the death from kuru of seven members of one Wanitabe section and six members of another (the sections each had approximately 170 members), these previously friendly neighboring parish sections closed their territories to outsiders, and especially to each other, a situation aptly described as "social quarantine."[15] They attributed their catastrophic losses to unavoidable social intermingling during the government census of August 1962 and to unguarded meetings in our anthropological fieldhouse between 1961 and 1963. The decline in the incidence of the disease by 1970 was consequently attributed to the vigilant defense of their social borders. By 1970 also a number of Wanitabe parishioners had moved south to settle with affiliates at Abomotasa, having sold their land to the government in 1969 for a planned cattle station. For the migrants, the land sale was a happy resolution of the intensifying conflict between these two neighboring Wanitabe parish sections. In the 1950's, when their groups were small and relations peaceful, the two sections exchanged wives and shared a hazy belief that they were related as the progeny of two brothers. By 1962, with a combined membership of 352 persons, their parish was one of only three with over 350 members. Following the split in 1969, no further marriages occurred between the two segments, who now saw themselves as independent entities. These events will be discussed in more detail in Chapter 9.

When the incidence of kuru increases, political animosities rise and Fore intensify their watch over vulnerable points of entry and exit in both body and polity. In wartime, threats to parish survival impelled warriors to guard territorial borders with bow and arrow, while the political watchmen drew upon all body orifices to protect group life. Certain members were consulted for oracular signs to be used to plan the day's strategy for defense or attack. They consulted the man who yawned, to see if he had yawned or not, the answer determining which of two tactical options they should take. They consulted a man who belched, one who urinated, one who broke wind, one who defecated, and one who itched under the armpit. From this wartime draft of all the armaments of the body, they could judge when to expect or carry out guerrilla activities along their exposed parish borders. Similarity in the symbolism of military defense and the strategies of sorcery is not accidental. Sorcery is a kind of hidden warfare, perhaps used more when government outlaws retaliation by formal combat.

The etiquette of eating also reflects concern for personal or group survival. Men reject food from a wife whose fidelity is in question, especially food given after dark, when contaminating menstrual discharge can pass undetected. Others pay particular attention to food while visiting certain, not all, parishes. Like the vigilance devoted to parish boundaries, niceties of human ingestion convey political sentiment, epidemiological awareness, and a belief in preventive medicine.

CURES

Despite precautionary measures, kuru sorcerers still strike. South Fore resort to various cures, an essential element of which is discovering the sorcerer's identity. The commonest divination technique uses the possum as a vehicle for supernatural revelation. The victim's husband, her brothers, and her husband's agemates and male co-residents place some of her hair clippings in one small bamboo tube. In another bamboo tube they insert the body of a freshly killed possum. Striking one bamboo against the other, they call the name of the supposed sorcerer and place the bamboo containing meat in the fire. The guilt of the accused is established if the possum's liver, the locus of its consciousness, remains uncooked.

Possums are inhabitants of the powerful spirit world of the forest, which the Fore view as an area of undomesticated energy. They are suitable messengers for the revelation of natural truths. Believed capable of transformation into human shape, they provide metaphorical clues about the human condition. Independent of humans, the oracular possum is morally neutral, unlike the pig, a product of human management whose flesh and fat provide therapeutic material. By reversing the expected order of things, the possum's uncooked liver indicates that all is not well. The diviners have visible proof of the commission of an unnatural act.

The contrast with Enga divination procedures is instructive. Fore practice swidden, or slash-and-burn, agriculture, but with a higher level of technical competence in land management than one associates with classic swidden systems. The soil is lightly tilled and worked into small mounds, and small work parties cooperate in the establishment of new gardens. In short, Fore horticultural techniques lead to the creation of a partially tamed ecosystem. At the same time, they make extensive use of wild fallow — and rely on the undomesticated possum as an environmental mediator. Enga, on the other hand, have been forced by the shortage of arable land in the Western Highlands to substitute skills for land, and they have created a tame ecosystem. Even the fallow cover they sometimes employ is controlled by direct Casuarina planting.[16] Enga appropriately consult human mediums to placate the agnatic ghost deemed responsible for illness. Enga ghosts are appeased when (thoroughly domesticated) pig meat is distributed to the maternal and agnatic kin.[17] The ghosts are believed to participate in the essence of the pig during its distribution.

After possum divination, then, the South Fore do not openly accuse a specific person of sorcery (for the uncertain identity of friends and enemies is an underlying issue). Instead, the victim's group may subject the suspected aggressor to a further test. In a gesture of apparent goodwill, they invite him and his co-residents to share a meal. If on their return home one of the visiting party falls ill, the sorcerer is unmasked, identified by the victim's ghost. A similar trial occurs prior to the victim's burial or cannibal consumption. Visitors invited to attend the ceremony approach and touch the corpse, which may suddenly discharge fluid; the ghost again is believed to have forced an involuntary disclosure of guilt.

The form of the divination trials has several interesting implications. The procedure parallels the ascribed method of sorcery: tests require some intimate fragment associated with the victim, yet can be performed at a distance. Men of the victim's residential group act as a Subversive Activities Committee, investigating political foes in another parish. The victim's ghost attacks the sorcerer with a reversal of power, issuing from the body's orifices.

The group undergoing the sorcery trial may or may not be aware that they harbor a sorcerer in their midst. Just as social groups include men of disloyal intent, a local sorcerer may carry out a private attack, revealing his activities to just a small number of intimates. This in-group cooperates with the sorcerer, refraining from incorporating into their own bodies any sub-stance that might counteract his powers. They do not bathe or take by mouth such "cooling" foods as pig fat, sugarcane, or water until they hear of the death or illness of someone in the enemy group. The "hot" work of the sorcerer is thereby reinforced by the self-restraint of his social intimates.[18] To avoid involuntary disclosure, members of a parish section called to undergo divination enquiries perform a ritual before leaving their home territory. As the men huddle in a group, one man runs around the perimeter, spitting premasticated wild ginger, a pungent forest product. Thus the parish section draws on the protection of ritual and medicinal encirclement. A divination trial allows both groups—the victim's and the suspect's—to determine the strength of their support. Divination trials are sometimes held in two or three parishes until adequate alliances form and the official judgment is pronounced.

The victim's kin also consult curers. Curers always reside in distant parishes, and in many cases belong to non-Fore groups such as Kukukuku, Keiagana, and Gimi. They are not members of the most suspect groups, neighboring parishes. Known as "dream men," they derive their powers from dreams and trance states produced by the rapid aspiration of tobacco smoke, and from the hallucinations caused by the ingestion of psychotropic plants.[19] Dreams, trances, and hallucinations provide knowledge inaccessi-ble to the ordered regions of the mind. The curer's powers circumvent mun-dane spatial and temporal restrictions. He can identify the sorcerer even though he is alien to the curer's social milieu. Foreign curers are assumed to be more powerful than those at home, for they generate forces that are effective over a greater social distance. As chapter 10 indicates, curers often belong to less sophisticated groups, and are thus seen as tapping the in-herent potency of a more "natural" way of life.

Curers' techniques, like those of sorcerers, vary in detail. In addition to providing the names or descriptions of suspects, curers dispense medici-nal aid. They supervise a meal of pork that they bespit with ginger and dream-revealed forest barks. They puncture the patient's skin with arrows shot from a miniature bow, concentrating on the heavy limbs and the ach-ing head, where kuru symptoms are most distressing. Aimed at revoking the sorcerer's acts, the curers' powers work by inversion and reversal. The curer transmits some of his internal goodness, treating both interior and exterior of the victim's body.

In summary, the complex behavior associated with sorcery and sor-cery accusations constitutes a political institution peculiarly suited to the organizational problems of South Fore society. A social system that encour-ages the continual improvising of individual and group relations also fosters mutual mistrust among men living at close quarters. Lacking the comfort of genealogical unity and prey to a catastrophic illness, South Fore believe that sorcery is endemic among them. Sorcery is a constant subject of discussion.

Political debates are conducted in a medical idiom. Illness, like warfare, endangers the viability of groups of doubtful cohesion. The kuru epidemic gives rise to realistic fears for survival, and the use of body imagery in sorcery beliefs accurately depicts the dangers to which Fore feel themselves exposed. Even during normal times, care should be taken to keep bodily emissions from falling into the hands of those with whom social relations are ambiguous. When several members of a small unit die, its integrity is threatened, and personal and group relations should be more closely regulated. Curers and watchmen protect and treat passages to the body and to the group. A leading social concern becomes the definition of loyal alliances among the living. Severe misfortune is interpreted as an attack by political rivals whose identity must be determined. Fore views about disease, then, both reflect and comment upon their social relations. As we shall now see, their views are appropriate also to a population on the periphery of Highland settlement.

IDEOLOGY IN PERIPHERAL REGIONS

Fore both explain events and regulate activities by ideas of invisible forces that have both tangible and intangible aspects. As we have seen, Ples Masalai are protected by the idea of spirit-caused illness, which acts as a mystical barrier against deforestation. Similarly, respect for the illness-causing ghosts of deceased kin ensures a period of garden fallow, and also gives legal title to particular tracts of land. The idea of punitive ghosts is also conducive to considerate attention toward the living. In addition, mature men are in competition for women, who are in short supply as a result of kuru. Sorcery is an expression of competitive struggle, which culminates in the necessary dispersal of reluctant colonists. As will be described in Chapter 10, Fore also draw upon two concepts of pollution to regulate the social order. The new skills of Westernized youths are said to cause illness among pigs, while the audacious behavior of women depletes the health of men. Both notions of chastisement provide more or less orderly agreement among the older men, the traditional power-holders, about the distribution of authority and the allocation of resources. This is an oblique approach to social control. Power is clouded in a melange of heterogeneous elements. Messages are implicit and many-layered. Little power is directly available to the establishment.

The Fore etiology of disease emphasizes malign human agents and disturbed social relations. It is a message with a heavy moral load, although human responsibility for illness is shared with spirits and natural forces. The world view implicit in this etiology falls midway between that of the Gnau, on the one hand, and the Enga, on the other. The Gnau, a small society in the Sepik Hills in northwestern New Guinea where organized hunting is still important, lack Big Men and specialized medicine healers.

Gnau interpretations of illness do not dwell on conflict between men, but point appropriately to spirit agents whose intentions or purposes are understood but vaguely, and therefore are free of responsibility or blame. Enga, as noted earlier, depend on cultivated rather than wild resources. They have a pragmatic disdain for the uncertain outcome of sorcery investigations preferring to ensure revenge by cutting down the enemy with axes. Disease and death are attributed to the anger of agnatic ghosts, who may be placated by controlled and orderly rituals.

Fore can be placed midway between these two. As noted earlier, they practice modified swidden agriculture and maintain a partially tamed ecosystem. Their skills exceed those of the Gnau, but unlike the Enga they have not substituted skills for land, which remains available to them on the southern boundary of their region. Thus, their horticultural system remains extensive, requiring the constant relocation of fields and a relatively mobile population.

Fore medical theory proposes a universe similarly subject to imperfect masculine constraint. Sorcerers, curers, and Big Men of moderate stature populate the landscape. Jousting for position, uncertain of the outcome, their attention since the advent of kuru and Western contact has shifted from protection of the environment to coercion of humans, which requires the invoking of invisible energies and the heavy hand of moral opinion.

In social systems like that of the Enga, greater control is exercised over the environment, and social power is more directly available. Enga use unambiguous methods for settling disputes (except, significantly, for Fringe Enga, where sorcerers are said to be present).[21] The Central Enga religious system has greater clarity than the Fore, and is less encumbered by regulatory functions. The locus of power and the means by which it is protected are more predictable and apparent. Among Fore and Enga, then, as among the Gnau, there is a fit between environmental and cognitive experience. The diverse beliefs of these three societies illustrate the effect of different ecological contexts on modes of religious thought.

IDEOLOGY IN TRANSITION

6

The Fore view of the universe presented in Chapter 5 applies to a particular point in time and place—the South Fore in the 1960's. That analysis, however, gave little inkling of the rapid and momentous changes that have recently transformed a way of life and the Fore interpretation of how it should be lived.

One clue to the social upheaval is the lengthening Fore catalogue of sorcery methods since 1951. The Berndts' stay in North Fore between 1951 and 1953 produced a list of seven types.[1] In 1957, when Charles Julius visited the South Fore, an area that had only recently come under Australian government surveillance, he noted no more than six kinds, many fewer than the twenty he had recorded for the sophisticated and wealthy Tolai of the Gazelle Peninsula of New Britain.[2] My own records from the South Fore in the following decade show sixteen kinds of sorcery. This increase cannot, I think, be attributed to differences in fieldworkers, but represents a real shift in experience and belief. Fore are themselves aware of the trend. Many discussions of kuru elicit the same historical sequence. "Kuru is a recent form of sorcery," people say. "In the past we had only a few ways to exact vengeance. First there was tokabu, then fighting with arrows, then yanda, then karena, and after that kuru." Sometimes a further detail is added, such as "Kai is more recent again. This began after the arrival of white men."

Fore attitudes toward ailments not caused by sorcery are also changing. Ghosts of the dead and the spirits inhabiting Ples Masalai were considered more lethal in the past, when the dead were buried in old gardens and their ghosts hovered for a time at the grave site before gathering finally at

Namougoi, the great spirit place for the Atigina region. Many regenerating gardens were thereby assured a period of fallow while the kin of the deceased labored to accumulate death payments due his mother's kin, age-mates, and others. Beginning with deaths of the last generation (around 1950), the deceased members of a line were in many cases buried in one location, with the common burial ground marked by a casuarina tree plantation. A few bodies were interred in their gardens, but with the dangers from departed ghosts having diminished, some gardens continued in cultivation.

Ples Masalai, too, have become less intimidating. Fore say that since medicines introduced by whites appear effective against some masalai-caused ailments, they have fewer reservations about cutting timber from restricted grounds. Moreover, Ples Masalai formerly were inhabited by spirits in human form. Nokoti, or one of his several manifestations, lived with his wife Igo'enabi in the middle of the forest. It was believed that he stole food from men, women, and children to use in his deadly poison bundles. Like other kinds of sorcery, Nokoti Kionei (sorcery caused by Nokoti) could be counteracted only if a curer or Smoke Man located the poison bundle where it was buried in muddy ground. This the curer did by swirling a fern frond in the air until one piece flew off and lodged on top of the hidden bundle. He then removed and untied the bundle, and completed his cure by rubbing the victim with reviving pig grease.

Some elderly men remember meeting Nokoti while cutting vines in the forest. They conversed with him, thinking he was just an old man from a neighboring parish. On returning home, they found that no one knew anyone who matched their description, and they understood it had been Nokoti. In those days, too, Nokoti sometimes stood at the divide between Atigina and the lowlands of Purosa, inviting the southerners to a distribution of food. The visitors arrived only to discover that their hosts knew nothing about the invitation. Nokoti had caused the confusion. Sometimes a party of men traveling in single file along a forest path arrived at a destination to find that the first, fifth, and eighth traveler had spoken to Nokoti, while none of the rest had seen or heard him.

In the last twenty years, Nokoti has lost his power to harm. The legendary meetings with this somewhat fearsome but loveable trickster have ceased. His disappearance coincides with the arrival of whites and the construction, beginning in the mid-1950's, of the Okapa–Purosa road, the first public thoroughfare in the region. Forest journeys now do not have to be made along narrow, secluded trails, sometimes shared by other people, and offer fewer phantasmagoria. Dialect groups are in more frequent contact, and diminished isolation has removed some of the unpredictability from intergroup negotiations. In addition, an increased population and changes in agricultural technology have resulted in the shrinking of the forest, while store-bought canned proteins have reduced the number of

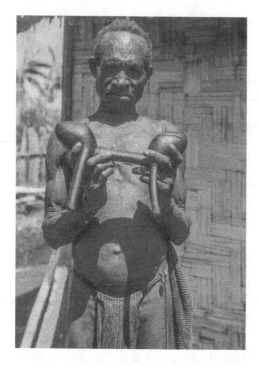

An old Wanitabe man cares for the vanished Nokoti's headrest.

hunting expeditions into the forest. The infant-wasting illnesses for which Nokoti was responsible have waned, as a result of the introduction of new foods and the cessation of warfare, which interrupted crop production and left the most vulnerable members of the population undernourished and susceptible to illness. As the Fore adopt new crops, metal tools, and gardening methods that do not lead to frequent relocation of fields, the ghosts that were concerned with garden fallow are said to be less threatening. The Masalai spirits who would have protected forests in the past are also less fear-inspiring.

The diminished powers of ghosts and spirits and the disappearance of Nokoti illustrate the oblique relationship between ideology and behavior. The Fore have modified their beliefs in a way that enables them to make necessary ecological adjustments while at the same time avoiding blasphemy.

THE CONTEXT OF IDEOLOGICAL CHANGE

Fore were never an isolated people. Located on the fringe of Highland settlement, they maintained contact with adjacent Highland groups to the north and Papuan Lowlanders beyond an uninhabited zone to the south. Producing salt, animal furs, feathers, betelnut, cane, and other forest materials themselves, Fore acquired stone axe blades from the west and north. From the Awa to the south, black palm bows were purchased with salt, traded internally to the west and north, and exported again on northern Fore borders. Their few pearlshells and amelia shells (Nassarius) were gained from the Papuans to the south, in exchange for tobacco and woven bags.

In addition, some internal commerce resulted from regional specialization among Fore inhabiting areas ranging from an altitude of 7,000 feet in the north to 3,500 in the south. Pandanus nuts from the elevated north were exchanged for taro in the warmer lowlands, while in the southwest women acquired bark capes and skirt fibers by sending amelia shells to the southeast. Local groups exchanged surplus food crops, such as yam or winged bean, that matured in different locations at different times of the year.

This was the situation until the early 1930's, when according to the accounts of elderly Fore men, there began an accelerating series of intrusions from outside the region and its traditional trade networks. Certainly

Forest trails were private property, entered at the visitor's risk. Photo by Dr. E. R. Sorenson, "The Edge of the Forest," Smithsonian Institution Press, 1976.

the most dramatic of these was the sound and sight of low-flying aircraft that passed overhead in 1933. In that year, joint exploratory flights by the Australian administration and the New Guinea Goldfields Company left from the Bena Bena region to survey what they assumed to be a mass of uninhabitable mountains farther west. What they saw in several flights across the Eastern Highlands were the fertile soils and teeming populations of the Upper Purari (Asaro–Bena Bena) and Waghi (Chimbu) valleys.[3] What the North Fore saw was a great shining bird whose noise was so awful that they fell in terror to the ground, not daring to look up again for fear they would all be killed.[4] South Fore also believed the thing to be a great Masalai-bird and when it had passed they ate rats with fortifying medicines to guard against impending illness.

During the 1930's, the intrusive phenomena arrived predominantly from the south. The first steel tomahawk, piece of cloth, saucer, and fragments of mirror entered the South Fore from Papuan groups to the south. A resident of the South Fore parish of Takai is reported to have traveled through the region some time in the late 1930's demonstrating the great utility of the new steel axe. Groups as far east as Okasa recall his visit. Some borrowed the tomahawk to cut trees, while others gathered the shavings from arrows fashioned with the new tool and ate them with medicinal leaves. Having thus acquired the cutting edge of the amazing axe, they felt what they later described as a new-found confidence that they would rise and overwhelm their enemies.

Some shreds of the new cloth, a potent red, came to Wanitabe, while other remnants were traded north to Fore at Yagusa and Kasokaso. Some used the cloth to revitalize their fighting shields, and others used it medicinally. They rubbed it with shells, bespat it with medicines, and fed it to the sick. Its power, they thought, derived from its manufacture by ghosts of the dead in Papua. The saucer and pieces of mirror were similarly believed to contain an innate power. The saucer was worn as chest decoration, and the pieces of mirror were threaded into men's hair, where their potency was visible as they flashed in the sunlight. South Fore continued to incorporate and append to themselves objects of power and value.

Although the distance between the southernmost Fore and the nearest Papuan populations was two days' journey through uninhabited terrain, the Fore, like the other Highland groups, had a normal trade and refuge span of about fifteen miles, a distance that could be covered in one day. Goods moved between trade partners in a series of small chainlike links, and political boundaries were recognized in narrow focus. "If we heard people speaking another language," the Fore said, "we fought them, and if our women ran away to people who spoke another language, we didn't try to retrieve them." At Wanitabe in central South Fore, people traveled no farther north than the parish of Pusarasa, about fifteen miles away, and they sometimes wondered if humans were responsible for the smoky fires they saw on the mountain ridges and grassland regions below them. The tangible world was said to end at the horizon. In the skies beyond the southern mountains lived the Creative Beings, originators of all things in the world. From them came plants, pigs, birds, humans, and all forms of wealth. When it thundered or the earth trembled, it was thought that the Creators had raised and shaken the corner of the earth, warning Fore of impending sickness and death. The myths of origin thus support the inhabitants' southern orientation, and indeed the first seeds of sweet corn, Casuarina trees, and an old variety of sweet potato are known to have entered the Fore region along southern trade routes.

The first recorded white men to enter the kuru region were the Ashton brothers, two Australian gold explorers who made several prospecting trips from Kainantu to the northwest during the second half of 1934. The first outside visitors the Fore remember, however, were not the Ashtons but a black man with a party of carriers who entered from Papua, coming as far north as Kamila. These visitors are said to have worn laplaps (cloth skirts), shoes, and shirts, and to have carried metal traveling cases, lamps, and a radio. The leader was so tall that "his legs hung out of the house at night" Fore brought his party food and firewood, and kept their distance as he directed. They watched in wonder as the hurricane lamp appeared to illuminate by burning water, the evening meal was cooked in metal containers, and woolen blankets were unfolded to make beds at night. The men left without conveying to the Fore the purpose of the visit. They, too, were probably prospectors searching for gold.

In the late 1930's and early 1940's, the predominant external influences changed in origin from south to north. New foods, new ideas, and new forms of wealth began to flow abundantly from northern trade partners, with the chain of connections leading back from the Fore through the neighboring Kamano to government and mission posts at Kainantu and the mission at Raipinka. Potatoes, tomatoes, cucumbers, beans, and several new varieties of sweet potato filtered down this route and into the Fore in advance of the government patrols which began in 1947. The next wave brought peas, peanuts, cabbage, onion, and pumpkin, after the first government patrols but still before 1954, when the first government Patrol Post in the Fore region was established at Okapa. With greater diversity in vegetable crops, periods of hunger were less frequent. There was a decline in breast swelling among adolescent boys, which may possibly have been a manifestation of malnutrition and which was treated by bloodletting with medicinal bow and arrow. Fore selected from the flow of new foods. A few people planted papaya, passionfruit, lemon, and lime. Mint, Hongkong taro, and manioc were unenthusiastically received, while several plants Fore describe as inedible grasses were grown briefly and discarded. Ni (Cyanotis, family Commelinaceae) a plant now the focus of public ritual consumption, was first served as a secret growth stimulant for pigs and young men. For a time Fore planted an improved variety of the black seed kinta, an item of value exchanged among maternal kin. This was soon displaced by small and large cowrie shells. Chickens arrived in two waves; as mentioned above the earlier variety, like human flesh, was deemed suitable only for women and children, while the second, appearing after 1954, was defined as food also for men.

South Fore heard stories of white men at Kainantu, and in the mid-1940's a Wanitabe man together with a friend from North Fore walked forty miles to the government outpost at Kainantu to see what lay behind the rumors.[5] In Kainantu they traded their Irish potatoes for a box of matches and then sat by the airstrip watching the passing scene. Suddenly a plane landed and they saw white men emerge from its belly. They returned home to report that the great birds seen passing overhead since the 1930's carried a kind of Being, as some Fore farther south already knew, having visited the site of a crashed Japanese plane at Awarosa in 1943.[6]

The first government patrol in 1947 passed rather quickly through the Fore region, but those who saw Patrol Officer Skinner believed him to be one of the Creative Beings, a view to which he lent credence by firing a cartridge into the ground, in an impressive demonstration of the power of firearms. The moment he left, the men ate rats with forest "medicines" to protect and strengthen themselves. With this act, echoing men's initiation rituals, Fore attempted to counter what they perceived as a threat to their monopoly of control. A parallel can be drawn with anti-pollution rituals, whereby Fore men cleanse themselves of the threat of female dominance. The sudden intrusion of creatures with astonishing skills suggested a similar inversion of the natural order.[7] Patrol Officer Toogood's visit two years later, in 1949, was more leisurely, and eastern Fore at Okasa and Yagusa offered his party vegetables, pigs, and women, acquiring generous quantities of cowrie shell in return. Adjustment to the new order apparently had begun.

Official accounts of these same encounters describe the enthusiastic reception given the patrol by the Fore, in contrast to the response in other regions of New Guinea. Indeed, Skinner's report of 1947 indicates that Fore assembled spontaneously in rows, ready for a census, having understood from their northern neighbors that this was the expected procedure. Skinner, however, believed a census at that time would be premature.[8] Toogood's report two years later notes: "It is a great pity that the staff position in this sub-district is so acute that the people cannot be visited more frequently, such is their desire and eagerness to cooperate and be recognized that the slightest suggestion is seized upon and executed in an effort to please."[9]

In the two decades before sustained contact with whites, then, Fore were engaged in lively innovation and modification of their environment. Old gardens were being more regularly seeded with Casuarina, a coastal transplant that replenishes soil and discourages unwanted regrowth. New varieties of potato, selected for their taste or prolific growth, displaced the old, with each new one eliciting special cultivation methods. Some species, said to have required the extra labor of mounding, were subsequently abandoned. The adoption of new food crops involved changes in environment and diet, as well as in the distribution of labor and its intensity.

By the early 1950's, Fore were beginning to respond to a different timetable, one established by the government, the missions (at Tarabo, Raipinka, and Kainantu), and populations to the north. This new sense of regularity stemmed from mission Sundays (or, in the case of the Seventh Day Adventist mission, Saturdays) and from the government requirement that one day a week be spent maintaining the roads then being built under government aegis. In addition, annual celebrations at the Okapa government station caused people to begin counting months and Christmases. "We didn't reckon in months and years," the Fore say, "we only counted by gardens." In those days, too, their agricultural calendar hinged on events to the south rather than the north: "We used to hear that the period of hunger had just come to an end at Awarosa," a Wanitabe informant said, "and we knew it would soon be over for us, too. We would hear that an Awarosa man had lifted huge sweet potatoes and bean roots from his gardens and had

Reflecting influence of Christian missions, men assembled before brideprice pray that the bride will not fall victim to kuru.

Men consider a brideprice while women look on.

invited the hungry to come and eat, announcing an end to the shortage of food there. Now we get the same message from the north, from the Keiagana at Taramo and Ke'fu, who tell the North Fore at Awande, and we hear it from them."

Objects and ideas had always filtered in from neighboring groups, but the direction and scope of outside influences and a local adaptations to them was something new. By 1960 wild boars had disappeared from central South Fore, although they were reportedly still present in the forests of Ilesa and Abomotasa, where during the rainy season they impregnated domestic pigs. By 1960, too, Wanitabe, Purosa, Agakamatasa, and Awarosa had traded bird-of-paradise feathers northwards for government-introduced breeding sows, while none of these new pigs had reached southwest Fore at Oriesa, Mentilesa, Kasalai, and Paiti. In 1962, people at Wanitabe began to plant cash crops. Peanuts were already growing, and the ground and fences were prepared for coffee. It was said at Wanitabe that people farther south who had not planted coffee would soon see the new Wanitabe wealth, their houses, goods, and machines, and they would shake and tremble at the sight, their livers spinning like tops. The new coffee groves were soon to alter Fore modes of cultivation, since unlike banana or pandanus, coffee trees demand continuous labor and cannot be left to care for themselves. Coffee owners felt reluctant to move far from this wealth; Fore were becoming more sedentary and would need to devise new forms of property transfer. The planting of coffee took South Fore one step further from classical swidden.

The pace of events had quickened in 1955, when the government road connected Okapa station in North Fore to Kamila in the South, and by 1957 to Purosa. Two missions settled at the end of the road, an American family representing the New World Mission at Purosa, and two New Guinean representatives of the Seventh Day Adventists at nearby Mougai Amusa. Government and mission edicts quickly brought a halt to warfare, cannibalism, and—for the next decade—to most indigenous ritual. The New World Mission would not baptize new polygamists. The Seventh Day Adventists refused those who ate pork, possum, rats, or snakes. Government representatives discouraged infanticide and child marriage, and the missions forbade the traditional privilege of premarital sex with matrilateral cross-cousins. Lutheran missionaries, with a base outside Fore territory, made occasional visits, during which they undermined indigenous beliefs by revealing the men's sacred flutes to women. Lutheran baptism also required monogamy, and while the World Mission allowed current polygamists to keep all their wives, the Lutherans insisted on the divorce of all but one. It was said by South Fore that the situation was even more restrictive for Chimbu, who were permitted sexual intercourse only on Fridays. The government and the Lutherans allowed Fore *singsings* (communal feasting and dancing) to continue, whereas they were frowned upon by the World Mission and Seventh Day Adventists. Fore men, seeing little distinction between government and mission authority, were prevailed on to cut their long hair, and to wash what they considered an enchanting patina of black body grease and soot from their faces and upper torsoes. This visible index of virility they had acquired during many sessions in the men's house, eating plant stimulants and hallucinogens and enduring the saunalike heat of a strong hearth fire. Not only did men relinquish the sweathouse rituals and all visible signs of them, but in many cases they abandoned the men's house altogether.

Domestic architecture soon reflected the new era. The stockades surrounding South Fore hamlets were pulled down in 1956, and houses were built in open clearings where individual nuclear families settled side by side in suburban-style rows. Married men cohabited for the first time with women they earlier had thought were dangerous and debilitating. The balance of power shifted further when the new British-style judicial system imposed by the Australian government sided with women who had been severely beaten by angry husbands. By the 1960's, Fore men were noting this legal change, which diverted their protective care from their sisters to their wives.

Along with modifications in behavior and thought, rapid biological adjustments were also being made. Although some diseases such as kuru had earlier entered the Fore region from the north, between 1930 and 1960's an unusual number of new illnesses traveled along the same path. Fore describe severe epidemics of measles and mumps in the early 1930's, and whooping cough in 1949, diseases for which they carried no immunity. The second measles epidemic in 1957 was milder. Like other Highland popula-

New-style hamlet, Awarosa, 1967. Photo by
Dr. E. R. Sorenson, "The Edge of the Forest,"
Smithsonian Institution Press, 1976.

tions, Fore suffered an outbreak of dysentery, which caused many deaths in 1943. Mental illness and liver disease are also said to have increased since the arrival of whites.[10] The Fore fear of illness following confrontation with new phenomena is well-founded.

Fore represent a southern projection of the general movement of Eastern Highland peoples toward virgin territory. Their close genetic relationship with northern neighbors suggests a recent migration from peoples in the Kamano region, with an earlier dispersion from Gadsup and Tairora.[11] The organized exchange of genes in marriage also has a northern orientation. A sample of three generations of marriages in Wanitabe parish shows that while group endogamy is high, more sisters are sent north rather than south in marriage, and more wives come from northern groups than from peoples to the south.[12] Although the northward orientation for intra-Fore wife exchanges has persisted, patrol reports and the Fore themselves indicate that since the cessation of warfare in the mid-1950's, there has been increased intermarriage with Awa, Kukukuku, Gimi, Kamano, and other non-Fore groups.

Although the South Fore still look to the north for wives and other valuables, they continue to move south. Indeed, the pace of movement is considerable. Some elderly men living at Wanitabe in 1962 were born at Keiagasa five miles to the north, but were living ten or fifteen miles south of Wanitabe at the time of the first government patrols. With the imposition of peace in the 1950's, many moved back north to Wanitabe. By 1970, however, some had moved again, this time to join a frontier group creating another finger-like clearing ten miles to the southeast. They return to Wanitabe to receive payments at the marriage and death of kin. Thus, as they work their way southward, Fore glance back to the north for present interest and recent history. The mountain ridges, rocky outcrops, and water courses of Fore legend are behind and above them, occupied by groups with whom they are rapidly losing intimate contact.

The body of legendary and recent history stands in contradiction to Fore myths of origin, which as noted, place the creation of all people, animals, and food in the hot lowlands to the south. This may be an echo of ancient history. As noted earlier, genetic relationships depict a similar polarity of forces operating on the Fore region. Fore thus occupy a strategic place midway between Highland and Lowland groups, transmitting food and artifacts both north and south. In the past thirty years, however, the Fore position in the regional scheme has been greatly altered. Until the end of the 1930's, Fore sent important items of trade in both directions, with many foods and objects arriving from Papua. By the early 1950's, the interest of peoples to the north in objects arriving from the south through Fore hands diminished. The new access of northerners to trade salt lessened their desire for indigenous salt of Fore manufacture, while peace and decreased hunting quenched the demand for Awa bows. The flood of new foods and valuables introduced by whites reached northerners first, and Fore began to occupy a distinctly inferior position in the regional mosaic.

As the hierarchy of northern populations over their southern neighbors became more pronounced, new surpluses and new forms of wealth dislodged existing status arrangements among individual Fore. Discrimination based on sex, age, and talent were known in the past, but new opportunities arose now for Fore who were not the occupants of traditionally favored positions.

CARGO CULTS

Cargo cults promising wealth for all twice reached South Fore, the first in the 1940's, the second in 1953–54.[13] In each case, the ritual technique for creating valuables, thought to have been acquired from whites, was "sold" by northerners to southerners, largely in return for pigs. The Kamano thus sold the technique to the North Fore, who brought it down to Wanitabe. There they persuaded the Wanitabe Big Men that participants in the cult could produce their own laplaps, knives, guns, and cowrie shells by a kind of homeopathic transformation. Local objects with a resemblance to the desired goods (small slivers of sharpened wood for bullets, pebbles and stones for small and large shells), were placed in a special "cargo" house constructed at the rear of the men's house, where women could not see it. The men ate hallucinogenic bark, smoked their pipes, and waited for the desired goods to appear.

The men from Kagu and Pusarasa in North Fore had demanded pigs as payment for their instruction. As they departed for home, they warned that anyone who prematurely entered the cult house would certainly die. The Wanitabe cult leaders conveyed the additional news that certain foods were now forbidden: yams, sugarcane, rodents,and marsupials. By eating only pork and sweet potato, they told women and youths, they would hasten the transformation of the goods.

From to time during the next few weeks the North Fore would visit Wanitabe, look into the cargo house, and assure the assemblage that the room was swelling with valuables. As a sample, they produced a small piece of cloth or a few shells "which they had no doubt purchased from the trade store at Raipinka," the Wanitabe leaders later commented.

> Nevertheless, we were eager for goods, and we killed more pigs to give them, and smoked pipes and ate bark until our throats were parched and our heads spun. Those who fell into a trance, who shook and whistled and fainted, we thought . . . had a special vision of the cargo, and we killed pigs and gave pork to these people, too. . . . As time passed, and the men from Kagu failed to return, and all our pigs were used up, we decided to open the door. When we found the house had no cargo but only

bundles of bark and sand and stones, people were angry with those of us who had listened to the men from the north.

Although they had failed in their own attempts to manufacture goods by this method, the Wanitabe leaders "sold" their ritual information to eager applicants from farther south and west. Disenchanted purchasers there are said to have responded with a variety of sorcery assaults against Wanitabe in the next few years, and the movement leaders felt frustrated by their failure. With the construction of our fieldhouse in 1962, the Wanitabe leaders believed that their cargo efforts had at last been realized. They took a proprietary interest in the building and its contents, and called it the Wanitabe "store."[14]

That the purpose of acquiring technology is related to the potential for dominance over those lacking similar skills is suggested by an incident which occurred at Pusarasa, in the North Fore, while a cargo cult was attracting adherents there. A man named Iogo covered his skin with red pigment and announced that he was a white man. Refusing to work, he sat on a platform, ordering people to cook his food and remove the scraps at the end of the meal. If he wished to travel about or visit the latrine, he avoided contact with the ground, demanding that trees be felled to assure him of an uninterrupted timber path. For a time people treated him with respect, even killing pigs to give him. When the promised cargo failed to arrive, his disillusioned supporters abandoned him, and he was unable to maintain his state of temporary "chieftainship."

These ostensibly egalitarian movements, promising equal access to the anticipated wealth, in practice resulted in the emergence of some individuals who were markedly wealthier than others, adding to the differences in status already created by the presence of Australian officials in the Highlands. Those who had failed to gain were perceived as disgruntled sorcerers, seeking revenge on those who had duped them and drained them of their wealth. The south was accused of sorcery against the more affluent north. This was the period—from the mid-1950's to the early 1960's—when the South Fore sorcery count rose from six to sixteen. It was also the time when exposure of Fore to new diseases, particularly kuru, created further patterns of social imbalance.

Not only did the number of sorcery methods greatly increase, in this period of emerging hierarchies, but the methods themselves were transformed. The classical forms of attack (tokabu, arrows, yanda, and karena) did not require the theft of a victim's body particle by a disloyal or envious co-resident. Nor did survival depend on divination to ferret out the culprit. Recovery from yanda and karena rested on the curer's ability merely to locate the buried poison. The sorcerer of old was not to be known. Nor was he subject to public appeal or private manipulation. This earlier view of sorcery accorded with the conception of the more widespread masalai- and ghost-inflicted injuries of the day. Dangers emanated not from competing fellow residents, but from spirits of the environment or from known forebears who punish faulty behavior.

Those who began to treat the pressing sorceries of the 1950's and 1960's are called Dream Men or Smoke Men. These men of wide repute replace the many lesser-known Bark Men and Bark Women of the past, who were residents of the victim's parish and used forest medicines in their cures. No longer residents of one's own parish, Dream Men characteristically arise in the border areas between language groups, along Fore, Kamano, Gimi, and Kukukuku boundaries, where patients now travel for consultation and cure. The Dream Men's great abilities derive from information revealed in dreams triggered by the ingestion of psychotropic plants and the inhalation of tobacco. The cure now requires divination to disclose the identity of particular enemies. While their reputation for the control of special powers and secret information remains intact, Dream Men acquire considerable wealth and, like cargo cult leaders, enjoy exceptional acclaim. These new kinds of Big Men are technicians of the new order. In Wanitabe, the Bark Men and Bark Women of old are said to have been impotent in the face of sorcery, and to have spent their time finding lost pigs or tending the Masalai spirits believed to be causing sickness in children and adults. They treated sick adults by heating bamboo tubes of mud taken from the offended Ples Masalai. Sick children are said to have been cured by mixing pig grease with their feces and leaving the sediment in the sun to dry.

The rise of Dream Men further underlines the ecological transformation of Fore society in the past two decades. Gone are the protectors of regenerating and primary forests. Nokoti has shrunk from the killer of ancestors to a meddling, now invisible trickster. Attention has been deflected from the concerns associated with older forms of shifting cultivation. Now men face one another in competiton fostered by intensive agriculture and Western contact. There has been a shift from the cooperative acquisition of wild game from the forest to the more difficult individual accumulation of domestic pigs. As an index of the change, the Fore say that in the time of Nokoti "rats were his children," whereas now "pigs are the children of men." Dream Men have emerged to cope with the now ubiquitous sorcerers, and, as the following chapters disclose, the powers and audience of both have vastly increased.

THE CRISIS YEARS

7

Between 1957 and 1977, some 2,500 people died from kuru, most of them adult Fore women. Socially, the pronounced sexual bias in kuru mortality is one of its most deranging aspects. The marked excess of deaths of females over males led at times to male-female ratios of over 3:1 in some hamlets and 2:1 for South Fore as a whole.[1] The late 1950's and early 1960's were crisis years, as Figure 2 illustrates.

Between 1957 and 1976, kuru killed approximately 400 women in the North and 1,000 in the South (see Figure 1, p. 00). In both North and South Fore, but most rapidly in the South, women were disappearing from the land.

The marital histories of fifty Wanitabe men, taken in 1962, show that among them they had contracted 76 marriages, or one and a half per man. Two marriages had ended in divorce, and 45 as a result of the death of the wife, 40 of them from kuru. Polygamy is rare, partly because Christian missions refuse baptism to men with more than one wife, but also because of the acute shortage of women. Big Men marry more women than others, but in the South Fore they tend to marry serially, acquiring only one wife at a time. Of 125 Wanitabe males over the age of 21, only three had two extant wives, and none had more than two. The position was in fact graver than these figures suggest. Sixty-three men had no living wife, ten had never married. That is, just under half the adult Wanitabe men were without wives in 1962. Women were particularly likely to succumb just after giving birth to a child, and the motherless nuclear family was a common domestic unit.

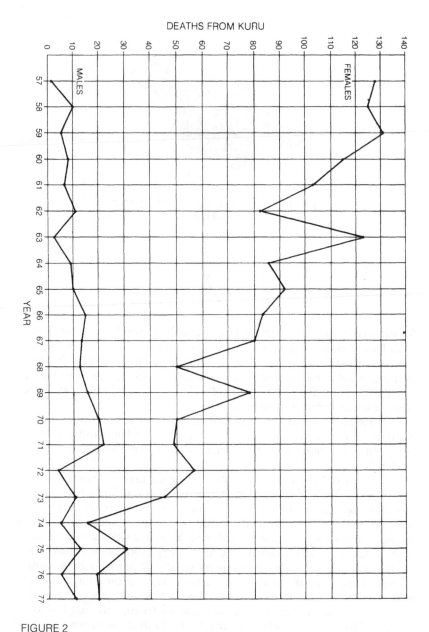

FIGURE 2
Annual Deaths from Kuru, 1957–1977

SOURCE: Adapted from Hornabrook and Moir 1970, King 1975, and Alpers personal communication.

There is scarcely a man in South Fore who has not lost a number of immediate kin to kuru. One Wanitabe Big Man has seen the death of his mother, his half-sister, four wives, one son, and one step-son. Pigo of Wanitabe, a man about 45 years of age, had three wives and three daughters die of kuru, while Anatu of Kamila has been deprived of his mother, four wives, one sister, one daughter, and one son. Oraka of Kamila, perhaps an extreme case, has seen the demise of three wives, two sisters, two sons, one son's wife, and three daughters, one of whom was married to Anatu. The genealogical records convey a sense of obliteration, yet the reality was even worse. Often a Fore man's closest female tie was to his kagisa sisters. They, too, were dying of kuru at an alarming rate, yet such relationships are not recorded in the parish genealogical registers.

The resulting demographic distortions have had a major effect on social behavior. Many men are forced to perform the roles of both mother and father for their remaining family. Of the 63 wifeless men in the Wanitabe sample, eleven have children under the age of five, and 23 have children between five and eleven. Some assistance may come from sisters and from brothers' wives, and a man fortunate enough to have a daughter among his older children may find in her some compensation for the lack of adult female labor. Small girls in such motherless families work long hours

Short of women, South Fore men perform many domestic chores.

in the gardens and struggle home each evening with tremendous loads of sweet potato and firewood. Men have also been forced to extend their own domestic activities into what traditionally was the woman's sphere. Not only do they continue to fence and clear garden sites, they now dig the ground, plant crops, weed, and harvest. Some men cook food and feed their own children, becoming progressively involved in women's tasks as the wives' capacities wane.

During his wife's third pregnancy, Noka, formerly a Wanitabe warrior of note, had abundant leisure in which to discuss Fore history. After the child was born, it became apparent that his wife had kuru. Depressed and afraid, she remained in their house for the following few weeks, her friends (her brother's wife, her husband's brother's wife) sitting with her to keep her company. Finally she emerged and resumed gardening, but her condition deteriorated so rapidly that Noka was obliged to accompany her to the gardens. As her walk became an erratic stagger and she could no longer safely carry the newborn child, she gave it sometimes to her twelve-year-old daughter to carry and sometimes to Noka. In the past, men were careful not to handle young children; the child's urine, it was said, drained a warrior's strength.[2] The girl, who would herself die of kuru eight years later, worked long and hard in the gardens, bringing home one string bag of food at the end of the day and often returning to the gardens for a second.

With his wife no longer able to coordinate her movements, Noka built a rough lean-to of grass and cane in the gardens to shield the sleeping child from the sun. When it woke and cried, he carried it to his wife, where as long as she could still sit upright she worked at digging the ground in a small area around her. Later that year, shortly before his wife died, when she could no longer provide the infant with breast milk, Noka took the child to the government hospital at Okapa. There, along with many other "kuru orphans," it was fed a nutritious diet of ground peanuts and powdered milk. While it is customary for Fore to adopt weaned children, there is little history of adoption of the newborn, and in the past many motherless infants died. This suggests both the recent onset and the breadth of the present emergency.

The prevalence of kuru has affected customs other than the traditional division of labor. In some instances, brideprice is withheld until the girl demonstrates her ability to survive long enough to produce at least one child. Marriage speeches directed to the recipients of brideprice often include directions for the distribution of the bride's death payment. If the bride survives only a short time, it is indicated, no one should expect further compensation. The assumption is clear: men of forty-five expect to outlive a girl of thirteen or fourteen. In the early 1960's, faced with a demographic emergency, the dimensions of which they grasped clearly, the Fore had recourse to a series of desperate remedies.

JOURNEY TO THE GIMI

During 1961 and 1962, Fore expended much time, material wealth, and emotional energy in a vain attempt to control the incidence of kuru. Their efforts began with a search for cures, the most spectacular of which took place in the Gimi, west of the Yani River. At Uvai, in the heavily forested central Gimi Valley, a man called Uwana proclaimed himself to be a curer of kuru, and between April and August 1961, over seventy Fore patients walked or were carried to Uvai for treatment.

Uwana was about thirty-six years old, slight in stature, and the father of three children. He did not speak Pidgin, and had no long-term association with white culture, although before marriage he had labored on the Goroka airstrip for about three months. He was not baptized and had no connection with any mission in the area. He had not seen the town of Kainantu, but had often visited the patrol post at Okapa and said he knew Fore and Keiagana territory well.

Uwana's first patient is said to have been his wife, who was pregnant with their first child when she showed symptoms of kuru. The cure came to Uwana in a dream, in which he was directed to make a miniature bow and arrow, using a sharp stone for the arrow tips. This is traditional equipment among Gimi and Fore, who let blood to relieve headaches and muscle pains, although Uwana changed the stone tips to fragments of glass. His dream revealed also the three kinds of bark he should use as medicine.[3] The first cures took place around 1951, when Uwana treated his own wife, the wife of a Gimi luluai, and the wives of an agemate and a classificatory brother, men with whom he lived at the time. It was not until 1961, he said, that the Fore heard of him.

The South Fore who traveled to Uvai for treatment said their affliction followed the taking of the February 1961 census—a mixed assemblage not of their own arranging—which gave their enemies an opportunity to steal the necessary sorcery particles. It is not clear where the Fore pilgrimage began, but by July 1961, kuru victims from almost every hamlet in Fore territory, and some from Keiagana, had left for Uvai. Walking in small parties, they crossed the mountain range with their husbands, infant children, pigs for use in the cure, and often their luluai or tultul. The luluai of Waisa, a Fore parish adjacent to Gimi territory, took his ailing fourteen-year-old son. Bilingual in Fore and Gimi, the luluai remained to act as entrepreneur, buying food from the Gimi and distributing it to the visitors.

The therapeutic method Uwana used at Uvai was the same one observed later in the South Fore. In a follow-up treatment at Waisa for the luluai's son, Uwana and two Gimi assistants took the youth to a small forest stream. There, Uwana pierced the patient's feet, legs, arms, shoulders, and scalp with his medicinal bow and arrow, until blood flowing from the

*Gimi curers treat
a kuru victim.
Blood will flow
into the stream
from multiple
puncture sites.*

boy's body colored the stream red. The luluai supplied a pig for the meal that
followed, and the assistant spat medicinal barks, ginger, and salt on the pork
and accompanying green leaves. Uwana prescribed sexual restraint for the
patient and close kin during the next few weeks, a rule said to have been
strictly observed at the Uvai "hospitals." During treatment, he also named
an enemy of the luluai, as the sorcerer responsible for his son's condition.

To cater for the influx at Uvai, Uwana and his kin and friends built
three large houses, which they called hospitals, small replicas of the government medical buildings at Okapa. An overflow of patient's families lived
in Uwana's own house. At the height of the activity, Uwana was unable to
treat all the patients himself, and he allotted some to the luluai Tete Ura
from an adjacent Gimi hamlet. Tete Ura built his own "hospital" and began
treatment, but by mid-July he had voluntarily relinquished his work, having
cured, he conceded, only six people. By August, Uwana was again stating

that he alone had the power to cure. Patients stayed in the Gimi hospitals for one or two weeks, and then they made the slow journey home.

Five months after the exodus to Uvai, it was possible to trace seventy of Uwana's former patients. Nine had died, 58 appeared close to death, and there were three complete "cures," the latter perhaps representing cases of faulty diagnosis, hysterical mimicry, or apparent remission. (In a small percentage of cases, kuru symptoms occur intermittently for several years, before the victim becomes incapacitated and dies.)

Uwana accepted fees for treatment. Some men could pay more than others, and by the end of August he had accumulated cash equal to about $210—in an area with no cash crops and at that time little source of monetary income. Uwana abandoned traditional dress. Instead of fiber garments, string-woven cloak, and head decorations of cassowary plumes and cowrie shell, he now wore a white laplap, T-shirt, and black felt hat. He stored his payments in kind (lengths of cloth, scissors, hinges, and knives) in a new vermilion-colored wooden case, where he also kept a reserve supply of medicinal barks. At this time, too, he gave up all work in his garden to become a full-time specialist. His next desire was to be appointed tultul, a title by which he was already locally known.

Several months after the "cures" at Uvai, it became apparent that the patients were not recovering. As news spread of their progressive deterioration, Uwana was called a fraud and a scoundrel. Traffic to Uvai ceased. In their frustration, some spoke of having Uwana jailed, yet they listened when he came through Fore territory in mid-September. He had given good medicines at Uvai, he said, and had provided real cures. When the victims returned to their hamlets, however, their enemies had attacked them anew. He declared that the kiap for the Okapa region had dispatched him on his present tour, and that luluais and tultuls were therefore obliged to support him. He claimed that the kiap had placed his knife close to Uwana's head as a sign of personal protection (an incident the kiap privately disclaimed). Thus shielded from Fore sorcerers and angry kin, Uwana added that he had been authorized to report the name of anyone who campaigned against him. He and his Gimi assistants traveled thus through Fore lands, treating patients and planting cordyline, a traditional taboo and boundary marker, to signal the end of kuru sorcery in the region.

In the following few months, several Gimi curers imitating Uwana's procedures traveled through Fore territory. They offered to treat again those whom Uwana had attended, and also sought out new patients. These itinerant practitioners gained little support, for by this time most of those who had journeyed to Uvai were dead, and Uwana was again in great disfavor. The Gimi medical orderly from the aid post at Uvai reported that the patients' kin were talking of reclaiming their fees, and that Uwana had returned to traditional dress.[4] In an attempt to revive his reputation, however, Uwana performed a public cure, treating the wife of his former assistant, the luluai Tete Ura.

While the Gimi connection quietly lapsed, the next few months witnessed the arrival at Wanitabe of several North Fore curers from Kagu. The Wanitabe medical orderly, whose position they openly challenged, provided the following account of their treatment. The curers were called to Wanitabe by Noka and his wife's brother, Walipo, both of whose wives now had kuru. Each man gave the curers a pig, which was slaughtered, and its blood poured into two bamboo tubes. Next, the men from Kagu asked to be presented with patients. Five women with kuru came forward, and two men suffering from the respiratory ailment karena. The curers, patients, and as many others as could fit, crowded into Walipo's house. The ailing women's skirts were removed, the two sick men were left fully dressed. The men from Kagu then spat chewed leaves on each patient's skin and followed this by rubbing the patients briskly with a bundle of leaves. Next they paused to drink from the bamboos, and sucking at the patient's skin above the ear and then at lower points on the body (kuru symptoms are said to progress from the head down), they spat bloody saliva onto a leaf plate. This, they said, was bad blood drawn from the sick bodies, and they handed the evidence to the medical orderly, commenting on the uselessness of his medicines for the matter at hand.

They called then for fat from the slaughtered pigs, and the medical orderly cut it for them so he could observe closely everything they did. He handed them a strip of fat (a traditional restorative), which they covered with dry banana leaves. Rubbing the bundle in ashes from the fire, they scuffed the package up and down the patient's skin. One of the two curers smoked as he worked, blowing smoke at the bundle, while his partner stated that pig grease was passing into the victims. Although the medical orderly could see nothing on the patient's skin, he thought he noticed the first man slip the fat from the bundle into his laplap. The curers then opened the leaves, showed that the fat was gone, and declared that the grease had surely penetrated the patient's bodies. Next they bound another piece of pig fat with three kinds of bark and hung this bundle on a rope tied to the roof of the house. They asked the patients to pull on the rope, and while the curer sat and the other stood, they sang a song. When the song was completed, they invited the audience to loosen the rope and see if any fat remained. One man in the audience opened the bundle and found it to be empty. The luluai of Kagu then made a speech saying that government medical orderlies had tried to treat kuru victims and had failed. Standing beside him, the Wanitabe orderly felt ashamed. The cure came to an end with the practitioners asking for the pigs' livers and intestines. They spat the pig innards with three additional barks and gave them to the patients to eat.[5] They then quietly disclosed the names of those responsible for causing each victim's illness.

The following morning the medical orderly found a second treatment in progress in an adjacent hamlet, and this time he placed a couple of his friends in the audience as critical observers. His friends reported, as he had previously suspected, that the performance involved sleight of hand. The pig fat was not secured in the banana leaves, but was slipped under the curer's laplap. When the treatment ended, the curer quickly moved the fat from his garment to his armpit, and the observers walked outside just in time to see him throw it into a nearby latrine.

The Kagu curers now demanded a big pig for themselves, declaring that the pigs killed on the previous day had been mean specimens, and that others had in fact consumed them. Two medium-sized pigs were killed, and the men from Kagu received two legs, along with one chicken and about two dollars (Australian) in cash. As they departed, they declared that the patients should expect to wait two months for signs of improvement. Walipo and Noka warned the curers not to spend their fees at the trade store, for they would be reclaimed in the event of failure.

It should be noted that the medical orderly's skepticism and the wariness of Noka and Walipo concern only the possible fraudulence or incompetence of the Kagu practitioners. None of the three men doubted that trustworthy curers exist. The medical orderly in fact remarked that curers

Curers spit medicines on pork to be fed to kuru victims.

with real power come not from the north, but from the Kukukuku region to the south, the direction to which the women's husbands in fact next turned. While it is reasonable to believe that some men are charlatans, there is, as Evans-Pritchard observes of the Azande, no incentive toward agnosticism.[6]

Sorcery beliefs belong to a body of theoretical tenets considered sacred, a point made during discussion of the Sorcery Bill in the Papua New Guinea House of Assembly in 1970. Sorcery has a kind of power of its own, the delegate said, which makes it work:

> Where this power stems from I do not know, but to say that if we neither know where the power comes from nor understand how it works, it is not enough to prove that it is not true. . . . Mr. Speaker, it is very difficult and almost impossible to believe in things which we cannot see with our eyes. . . . In all churches the members are taught to believe. Belief is the very root of the churches. . . . Sorcery . . . works on the power of belief. . . . The whole thing behind all the performances of sorcery is belief itself. . . . The very belief the person had in these things causes them to happen as he expects.[7]

The failure first of Uwana and then of the men from Kagu did not lead the Fore to scrap their beliefs in the way cures are effected. That alternative is not only unthinkable in the sense Evans-Pritchard suggests, it is also intolerable, since it implies a lack of design in the universe. Just as the sick travel hopefully from physician to physician in the West, the Fore continued to search for effective curers before it was too late. An incurable illness in Western society is one for which there is at present no known therapy. We do not live with the idea that a cure will never be found. Some deaths occur because of the absence of a cure at a certain place and a certain time. In primitive society, it is the place but not the historical moment that is wrong. Sorcerers exist; the only challenge is to discover them. In this sense, both societies are equally empirical, their empiricism built on the assumption of a discoverable order in the cosmos. Failure to cure does not undermine the assumptions of the medical system.

In seven months between late 1961 and early 1962, Walipo and Noka together made fifteen attempts to free their wives of kuru, including six major cures, with the expenditure of three pigs, several fowl, and about $17, a considerable expenditure where women and thus pigs were few, and cash crops almost nonexistent.

Not all men consult diviners when family members fall ill. For several other kuru cases in the same hamlet at this time, no countermeasures were undertaken. One such case was that of a ten-year-old boy, another that of a woman blind for many years before she got kuru. A third was that of a fifty-year-old woman who had experienced intermittent symptoms for more than a decade. While her deteriorating condition in 1962 gave rise to no divination procedures, the first appearance of symptoms a decade earlier, when she was still a potential childbearer, had led to political conflict. As the analysis of Fore disease categories in Chapter 5 hinted, the need for an active response to illness depends on the victim's status in the community. Divination ceremonies were deemed necessary by Walipo and Noka because they were men of considerable reputation, known locally as tultul and luluai although neither had an official title. As men of stature, they had further to fall. Being deprived of wives (the "hands of men") would force their withdrawal from the generous food presentations that had raised them above the level of "rubbish men."

Since curers identify the person responsible for the victim's illness, the rounds of kuru treatments and divination tests gave rise to new tensions, which unsettled the course of daily life. Groups of men began to arrive for sorcery discussions carrying arms. Waterholes were guarded throughout the night, and paths through hamlets were rerouted to force all travelers to bypass the hamlet. Careful observation of travelers would not have provided sufficient protection; while passing through a hamlet they could snatch up sorcery items with their toes. Worse, sorcery accusations showed that men living together in one parish, even in separate lines of one section, harbored mutual suspicions. To the often expressed fear of extinction through the loss of women's reproductive powers was now added a fear of internal disruption so great that society itself was in danger.

THE KIBUNGS

8

1961 ended and 1962 began in the South Fore with little perception of gain. Indeed, people spoke of a sense of slippage, an observation that epidemiological records would subsequently confirm. At the same time, kuru in the North Fore was stable or declining, another fact of which Fore were aware. They attributed the improved situation in the North, particularly the more even balance between men and women, to the social countermeasures taken there since the 1950's, notably the public meetings held in 1957 to denounce sorcery. In an attempt to duplicate this achievement, South Fore called a halt to further cures, and the succession of treatments sought throughout 1961 and most of 1962 gave way to Quaker-style mass meetings known in Pidgin as *kibung*. People in the North, it was said, had curbed the mutual aggression that had been causing their ruin; men in the South should do likewise before it was too late.

From the end of November 1962 to mid-March 1963, hostile parishes gathered in groups to discuss the emergency, to demand the outlawing of kuru and repair of the sexual imbalance. Reputed sorcerers made public confessions of their past activities, and Big Men appealed to sorcerers still in hiding to come forth and relinquish their evil practices. All other social events came to a halt.

Orators at the opening kibungs reaffirmed the Fore belief that kuru results from the actions of sorcerers in their own society. The kuru epidemic would end if unity replaced factionalism, if this pernicious form of concealed warfare were ended. The warfare Fore had known in the past had had a self-limiting aspect. Opposing sides had arranged peace ceremonies when

100

the toll of deaths reached a certain limit of propriety. Many Fore stories about the origin of material objects or animals illustrate the theme of rational preservation of the species. The first bow, for instance, strung with the cord on the back of the arc, is said to have provided deadly aim. Borrowing the bow from his father, a young man felled the inhabitants of an entire men's house. Hearing this, the father took the bow from his son and attached the cord to the other side of the wood. The young man tried the bow again. The first arrow misfired, a second pierced his opponent in the hand, and only the third caused death. "This is proper," the father said, "If you had continued as you began, whom would we fight against in the future? Who would have remained to produce children? Humankind would have been destroyed." Lectures at initiation also emphasize balanced redress: "If you want to avenge a death," the young men are told, "kill just one man or shoot one of his pigs. If you can't find a pig, his dog will do. They are, after all, the children of men. You may even take something very good from his garden and eat it, but stop at that."

Kuru sorcerers plainly had exceeded all such bounds, and at the public gatherings they were reproached for this crime against society:

> Why are you men killing off all the women, stealing our feces
> from the latrines to perform sorcery? We women give birth to
> you men. Try to find one man who is pregnant now and show
> him to us. Or go and search the old burial grounds and bring us
> the skull or bones of one man we women have killed. You
> won't be able to find any. You men are trying to wipe us out.
> (Speech of a woman of Kamila, December 4, 1962.)

The sexual selectivity of kuru exacerbated the Fore variant of male-female hostility common in the New Guinea Highlands. The Kamila

Wanitabe Big Man addresses a kibung.

woman's speech caused discomfort and shame among the men in the audience, as did that of a visiting Awa, the tultul of Agamusa. He, too, spoke of
the enormity of the issue:

> We men from the other side of the Lamari River are good
> people. All men are in fact the same. We don't have the hair
> and skin of dogs and pigs. Even the tetegina ["whites"] are the
> same as the rest of us, they just have skins that are red. Yet you
> Fore are evil people, always working at sorcery. Why don't you
> live like the rest of us? No one causes kuru the way you do.
> Will you finish off all your women before you stop? Where will
> you get women from when that happens? If you try to steal
> women from us, we'll cut your necks and throw your bodies in
> the river. (Speech of December 22, 1962.)

The death rate from kuru at Wanitabe in 1962 was almost three times
that from injury in war in the past (see Table 2, p. 65 above), a dreadful
measure that competition had reached abnormal, maladaptive levels.
Moreover, a sample of Wanitabe genealogies shows that 104 men but only
27 women had died as a result of war. Kuru sorcerers were plainly killing
those on whom they depended. Speakers raised the possibility that the
South Fore would soon become a wasteland:

> Men don't have vaginas from which they can produce children.
> Where will you find wives from in the future—if women are
> completely finished? Look at the bush growing up around us
> where we once had lines of people working in their gardens.
> You men want to plant coffee now to begin your own business.
> Soon there will be no one here to look after it. (Speech of a
> young man of Wanitabe, December 4, 1962.)

Every day for three-and-a-half months, in one or another place in the
South Fore, groups met to outlaw further acts of sorcery. The North Fore
held similar gatherings. The host parish invited others in the vicinity to
attend, and men traveled from meeting to meeting in their home region.
While they were predominantly masculine affairs, women of the host parish
took part. The devastating incidence of kuru was an affront to group norms,
and speakers proposed some fundamental principles to which all Fore could
subscribe. The assemblies provided an occasion for the affirmation of solidarity following a period of divisive cures and divinations. Just as peace
ceremonies follow the discordant skirmishes of war, the kibungs brought
together hamlet and district groups divided by suspicion and fear in the
shared resolve to end kuru sorcery. The two kinds of meeting have many
elements of ritual in common: the sharing of tobacco, the pouring of water
on former enemies, and the planting of cordyline to signal a barrier against
further aggression. Some speakers explicitly drew the parallel: "We are

calling for an end to kuru sorcery, just as we have abandoned warfare" (kibung at Wanda, December 2).

As the days passed, there was a progressive quest for social agreement. At the gatherings in early December, representatives of the host group called for sorcerers to come forward and identify themselves, to pledge that henceforth they would no longer resort to the impulse of envy or the desire for vengeance. One or two self-proclaimed sorcerers would then confess to such hostile acts, admissions that appeared to unsettle the audience. Some young men who had doubted the presence of actual sorcerers in their midst became very disturbed, as the following report from a young man of Wanitabe indicates:

> I sat listening to the older men saying that kuru was the product of their hands, that it was the result of sorcery. Then I felt a hot sweat break out all over my skin and I stood up and delivered a speech to them all. I said that I had listened to them and had it from their own mouths that kuru was the work of sorcerers. It wasn't my idea. I was only reporting back to them what they had said. So if it came from the hands of men, men could put an end to it. They should therefore throw water on the bodies of all the Kamila women present and publicly swear an end to further sorcery against them.
>
> They listened to me, and no one replied. They were all ashamed, and they bowed their heads to the ground, their hands scratching around in the dirt. (Report on a Kamila kibung, December 3, 1962.)

The women, too, were resentful and upset, as another man's report shows:

> The men gathered at Kamila to talk about kuru. They turned their hands palm upward and confessed that they had killed women with those hands. When the women heard this, they began to cry. I asked the women if they thought they had a sickness, or whether men had performed sorcery against them.[1] One woman said: "We don't really know. Perhaps we have a sickness, or perhaps men are responsible. Our only knowledge is about giving birth to children. We don't think about making sorcery. Sometimes we have thought we might be suffering from sickness, but the men have now spoken and admitted their part. There are so many men and only a few of us women. Why are the men killing us off? A long time before 'red' men came, they began this sorcery against us." The men were ashamed when they heard her say this. (Report of a young man of Wanitabe at a Kamila kibung, December 5, 1962.)

As Victor Turner observes, severe natural misfortune precipitates a crisis in which confessions of guilt are made by those who feel they have broken some crucial norm governing the intercourse of the living with the living or of the living with the dead.[2] Ritual emerges as a result of the "moral discomfort" of the group when confronted with a breach in the natural order. In ritual gatherings, common values are stressed regardless of particular loyalties and interests. Public confession also permits the disclosure of ill-feelings in a context of healing ritual forces. Individuals can purge themselves of rebellious wishes and emotions, and willingly conform once more to public mores.

On some occasions, speakers referred directly to alleged acts of sorcery by particular men in the audience. In contrast to the testaments of the guilty, these discussions created no excitement. People commented that it profited no one to dig up old history. The sprinkling of water on kuru victims, a component of some divination rituals, also had a different impact in the context of a kibung. As a divinatory technique to expose the guilty, suspects were asked to approach kuru victims and shower them with water. If at that moment a victim fainted, urinated, or broke into a sweat, the defendant was in real danger. Men witnessing the ritual, weapons at hand, might set upon the unmasked villain. During the kibungs, however, a woman's collapse evoked much greater restraint. Quietly taking the suspect aside, the victim's kin attempted to change his thinking by measured reason. If he had manufactured the kuru bundle that was killing the woman, they told him, he should remove it now and relieve her of her distress.

Kibungs provided a forum for purging by confession. They also gave expression to a more general note of self-deprecation. Speakers not only called for an end to reprisals, they belittled many Fore activities and pursuits. Recent behavior had been uninformed, self-destructive. People should not look for the rewards of secret aggression, but should direct their energies toward the activities promoted by the government, such as planting coffee or peanuts and sending their children to school. They should concentrate on the future, rather than dwell on bitter events of the past. Catherine Berndt had observed similar expressions of self-denigration among the North Fore in 1952. She interpreted them as an attempt to protect, by seeming to repudiate, values and practices that Fore felt were vital to their continued existence.[3]

Fear of whites and the desire to protect putative traditional values were themes that continued to emerge throughout December. Every kuru death was the sign of an imperfect conversion to official rules, proof that Fore still harbored sorcerers in their midst. This raised fear of punishment, which was met by the call to adopt a more Westernized way of life. At the same time, each new death demonstrated that the continued activity of sorcerers was causing hurt only to themselves. The ultimate solution to the problem, they felt, was to reconstitute the supposed allegiances of the distant past.

By mid-December, the desire to return to the past became explicit as orators stressed the origins of their present groups. At Igitaru on December

16, having distributed tobacco and food to all group representatives present, the host luluai began his speech. In the old days, he said, their ancestors had not been troubled by kuru. Those were good times. Men must now revive those days and relinquish kuru sorcery before all the women disappeared. The people present constituted one big line called Tamogavisa. They should think of this common bond and forego their internal disputes. At this point some young men called out: "What is Tamogavisa? The name of a mountain or tree or something?" The luluai replied that it was not the name of a mountain or a tree, but their own district name. The luluais of the constituent parishes arose then and said: "We are men of Tamogavisa. In the past, our ancestors lived together in peace. Now we can follow the example set by our ancestors."

In the following days, similar expressions of unity were voiced throughout the South Fore. At Ivaki, representatives from parishes of this southwestern fringe made the following declaration: "Our ancestors were the same. We living men are the ones who split apart and gave separate names to our groups. At this kibung let us adopt the customs of our ancestors. We will stop making kuru on our own people. Ibubuli [another district association] is our all-inclusive name." Thus, the plea for a return to the unity of supposedly less divisive times was again accompanied by the speakers' acknowledgement that their own behavior has given rise to present troubles.

It should be noted that the assembled men are not being asked to forgo sorcery as a technique for punishing enemies. The discussion seeks rather to enlarge and redefine the participants' moral boundaries. Moreover, the impetus for the discussion comes as much from fear of disregarding government wishes as from the desire for internal harmony. The tultul of Wanda commented that in the early days of government contact, Kamano disobeyed orders and were punished for their lack of cooperation: "Now they obey the tetegina. Here in the Fore it was different. We showed pleasure when the missions came among us and were enthusiastic about the new ways. Yet kuru sorcery runs like a river underneath our society, a sign of our lack of response to government commands. What will the kiap say when he discovers this?"

Fear of official punishment continued to gather strength. The tultul of Wanitabe's speech of January 9, delivered to three hundred people representing nine parishes, is typical of many at this time. The luluais and tultuls, he said, suspect that Fore continue to perform sorcery to defy them in their role as surrogate "white men," to express hostility to required work on the public road, or to the government demand for pigs and vegetables in Christmas celebrations at the Okapa patrol post. The kiap has announced that kuru is a kind of sickness, but Fore know it is the work of sorcerers. The tultul fears the kiap's reaction when he discovers that Fore are really responsible: "We luluais and tultuls can tell him that this is so, unless you ordinary men stop doing it. He may deal with us the way he dealt with other recalcitrant people. For our own good, let us concentrate on the new things [cash crops] and give up the old ways [sorcery]."

In the next few days, the leaders' scheme to force sorcerers out into the open became more concrete. It was announced that the luluais and tultuls would return to their home parishes and state that they now had concrete evidence of on-going sorcery. The kiap could then send government tractors down the road from Okapa to collect all South Fore men and take them to some distant place. There they would remain, punished by hard labor. If kuru ceased during their period of banishment, it would be indisputable proof that the affliction was caused by men. If not, kuru was simply a kind of sickness, and they would be permitted to return. A Wanitabe woman spoke for the victims: "We women will ask the kiap to send you men away to an uninhabited region. We would be pleased to do it. The women feel no pity for you in your time of exile."

The leaders returned to their home groups, but as the day approached for their march to the patrol post, the plan seemed to evaporate. Instead, it was suggested, good men could remain at home and only sorcerers would be sent away. Good men were those assembled at the present meetings. Those still hiding at home—the physically deformed, those covered with dirt—they were the guilty ones. People must drag them into public view. They must be forced to join all the innocent and good people who had gathered together. This plan, too, failed to outlive the oratory that proposed it.

The question of the disease's origin was still a focus of interest, sustained by conflicting Fore and Western interpretations. The logic of the Fore position was presented with ingenuity by numerous speakers. One man noted that whites say kuru is a kind of "sickness," a category of ailment Fore attribute to masalai spirits of the forest. But women, he pointed out, the main victims of the disease, do not spend their time in the forest. Only men do. Therefore, kuru could not be a sickness. Another speaker noted that at kibungs held in 1957, they had all agreed that kuru had begun in the Keiagana hamlet of Uwami. Yet he had recently visited this place and found people at Uwami to be free of the disease. Moreover, people there were not even short of women. Perhaps this story of the beginning of kuru was a cover for the real culprits, the present assemblage, the men of the Atigina district association. It was this district, he said, which was now suffering the highest incidence of the disease and had the fewest women.

Another speaker pointed to the victims' age and sex, arguing that if kuru were a "sickness," some men would get it too. So would some infants still at the breast, or toddlers just beginning to walk. Instead, kuru fell upon young women, or women with three or four small children. That was not a random spread, but evidence of the selective aggression of certain sorcerers. The tultul of Mentilesa declared that Fore were pursuing behavior they had learned during initiation: "You men were told then not to disclose your secret plans to fight the enemy, or the identity of those making sorcery bundles. That is what you are doing now, but you must stop it. Speak out and tell the truth." Later, he rose again: "You are running this kibung the wrong way. You have everyone mixed together. You should separate the mature men from the young boys, those who know all about sorcery from the uninformed. When you have these two groups separated, the older men can point to the youths they have entrusted with this information, and you will have isolated those who are the likely sorcerers."

At Purosa, where kuru had most recently appeared, speakers noted its late arrival and suggested they expend their energies tracing the particular route by which kuru had entered their region. If they could work their way back along this path of entry, conveying the information acquired to each group as they went, they could send the thing back the way it came.

Acceptable values of both past and present were most clearly expressed in a ritual toward the end of January. The men of Ivaki gathered one night to confess their acquaintance with all forms of sorcery. Each man stepped forward, listed his past acts of sorcery, and then thrust his right hand (the "strong" hand of aggression) into a dish of soapy water, swearing to abstain from such activities in the future. When all had thus washed away their crimes, they sat down to a meal together, using plates and spoons, articles which were rarely used by any Fore at that time, but which had been introduced to Ivaki by a missionary working nearby. The next morning they met again. Orators noted that kuru had eroded their group loyalties. Old hostilities must be forgotten, and all present should bear in mind that they belonged to one ancestral group. They then clapped hands to signal an end to mutual aggression. Their ritual had combined the symbolic adoption of elements of the new culture while recalling the wider allegiances of the past. Themes of broad unity and rituals of harmony continued to gather strength throughout January.

In early February 1963, the government took another census of the South Fore region, hoping to record all kuru deaths and any new cases since the previous year's count. Following the census at Wanitabe, it soon became apparent to all that three new cases there had gone unreported. No further kibungs occurred in this area, and the last reported meeting came from a fringe area in the southwestern region on March 10, 1963.

Why did the kibungs suddenly end? The appearance of new kuru cases in several hamlets at this time may have forced people to reconsider the effectiveness of the gatherings and the sincerity of the participants. Hollow pledges of friendship given at truce ceremonies while secret alliances were being formed for future attack were deceits familiar to all. Indeed, the strategy of much intergroup aggression requires men to act in secret: the sorcerer who works in hiding and who must be revealed by divination; the "sweet talk" man who quietly proposes to a member of an enemy group that he betray one of his fellows; the avenger of the wartime death of an ally who is awarded his payment at night to conceal his identity from the second dead man's kin. Aware of all this, orators at the waning kibungs had urged their listeners to speak without reserve. Confession had tumbled upon confession as the bereaved men absolved themselves of guilt. How could they now explain the new kuru cases that began to appear?

AN ECLIPSE OF THE SUN

The kuru kibungs may be better understood by considering briefly a separate emergency that the Fore had endured a year before these gatherings began. This earlier crisis was precipitated by a predicted eclipse of the sun. Despite the dissimilarity of the triggering circumstances—a meteorological event and a decimating illness—the Fore response in each case reflects their concern with an immediate threat to their survival. In addition, a common theme is the need to come to terms with the situation introduced into their world by the arrival of white men and their government.

Late in 1961 rumors of an impending total eclipse of the sun spread throughout the Eastern Highlands. News of the eclipse, originating with broadcasts and press releases issued by the government, was intended to assure the population that the event was a natural occurrence which would last only a few minutes. People were warned not to look directly at the sun during the moon's transit, because of the risk of injury to the eyes.

By January 1962 South Fore were discussing the event that would take place on February 5. Despite the emphasis in government announcements that the eclipse would last for but two and three-quarters minutes and that there was no cause for alarm, Fore were convinced that the eclipse posed a serious threat. Each South Fore parish constructed one or two huge refuge houses, large enough to accommodate the human and animal population of each hamlet, along with stores of firewood and food. Roofs and walls were strengthened to withstand the great sheets of ice expected to tumble from the skies. Since the survival of the pigs was uncertain, many pigs were slaughtered and a flurry of debt payments occurred. This pragmatic approach to endangered assets had the added benefit of canceling the strain on the goodwill of those who hoped to endure the calamity together. Reports were current by mid-January that the eclipse would last two or three weeks. The general atmosphere became one of excitement and tension. January saw several acrimonious incidents. Wanitabe leaders publicly reprimanded youths for their insubordinate behavior, and men from Wanitabe and Amora fought with bows and arrows over a vagrant pig.

Toward the end of January, South Fore laborers returned suddenly from the coffee plantations where they were employed near Kainantu and Goroka. They carried with them blankets, kerosene lamps, flashlights, sunglasses and canned food, in preparation for the ordeal to come. Mid-January also saw an increase in religious activity. Most people of Wanitabe parish by 1962 were nominal members of the World Mission based at Purosa, six miles to the south. Wanitabe residents had built a small bamboo church on parish territory, and several men who were appointed mission representatives (Pidgin: *bosboi*) had been schooled in Bible stories and in the new morality, which they were directed to transmit to their fellow residents. Some of these mission evangelists now stated that the unbaptized would certainly not survive the eclipse, and wishful Fore suggested that all kuru sorcerers would die. For months the bamboo church had stood empty and unused. Suddenly in mid-January, morning church services commenced. Each day the sound of the conch shell called people to gather for an hour, after which they departed to work energetically in their gardens, preparing the food and firewood they would later heap inside their houses.

Last-minute preparations on February 4, the day before the eclipse, had all the appearance of a mass baptism (or an imminent census). Hair was cut, faces shaved, bodies washed, and all but the aged appeared wearing some item of Western dress. By trading chickens, money, or bamboo with the missionary at Purosa, a number of men had acquired neckties, which until then had been reserved to designate the office of mission bosboi. Parish members from outlying houses moved into the hamlet square, where all the buildings had recently been reinforced. In the early afternoon, hamlet residents gathered to cook and eat a communal meal. An afternoon church service began at 4 P.M. and ended at 5:20. That evening when residents of Wanitabe went to bed they took their pigs into the houses as usual, but on this night they also took in their chickens.

Refuge houses under construction before eclipse.

Men prepare for communal meal before eclipse.

At 7 A.M. on the morning of the 5th, people hurried to chop more wood and collect more water and food. At 8 A.M. the light began to fade. Shouting to one another and calling to their children, they ran to their houses, barring the doors. Mothers reprimanded children who attempted to leave. Many people wept.

Because of heavy cloud cover, the total eclipse was not evident. After a few minutes of twilight, illumination steadily increased, and by 9 A.M. full daylight had returned. Most people remained in their houses until noon, when they emerged to assemble for another prayer meeting. After singing a few hymns, they returned to their houses, emerging only at 4 P.M. to cook a communal meal. In the week following the eclipse, few people went to the gardens, for every house had food and firewood in plenty. No apparent harm had occurred, yet no one was certain that it was not yet to come. Daily church meetings continued for the next few days.

Ambiguity toward the white intruders appears crucial to an under-standing of Fore behavior. In view of their evident technological superiority, the outsiders' prediction of the event was accepted. Yet Fore mistrusted assurances that the eclipse would be brief and inconsequential. The eclipse was a cosmic event, apparently controlled by the white men, the purpose of which was uncertain, and therefore alarming. Fore responded to news of the eclipse by preparing shelter and food stores to tide them over an impending disaster, while at the same time embracing the religion and ritual of those who appeared to control the event. Recently deprived of the security of much of their own ritual, they observed the new behavior as best they could. They held church gatherings, sang hymns, and said new prayers. Washing, hair-cutting, the wearing of Western clothing, were outward signs of mission community membership. Neckties were perceived as amulets with even greater promise of protection.[4]

The Fore were not alone in expressing anxiety about their survival and the character of colonial relations. Similar reactions to rumors of the eclipse occurred in other parts of Papua New Guinea. The period of the early 1960's was throughout the Highlands a time of widespread malaise. The world price of coffee, a crop introduced by Australians, had dropped, and Chimbu coffee producers sent delegations to Port Moresby to protest, convinced as they were that white buyers were deceiving them.[5] To add to the confusion, 1963 saw prolonged dry spells over much of Australian New Guinea,[6] which disrupted the agricultural calendar of many Highland populations. Fore said the drought would terminate with a great cataclysmic event.

As we saw in earlier chapters, Fore express social relationships through reciprocal exchanges of goods and services. Without reciprocal exchanges, harmonious relationships cannot exist. From the point of view of the Fore, they had provided whites with territory, food, and services, and they expected a reciprocal endowment of valuables. At the behest of the missions, they had abandoned a major part of their indigenous ritual and song, and had rapidly tailored their way of life to suit the requirements of mission membership. In return they expected knowledge they could use to induce the gods to favor them as they had favored the whites. They now began to experience disillusionment. Their attempts to acquire wealth as an automatic consequence of a relationship with the newcomers had failed, as had the cargo cults, and they were in doubt about the relationship itself.

Fear of the eclipse and of the kuru epidemic thus provoked similar responses from the Fore. In the days preceding the eclipse an apprehensive population gave vent to personal and group hostilities. As the predicted day approached, acrimonious encounters gave way to rituals of unity in church meetings and communal feasts. The initial response to the rising incidence of kuru was to pursue activities (divinations, sorcery, accusations) that provoked hostility. In time, the main theme of kibung ritual and oratory changed to a pledge of mutual support in a future that seemed uncertain for all.

The discomfort of the colonial encounter was the backdrop common to both situtations. The Fore were still seeking to define an approach to the aliens in their midst. From the time of the cargo movements, Fore had been attempting to explain and gain control of their altered situation. They were forced to adjust to the problems raised by the encroachment on their universe by powerful outsiders. The predominant note in both the kibungs and the response to the eclipse was one of foreboding, a fear of loss. Food supplies were endangered, in one case through the loss of women, who were the gardeners, and in the other as the result of cosmic destruction. In both, the entire population was threatened with extinction. These are themes that stem from the domination of one culture by another.

THE END OF THE KIBUNGS

One can understand why, in February 1963, the Fore were slow to report new cases of kuru to government officers. The three new victims at Wanitabe were evidence of continued sorcery. To report them would reveal their imperfect compliance with the government's wishes, and would constitute another public disclosure of themselves as the guilty people. As a further security, the luluais of Wanitabe and Kamila now delivered a new message. (Wanitabe and Kamila had experienced the highest incidence of kuru, and their leaders had been the most energetic in sponsoring kibungs.) It was now their considered opinion, they said, that kuru was indeed a sickness, and had nothing to do with sorcery. The evidence for their new position was as follows:

1. Several self-confessed sorcerers, whom they named, had attempted to perform kuru sorcery as an act of personal vengeance and had failed. The same men had succeeded with other forms or sorcery.
2. They had had the same experience themselves. Their own kuru bundles were without power.
3. Fore were taught at initiation to avoid excessive reprisals. Kuru went beyond the bounds Fore typically observed.
4. In recent journeys to border areas at Intamatasa and Umandi, they had seen several very old women with kuru. People in this age group are not the objects of sorcery.
5. The Kukukuku had advised them not to rub the legs of the deceased while mourning, for the disease was spread this way.

For all these reasons, kuru was without doubt a sickness, and therefore could not be caused by men. Their statement should be reported to the kiap, and he should be asked to find a medicine to cure it. For their part, they would put an end to the kibungs.

This somewhat self-conscious recital had a persuasive logic, but advanced no new ideas. Delivered as the first post-kibung cases were confirmed, the speech appears to be a change of tactics, an attempt to avoid punishment by denying involvement. In the kibungs Fore had expressed their cumulative fears of the strangers who now influenced their lives.

Despite their attempt to conceal it, this still appeared to be an important concern. On the morning following the luluais' speech, Wanitabe resumed early morning Christian services. They sang hymns and listened to a Bible story told by the World Mission bosboi, and in the following week there were reports from Fore farther south predicting a recurrence of the eclipse, a previous index of their uncertain relationship with white culture.

The question of why the kibungs came to an end may also be answered by asking it another way. What did Fore hope to achieve by holding these large-scale gatherings, and to what extent did they succeed?

Following by a year-and-a-half the mass exodus of kuru patients to Uvai, the meetings ended the disruptive search for the locus of ill-will, for the perpetrators of the epidemic. Month by month, Fore had participated in a vast morality play, attempting to expose the motives for human behavior, the envy in men's hearts. Declaring a halt to unending retribution, the kibungs spoke instead of basic allegiances, of the positive values of community life.

Groups assembled at this time in structural units wider than those elicited by any other social task. Those misty entities, the district associations, had fleetingly emerged. Their little-used names (Tamogavisa, Ibubuli, Atigina) were cited in public, and constituent parishes duly acknowledged their joint district membership and myth of common origin, providing themselves with the symbolic unity of shared history. That they were tangible communities was demonstrated as each parish hosted a separate kibung, which other parishes in the district attended. While representatives from parishes outside the district were often present, the debates drew attention to their status as observers. Like speakers at a national political convention, orators tried to overcome in-group competition by appealing to broader loyalties. The idea of the punitive white man, based on a realistic assessment of the unequal relationship, provided a strongly unifying theme.

In the kibung discussions, orators indirectly presented what amounted to significant demographic and epidemiological data. At each gathering, hosts assembled their dying for the visitors so they might enact rituals of ablution, with the remainder of the host community seated separately in the background. In this way, groups provided one another with current information on their woman power and thereby their wealth in pigs and gardens. The availability of marriageable girls was also conveyed without need of direct questioning. In the past, the postinitiation parish tours of new initiates periodically broadcast similar data on marriageable young men, and also served to acquaint the youths with the regional cohorts to which they belonged. At the kibungs, then, the human and material resources and current labor problems of particular localities became shared information.

Their analysis of social problems, which dwelt on the age and sex of sorcerers and victims alike, similarly served as a kind of intelligence-gathering on a regional scale. Groups projected gross census information about health and disease, and more refined data on the fluctuation of population cohorts. Like the National Center for Health Statistics in the United States, kibungs supplied information that permitted a collective solution rather than an individual approach to problems of health. Small groups collected information and measured their survival responses as part of a larger aggregate. Their demographic overview spanned more than a decade.

Kibungs can also be viewed as lessons in disease causation and in epidemiology. Some discussions examined small outbreaks of diseases other than kuru. An infectious disease that had occurred after the return of patients from Uvai, for instance, was said to reflect the purchase of Agai'ikio, a new kind of sorcery from the Gimi (See Table 1, p. 60). Its clinical quirks were noted and encapsulated in a theory of causation that related the symptoms to activities of aggressor and victim alike. (The poison used in the new sorcery is said to fly across the gap between the sorcerer's opened bundle to the victim's mouth as the latter smokes his pipe. Of perhaps more relevance for the experience of Fore pilgrims to Uvai, the poison may also be transmitted in a handshake.) Although their taxonomic distinctions differ from those of Western medicine, Fore sorcery categories are an inventory of their medical afflictions, and in public debate they were arriving at some consensus on the nature of each condition. Similar discussions in the past had shifted kuru from the general class of bizarre behavior to a sorcery category of its own. Diagnosis emerged in joint discussion. Clinical and epidemiological observations merged with political perceptions to produce a true community medicine.

The kibungs may also be placed in a calendrical context. Taking place between December and March they coincided with the wet season, a period of general agricultural slack and a shortage of favored foods. In February, the so-called hungry months come to an end. The new sweet potato crop is mature, and in March as the Obei tree bursts into red flower, the fruit of red pandanus is ready to eat. In past years at this time, South Fore had observed Kinomiyena, small rituals of regeneration and friendship.

On such occasions, a host parish or parish section would announce its readiness to hold the rituals, issuing invitations to kin and friends in surrounding areas. The focal point of the ritual was a protective ceremony for the health of the hosts. In contrast to the order at most social events, during these rituals the children were the first to eat. Male children were fed first, followed by female children and all pregnant women. Men bespat the food with the leaves of Ni, a red plant whose "cooling" powers, like those of pig fat and sugarcane, would ward off "hot" illness in the dry sunny months to come.[7] In some years, news of high rates of infant deaths in surrounding regions led to more extended protective rituals.

Visitors who arrived with gifts of rat and opossum received similar gifts of rat, opossum, grubs, and pandanus fruit in return. This they took home to their own children, their wives, and wives' parents. Some men remembered their married sisters now living in distant parishes, and sent food to them. The remaining abundance was then set aside to purchase women. Food was offered to the parents of marriageble girls; if a girl's parents accepted this gift, they had agreed to a marriage contract, and the donor of the food then set about assembling the true brideprice.

In 1963, the rains decreased and the red pandanus ripened while residents of Wanitabe were still preoccupied with kibungs. Although they had been alerted by news of infant illness in surrounding communities, they had no time this year to hunt for rodents and opossums for the full ritual complex. Instead, a truncated ritual occurred, the eating of *Ni*. Early one mid-March morning, a hamlet of Wanitabe parish fed sugarcane to their children and pregnant women and sprinkled them with water. Two men, each holding a stick of red sugarcane, ran around the assembled group. As they ran they said "You, sickness, go away to some other place and leave us alone," and then hung the word-impregnated cane at the north and south hamlet entrances.

The full Kinomiyena ritual was thus a kind of harvest festival, providing annual ceremonies of healing and regeneration and facilitating the extension of bonds among friends and kin. Like the kibungs, the Kinomiyena rippled through the South Fore, as different groups acted as hosts. The rituals provided for annual distribution of surplus food, as well as the preventive health care of particular communities.

The kibungs, in contrast, were directed at the greater demographic and economic emergency unsettling the entire region. Sweet potatoes, pigs, and women were all in unusually short supply, and social life was at an impasse.[8] "See how few pigs we have," the men observed. "Think how many women the sorcerers must have killed." Moreover, these were not the first great emergency kibungs the South Fore could recall. Mature men sometimes referred to two earlier anti-kuru kibungs. In the first, held sometime in the 1940's, men ran around the circumference of their grouped women, planting a symbolic barricade of cordyline leaves. In 1957, they had followed different procedures. Sorcerers had exhibited the kuru bundles they used in their work, and had poured pig fat on the bundles to neutralize their potent heat. The tultul of Mentilesa recalled that these measures had allowed them a period of reprieve. "For a short time, there were plenty of young girls, and we set them aside for marriage. You men should do the same thing now, and kuru can decline again," he said in 1963. These three reactions tell an epidemiological story of their own: the heightened concern for sorcery-related illness by 1957, which led to methods of disclosure, and the sharp decline in kuru mortality between 1958 and 1962, documented in Figure 2, p. 90 above. Two of the three kibungs coincided with peaks in kuru mortality rates (as Figure 2 shows). The kibungs can thus be seen as responses to the demographic, economic, and emotional distortions that arise approximately once a decade in small groups experiencing differential fertility and survival.[9]

Kibungs convey mutual vulnerability. Competition is absent. There is no exchange of pigs or wealth, only the symbols of truce and communion—sprinkled water, the clapping of hands, and shared tobacco. The focus of kibungs is on human survival. The major themes concern illness and social cooperation. Excessive competition leads to social disintegration; it endangers both predator and prey. Primitive medicine is known for giving greater attention to social cause than to practical therapy, a characteristic sometimes considered to be a weakness.[10] Yet it might also be argued that human survival depends on the successful organization of cooperative groups. The major concern of Fore during the dysentery epidemics of the 1940's was with the collapse of organized labor. Crops rotted unharvested while survivors struggled to bury their dead. A most urgent theme of the kibungs, too, was the fragile state of a society experiencing an atrophy of reciprocal support. Orators asked men to curb those passions which, if left ungoverned, would destroy any moral community. They offered immunity from prosecution to those willing to pledge membership in a cooperative society. The underlying pathology was both social and medical. Those suffering from kuru clearly have a kind of illness, but one caused by a derangement of human motivation. The danger for society lies both in the loss of group members and in the drain on mutual trust.

Kibung orators conveyed messages of social unity, pledges of a hiatus in aggression and in self-defeating competition. For three-and-a-half months, Fore reconstructed their shattered social networks, giving them a hallowed imprint. Faced with three new kuru cases as their season of communion ended, the leaders of Atigina district not only could not afford to report their failure to the government, they could not afford to acknowledge it to themselves. In mid-March, when the new sweet potato crop matured and the luxury pandanus ripened, the kibungs came to an end. Wanitabe resumed intensive social exchange and cooperation with neighbors and kin. In the month between mid-March and mid-April, there were sixteen large distributions of wealth. Eight of the payments (for births, marriages and deaths) occurred within Wanitabe, and eight with outside parishes. In addition, there were three exchanges of surplus food with the parishes of Amora, Kamila, and Kume, fellow participants in the Atigina kibungs. Several large work groups formed to build fences for the new Wanitabe coffee gardens.

The kibungs were directed at the impasse caused by random illness and aimless ill-will. Sanctified attention to orderliness opened the way for peaceful, small-scale exchanges of wealth and labor among members of the Atigina district, a process provided for in normal years by the rituals of Kinomiyena. In 1963, the larger society was patched together by a great crusade for public health and moral rearmament. Once again the Fore had attempted to redefine their troubled relationships with one another and with the colonial administration.

STATUS AND THE SORCERER

9

When I returned to the South Fore in 1970 after an absence of seven years, it was apparent there had been a shift in political affiliations. Close alliances between some sections of Wanitabe parish had dissolved. Parish segments that as recently as 1968 had joined to present pigs to neighboring groups were now estranged. By 1970 Wanitabe, once one of the largest South Fore parishes (352 members in 1963) had split in two. The constituent segments had emerged as parishes in their own right, resumed their precolonial group titles (Wanitabe and Nabu), and abandoned the theme of the past decade that they were descended from two brothers. Moreover, one Nabu line had just left the area to settle with kin and friends in the southeast frontier parish of Abomotasa. Wanitabe men said they had rid themselves of a pack of bad sorcerers.

The break was not without warning. A history of sorcery allegation and counterallegation between the now severed groups dates from at least 1963, when members of a Wanitabe section were asked to attend a divination test at Nabu. They had attended, some protesting that as affines they were ashamed to be under suspicion. Fearing the day's outcome, they had performed a ritual before crossing the boundary between the two territories. One man beat the earth with pandanus leaves and spat ginger as he ran around the perimeter of the group, conveying an image of political unity they did not have. The inquiry passed without disaster, although one Nabu kuru victim fainted as a Wanitabe suspect sprinkled her with water, a sign later cited as evidence of his guilt.

Between 1963 and 1970, adult mortality in the two groups had been

117

severe, and many of the deaths were said to be the work of sorcerers in the other camp. Nabu had experienced 25 kuru deaths (twenty female and five male), while Wanitabe had lost fifteen women and five young men. In addition, Wanitabe complained that a recent epidemic of respiratory illness had depleted them of five Big Men whose ritual knowledge had helped coordinate their group's activities. One elderly survivor suffering from karena, the disorder that had carried off his companions, alleged that the health problems at Wanitabe dated from the 1968 pig festivals, when Nabu men had slipped poison into the rice they had eaten together.

Several Nabu Big Men had also died. In the past, this would have been the moment for armed combat. Instead, Masanta, a young Wanitabe man, went to court. There he told a story of the aggression now occurring between members of the generation that had replaced the recently deceased elders. Masanta's father had been one of the elders to die, and he blamed Nabu. A few months after his father's death, he told the judge, he had encountered a party of Kamila men at the local trade store. They were buying rice and canned meat for the funeral of a Kamila resident. Not knowing their purpose, Masanta had said: "Why are you buying all this food? Are you opening your own trade store or something?" Alerted by the question, the men of Kamila concluded that he had caused their kinsman's death. He had performed sorcery and was now drawn to hear confirmation of his crime. That night some men from Kamila and some from Nabu met and decided to do away with the aggressor. Masanta was the cause of many deaths at Nabu, they said. They offered a bribe to Masanta's cousin (his mother's brother's son) at Kamila, giving him some karena poison for his kinsman's food. The cousin instead informed the Wanitabe Big Men, bringing them the poison as evidence. The intended victim shortly heard of the plot. His shock was so great that he felt his liver rise inside him, ascending as if to block his neck. The men of Wanitabe sent a message then to Kamila and Nabu, calling them to a meeting where they could try to straighten out the whole affair.

The men of Nabu, who arrived first, came armed with bows and arrows. When the others appeared the fight began, each side tearing up fence posts to add to their armory. The local schoolteacher, a recognized neutral from coastal New Guinea, separated the two parties, and the day ended with compensation for damages. Each injured man indicated the opponent who had spilled his blood, and the assailant paid him $10.

Soon after this Masanta's wife, Nagano, complained of head pains and poor physical coordination, the first symptoms of kuru. Nagano saw her assailant in a dream, but Masanta already knew where to look. Taking $20 from the sale of his coffee beans, he offered the money to his enemy at Kamila, suggesting that he reveal what he knew of the matter. The man accepted the money and admitted that he, together with one other Kamila man and three men from Nabu, had performed kuru sorcery against Nagano. He described the location of the sorcery bundles that were causing her illness. Masanta and some other men from his line subsequently found three kuru bundles, which they dried in the sun and cooled with pig fat. Then they waited. The victim did not improve. Angered at this outcome, Masanta began court proceedings.

During the trial, which took place in July 1970, the five men admitted their part. Having revealed the location of their kuru bundles, they now declared themselves free of responsibility. The (New Guinean) judge jailed them for five months. In addition, he confined Andokaba of Nabu for his part in the earlier karena plot. At Wanitabe, people said that Masanta's life now depended on his little hunting dog. The animal was not only a good business investment (its pups selling for $10 apiece), it was also Masanta's mouthpiece. The dog would bark as assailants approached, and it was considered to be Masanta's only protection against tokabu killers from Nabu.

The court hearing was an official confirmation of the long-standing deterioration in Wanitabe–Nabu relations. For more than a year visits between the two groups had ceased, with the obligatory payments between affines and matrikin being delivered by neutral third persons. Mutual assistance in assembling death payments, as well as marriages between the two groups, had also come to a halt; Wanitabe men now arranged marriages within the remaining sections of their own parish and sent their sisters as brides to the neighboring parish of Amora.

Early in September, Andokaba returned from jail. Relations between Nabu and Wanitabe were extremely strained. People were reluctant to walk the road between the two territories when the sun stood directly overhead. Many victims of tokabu, it was said, lost consciousness at this hot, shadowless moment of day. If travel was unavoidable, it was best to proceed on cloudy days or borrow an umbrella and keep to the protective shelter of occasional trees. One morning, a party of youths about to leave Wanitabe to work on the coast burned all their tattered old clothes. Nabu kuru sorcerers, they said, might misuse these material extensions of themselves.

In this atmosphere of mutual distrust and vigilance, on the evening of September 9, Nabu men sent word that Masanta's dog was stealing their chickens. If it happened again, they warned, they would take Masanta, whom they referred to as the father of the dog, to court. Early the next morning Masanta took his ailing wife to the government hospital at Okapa. In the terminal stages of both kuru and pregnancy, she now required help to deliver the child. During Masanta's absence, a message arrived from Nabu. Andokaba has just shot Masanta's dog. Wanitabe men found the body at the Wanitabe–Nabu boundary, a tuft of chicken feathers in its mouth as evidence of its marauding habits. Wanitabe gathered to mourn for the dog, and some who had eaten possum discovered by the little hunter expressed their sorrow. They brought gifts (a small towel, a piece of cloth) to be buried with the corpse in Masanta's garden. As a temporary measure they built a shelter for the dog and its gifts and awaited Masanta's return. What would he do when he heard the news? At this point in the conflict I left New Guinea, so I cannot report what happened next. Masanta, however, had said that when Nagano died, he would quit Wanitabe and this region of sorcerers, and spend some time working on the coast. Nagano's father expressed the opinion that when the current episode was over, people could call for another kibung and again declare a state of truce.

Expressions of outrage thus flow back and forth between individuals and groups, a measure of their differential fortune and survival. Sorcery arises to balance accounts. Sorcerers are the aggrieved, out to settle debts. Without recourse to diviners, victims know who harbors grievances against them. Women dream of rejected suitors and would-be lovers, while men take stock of others who have suffered injury at their hands. Thus, adulterers who take runaway wives expect retaliation from the abused husband, while great fighters think of sorcerers rising from the ranks of the unavenged. A Waisa Big Man blamed Gimi sorcerers for the kuru death of his son, for he had killed many Gimi warriors prior to the government-enforced peace. A leader from Purosa was more particular, matching clinical, epidemiological, and political detail. His son was deteriorating rapidly. He might well be dead within three months of the appearance of the first symptoms of kuru. His own unmet war debts lay among groups to the south—at Ilesa, Awarosa, and Agakamatasa. Since people in this hot southland were said to die more quickly and at an earlier age than those farther north, the sorcerers in his case were surely from there. Moreover, his son was now the age of those he had formerly killed. Someone was settling an account.

Of the mounting sorcery cases in the late 1950's and 1960's, those which were pursued most vigorously and were most widely discussed involved Big Men, as the above examples illustrate. Tables 3 and 4 present a

TABLE 3
Sorcery Cases by Sex and Cause of Death

		Male	Female	Total
Sex of sorcerer		47	0	47
Sex of victim		9	38	47
Cause of Death:				
	Kuru	2	35	37
	Karena	5	0	5
	Unknown	2	3	5
Intermediaries reported		6	0	6

summary of 47 cases about which I could obtain detailed information from the Fore, who, in recalling some cases and not others, in effect selected the data in the table. In 11 of these the main actors (whether accused or accusers) were luluais or tultuls, that is, Big Men whose fortunes are intertwined with those of their supporters. Table 3 also indicates the value of women to important men. The sorcerers are all males. No women appear among the accused, despite the theoretical possibility allowed by Fore that angry women might poison their husbands. But adult women constitute 38 of the 47 victims. For any man to lose his wife is for him to lose the very foundations of his existence, since women provide both children and the main labor in subsistence agriculture. And food is also wealth. A Big Man whose wife falls ill immediately senses his imminent decline in status. Without gardens and pigs he has nothing to exchange. Fore say that to lose a wife is as painful as having hair plucked from the nose. It is the husband of the sick woman who is perceived as the true victim, for it is his status that is under attack.

TABLE 4
Motivation for Sorcery and Residence of Sorcerer

Motivation for sorcery:	
Widower kills wife of another	33
Jilted husband kills own wife	4
Kin of male war victim kills son of killer	2
Frustrated suitor kills desired woman to punish her brothers*	1
Male sorcerer kills male victim as group reprisal	1
Man kills woman in reprisal for mother's death	1
Man kills woman in reprisal for brother's death	1
Man kills wife of father's killer's son	1
Unknown	3
Residence of sorcerer:	
Husband's parish	21
Other parish	16
Unknown	10

*Allegedly the cause of the first case of kuru among Fore.

Table 4 confirms the significance of wives to Big Men, or would-be Big Men, in another way. Note that in 34 of the 47 cases, a widower is accused of killing another man's wife. Men speculate freely on the motives activating widowers. A man's wife may die of kuru, they say, leaving him alone. In time he is unable to make public contributions of food and pork, and he begins to dwell on his miserably reduced condition. He steals a fragment of skirt or a strand of hair from a co-resident woman and gives it to her husband's enemies. He deliberately chooses a woman who is a strong worker and a fine gardener, and awaits the satisfaction of seeing her die of kuru. Or perhaps the victim's enemies bribe him to steal the fragment for them. Envy is a strong motivation. Married couples walking about together induce a widower to to think: "I once walked about like this with my wife, but now she is dead and I am a poor worthless individual. This married man can join the ranks and become as impoverished as I am." And he steals the material the sorcerers need to kill this desirable woman.

Big Men are not the only ones who lose their wives to kuru, although Fore think the wives of such men are particularly vulnerable to the disease. This may be because Big Men are in a position to pursue sorcery accusations more thoroughly; or perhaps their wives had access to more cannibal meals and were in fact more vulnerable to the disease. In any event, Fore say it is always the best women who are dying. When such women die, their distressed husbands suspect recent widowers who had themselves aspired to be Big Men. Thus the drama of accusations involves men in their political maturity jousting among themselves. The killers are not interested in eliminating the aged or the very young, but go to the demographic heart of the population, women and men in their working and reproductive prime.[1]

This contrasts markedly with the image of sorcery Fore convey in other contexts, such as the kibungs. There, orators portray sorcerers as physically deformed, covered in dirt. They refrain from washing, drinking, or eating cold foods, thereby avoiding those acts which would counter the hot effects of their evil work. They are the negative of all that is fine, trustworthy and good. Not born of women, they spring from trees, stones or holes in the ground. Envious and impoverished, they are "rubbish men," *alu kina*. Unhindered by the moral rules governing the rest of society, they raise the specter of anarchy and randomness in human experience. Alu kina are a danger to the community, and their behavior is creating a land of the poor.

When people at Wanitabe were asked to name alu kina in their own community, they identified four men who were physically afflicted—one blind, two facially disfigured, and one with a war-damaged knee. This last injury ranks second in seriousness only to the mortal wound of an arrow in the armpit. A damaged knee impedes mobility and spoils the image of the Fore male as an upright, majestic tree. One female achondroplastic dwarf was also cited. None of the Wanitabe alu kina had ever married and, on the face of things, might be considered to harbor some resentment. Yet none to my knowledge had ever been accused of sorcery. The conception of the sorcerer, then, encompasses a number of different ideas contained in the morphemes *kio* (hidden) and *alu* (rubbish). What do Fore mean when they speak of sorcerers alternatively as *alu kina* and *kio yagala* (rubbish people and hidden men)?

Kio yagala characteristically work in concealment. The Fore initiation rituals teach that knowledge is power, and that secrecy prevents the sharing of power with others. It enables the elders to command the young, and men to control women. To reveal information is to defuse it. Yams will not flourish or the rains fall unless the owner of the garden magic utters the spells in private. Once shared, their strength is diluted and they are not a secure base for personal advantage. Secrets should be shared only with equals. The occupants of a men's house thus share knowledge of the location of *kio kabei* (hidden doors). They must all know how to breach the place in the wall where the bark covering masks weakness in construction, for this element of surprise is all that will save them when the enemy sets fire to the house and waits to slaughter them as they emerge from the entrance. Sorcerers similarly keep tight rein on news of their secret activities, for few people have an identical interest in the outcome of the deed and the reputation of the actors. In the final analysis, agemates are the only safe male confidantes. They are equal in status and do not compete with each other. Information entrusted to agemates is as information committed to oneself.

Kio yagala are sorcerers in their power dimension, the performers of "hot" work. They cook things to ashes, tap the heat of the sun, and energize their poison bundles with the heat of the fire. The real potency of sorcerers, however, lies in the secrecy of their performance, in particular skills carried out in seclusion. Unveiling is the only counter to such private power, and this requires an opposing investment of time and wealth. The identity of the malefactor can be learned through intimidation and bribery. Counterknowledge comes from dreams, visions, and revelations provided by spirits of the sick and the dead. The common theme of consultations with curers, group inquiries, and kibung debates is disclosure. Sorcerers are encouraged to show and to tell. They confess, they raise their "strong" hands, they allow their sorcery bundles to be seen by all. Publicity defuses the danger of special information, and averts the emergence of a privileged elite.

Kio yagala superficially resemble normal men. It is their interior that is the locus of corruption. South Fore say that doctors involved in kuru research should go directly to the heart of the problem, the wickedness of their enemies. Failure to cure kuru results from the misdirected efforts of Western medicine, which focuses exclusively on medical therapy. Modern technology should be applied instead to improved intelligence gathering, to detecting the covert operations of those who endanger the general welfare. In the early 1960's, Fore suggested that a photograph of the entire male population would reveal the guilty, who would be seen holding a kuru bundle in their "strong" raised hands. By 1970 further exposure to medical research had led them to the hope that if properly used, the ophthalmoscope could reveal the sorcerer's rotting interior.

Alu kina, in contrast, represent sorcerers in what might be called their weakness dimension, their image as men of reduced status. They are the filthy old men absent from the kibungs. Their refusal to exhibit themselves and to share food with others marks them as persons deficient in some fundamental aspect. By absenting themselves from the ritual, they have failed to demonstrate a commitment to the human community, and are therefore not to be trusted. Alu kina are marked by an additional impediment: they are generally referred to as elderly, although specifically identified rubbish people are not in fact always old. *Alu* refers to a burial place, a dangerously contaminated location, and by extension to the aged, those near the grave. Alu kina, then, are people of another kind. They border on pollution. They are people of inferior status.

Alu kina show no respect for the rules of society. They eat food prohibited to men of consequence. Men who disregard the forbidden things are a disgrace to themselves and a threat to the social order. They merit the humiliations that fall upon the lowly. Men become alu kina by one particularly perilous route: residing with their affines. Affines exchange gifts of wild protein, food taboo for men in their early maturity. Co-residence with wife's kin is said to lead to the constant consumption of tabooed foods, loss of strength, and rapid senescence. Better to live apart from affines and send them gifts of possum and cassowary, thereby avoiding food violations and the loss of esteem that comes from inevitable dependence. A man who resides with his affines may be obliged to perform bride service, that is, to labor for his wife's father. Although he gives a smaller brideprice and gains access to land, the contaminating aspect of living with affines is the danger of enslavement.

In the past, a man who shot a wild pig sent it immediately to his wife's brothers. "We didn't slaughter it or cut out its belly. We didn't even touch it with our hands. We just put a rope on it and sent it to our affines. We thought that if we ate it we would become weak and scrawny, just like the pig." These ideas encouraged the transmission of gifts, and were also an implicit comment on the Fore view of affines. At Wanitabe men now call wild pig alu kina, and view it with considerable disparagement. It is food appropriate for social inferiors: women, children, and very old men.

Thus alu kina—the weak, the old, and the physically blemished—belong to a category kept in place by rules of priority and social exclusions. They are not specifically accused of sorcery, for they are visible and their particular identity requires no divination. Kio yagala, by contrast, must be identified in a political contest that tries the strength of both victim and accused. The outcome of divinations are frequently ambiguous, supplying the names of groups rather than specific individuals. Moreover, Big Men tend to test a case again and again, trying different divination procedures and different audiences. At some point in the search, they assess the degree of support their campaign has aroused, and if it is sufficiently strong, make an accusation. This sick person often provides verification by viewing the sorcerer who has caused her illness in a dream. As the statistics show, the accused are already losers and sufferers to some degree. Finding themselves unable to muster political support among fellow parishioners, they may migrate out of the area. As emigrants, they move one step closer to the category of the dispossessed, a confirmation of their identity as rubbish people. The status of those who remain is enhanced. The remaining leaders see this departure as the culling of undesirables from their midst, and a justification of the initial challenge.

Men rail at the presence of sorcerers, yet in a sense the sorcerers' motives are understandable. Reciprocal aggression is an outgrowth of prior victimization. Sorcery proposes an ethic of competition in which one's opponents are always venal. In pursuit of status, Big Men manipulate the behavior of women, plants, pigs, and one another. Like the sorcerers who cut them down, they are loners existing in a competitive environment. Few join the search parties for sorcerers other than one or two members of the victim's own line. Affines and maternal relatives are doubtful props. Your wife's mother is probably frustrating your desire for children by supplying her daughter with abortion-inducing plants. Your own ambivalence toward matrikin is tested in wartime. Upon wounding a matrilateral cross-cousin (mother's brother's son) in the confusion of battle, you rush to soothe him, rub his legs, and express regret for this untoward incident. Privately, the accident might trouble you hardly at all. The enemy resides neither in your own line nor in the paired lines of the amikina, but as Table 4 indicates, the limits of support are narrow indeed. At least half those accused of sorcery are members of the same parish and may thus belong to affinal groups. Sorcery is an ideology of estrangement, a severing of intimacy among formerly collaborating groups. In periodic sorcery campaigns, parish groups redefine the limits of political allegiance. The parish thus rarely exceeds 350 members, and divests itself of potential Big Men, averting the instability that arises when small groups become top-heavy in leadership. The irony of the situation lies in the fact that some accused sorcerers may gain in reputation and wealth (through bribes) as a result of their identification, and thereby gain esteem in their own and in allied communities.

When Fore speak of sorcerers as both kio yagala and alu kina, they convey a notion of some complexity. As kio yagala, sorcerers have the power to kill, that is, to diminish the stature of an opponent. Their power is recognized, but not acclaimed as a public good. The symbolism of the behavior of kio yagala shows them to be practitioners of misbegotten work. Fired by envy, they are thought to heighten their condition by acts of voluntary abstinence. They labor in secret, forgoing companionship until their destructive task is done. They go without sex, and deny themselves the most desirable, cooling, and regenerating substances—pork, sugarcane, and water. Already bereaved, kio yagala activate their powers in the heat of extreme deprivation. They are the essence of anti-social, anti-life-sustaining forces.

The attempt by Fore to combine an image of power with one of denigration conveys an ambiguous message. Sorcerers are powerful and simultaneously inferior beings who suffer from innate drawbacks. The jealousy of kio yagala is a danger; on the other hand, alu kina are not rivals for political space, and their envy is of little consequence. Alu kina, like women, are perceived as odious rather than truly threatening. No amount of self-denial by them will overcome their lot. By referring to sorcerers as rubbish men, Big Men seek to discredit political rivals both in their own community and in a more general sense. Like other New Guineas highlanders, the Fore admire the display of power; yet the dual image of the Fore sorcerer indicates an attitude of both respect and contempt. It is a debate Fore are having themselves. Tyrants arise and sorcerers acquire status, but secret power is not to be condoned. Malice, greed, and corruption exist, but they should not be unduly rewarded. Fore sorcery discussions publicly propose that married men are the victims of lawless assault, or that disloyal parish residents undermine the survival of the group. Sorcerers fill the ideological space occupied in some societies by the figure of the Anti-Christ. Devils in human form, dragons of chaos, they are rivals for power and enemies of the accepted social and moral order.

Thus Fore sorcery is a kind of political epidemiology, which fuses ethical and economic considerations. It is a public play among political rivals. It admits the force of envy as a human sentiment and allows that it is a force difficult to contain. At the same time, the pursuit of sorcerers contributes to an economy of redistribution. Although tied to accident, illness, and other apparently random events, the resulting diffusion of wealth conforms to a pattern. Wealth is siphoned from those who have to those who have not. Big Men spend more time and wealth hunting for sorcerers than do men of lesser means, with their riches fanning out in bribes and fees to those they accuse and those they consult. Their major payments go to curers in peripheral and more economically deprived areas to the south and west, contributing to the emergence of Big Men in those regions. Some status accrues to the accuser from giving things away, but this transmission of wealth differs from reciprocal gifts between allies and kin. It is a one-way expenditure, in which the donor constructs no following among the indebted. The cry "sorcery" is the pained diagnosis of the downwardly mobile individual who is experiencing an event that is diminishing his status.

The hunt for sorcerers nevertheless distributes wealth in a manner appropriate to a society with a partially intensive system of agriculture. Frequent interruptions limit productivity, while the kaleidoscopic changes in parish membership hinder large-scale, long-term ventures. In fluctuating rhythms of work, men spend time attending to the fruitfulness of their women and gardens, and some in contests for public esteem. The idea of a perverted human opponent has recently replaced the Pucklike Nokoti. Nokoti represented less competitive times. Living in the forest with his wives and children, he sometimes hindered and sometimes helped the people he encountered. Current hazards are more invisible and dangerous. Success rests not on the goodwill of forest spirits or the blessing of ancestors, but on the strength and skills of lonely men locked in serious combat.

The tone of sorcery discussions is highly moralistic. Kibung orators speak movingly of their desire for a better world. Men should turn from the "hot, red" things of the past (sorcery) and cling to the new "white" things of the future (education and business). This would produce a generation of young men ignorant of the means of destruction, and their land would flourish in health and plenty. The kibungs were a visionary interlude. At other times Fore proposed the idea that disease results from a failure in the balance that allows men of disparate interests to live in one community, in relationships of mutual aid and of parasite and host. In 1960, one Wanitabe Big Man argued against the slaughter of an entire Waisa line when a divination test revealed evidence of the men's guilt. They might readily kill the whole group, he said; the visitors were unarmed, and Wanitabe men had them surrounded. But who would then remain to remove sorcery bundles? Like the young man with the first bow, they might eliminate those on whom they depended. They had faced again a recurrent problem: how to accommodate private desires to social needs.

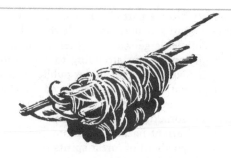

POLLUTERS, WITCHES, AND SORCERERS

10

In the peak years of kuru mortality, luluais and tultuls complained most loudly of their victimization by ordinary men, illustrating a general principle of social hierarchies that the weak are believed to endanger the strong. The Fore idiom of misfortune is that of the vulnerable male assaulted by forces beyond his control. Varied in origin, the agents of depletion aim their attack in a single direction; women endanger men, youths their elders, while the physically impaired burden the productive members of the community. Sorcerers, characteristically described as widowers, eliminate the wives of more fortunate men; striking at the mothers and pig-raisers, they doubly diminish the capacity of their opponents to maintain their monopoly of available status and power.

This theme of weakness sapping strength runs through the Fore universe in two dimensions. Geographically, Fore believe that mystical dangers emanate from the sparsely settled regions to the south. In relational terms, Fore hold that less prestigious individuals in their own personal networks threaten their survival. This chapter presents the Fore assessment of the obstacles in the universe, and suggests that fear of sorcerers and similar ideologies of anxiety conform to more general patterns of human behavior.

RELATIONS OF DOMINANCE

While sorcery accusations reflect serious conflict, the concept of pollution regulates less urgent affairs. Pollution as a cause of long-term debility rather than sudden death, is a notion widely reported through New Guinea. The

Fore fear of contamination by women is not as profound as in some New Guinea societies. Nonetheless, during menstruation and childbirth a Fore woman must retire to a seclusion hut at the edge of the hamlet, poised between the residential community and the dangerous outside world. Her seclusion there is a sign of the half-wild condition brought on by the natural functions of her own body. Other women bring her food, for if she visited her gardens during this period of isolation she would blight all domesticated crops. Nor should she send food to her husband: ingesting food she had touched would make him feel weak, catch a cold, age prematurely. In a word, he would suffer the consequences of pollution, an energy-draining respiratory condition leading ultimately to karena. A husband who suspects his wife of infidelity therefore hesitates to take food from her hand after dark, fearing an admixture of menstrual discharge. Such fears are most prevalent among older men with relatively young wives, a situation in which many remarried kuru widowers find themselves. Their anxiety is understandable, both because respiratory illness has a reported incidence of 56 percent in New Guinea subjects over age sixty,[1] and because marital discord is usually more severe when there is a marked age difference between husband and wife. The aging husband attributes respiratory difficulties to his inability to contain the sexuality of his young wife, which leads to the threatening idea that he is losing this resource to male competitors.

The dangerous universe of women includes a man's wife and other sexual partners, but not his sister, whose sexuality is the disciplinary problem of another man. Moreover, a sister's reproductive organs bring her brother prestige and wealth in birth and initiation gifts from her husband. In the past, a wife's exodus from the birth hut required ritual protection for the endangered husband. Mother and child were rubbed with the singed fur of wild opossum (the protein gift to her male kin), and as these beings-in-transition re-entered the community, the husband climbed a tree to rise above the cloud of reproductive contamination.

Male-female disputes involve issues of authority. The ritualized relations between men and their wives are repeated lessons in discipline. The lodging of an opponent's arrow in a man's buttocks (the body part his wife is entitled to consume) informs the husband of his wife's supposed disloyalty. On his return from such an encounter, he chastises her for the injury, as a sign that he knows her every movement. The birth of a deformed or stillborn child, held to be the women's sole responsibility, is a greater offense. Her husband and the men of the hamlet denounce the event as a great pollution, an affront to male norms of biosocial control. They punish the mother by killing one of her pigs, and rail at their need to undergo painful rituals of purification. Their noses pain, they say, from constant bloodletting, and the contaminating "smell" of this semi-human progeny has weakened them all. The cleansing rituals re-enact those of initiation, the performance which transforms youths dependent on women into mature, pollution-prone adults. In both bloodletting rituals Fore ram sharp canegrass into their nostrils to rid themselves of foul female "smells," in a cultural mimicry of female menstruation. While the men renew themselves in forest seclusion, female matrikin (mainly mother's brother's wives) eat the stillborn child, a source of protein not contested by men. The conflict may take a more serious turn. A husband assaulted by his wife observes ceremonial mourning, as described earlier (p. 48). Overt rebellion by a female causes symbolic death for the male. The husband and his agemates rub themselves with the ashes of mourning and demand pork from the repentant wife's kin.

Pollution, however, is an idea for the control of subordinates and threatening outsiders in general, and is not an exclusively sex-linked phenomenon.[2] This becomes apparent as Fore spontaneously apply the notion to novel situations. In 1947, the South Fore purified themselves following the appearance of Patrol Officer Skinner and the first Australian patrol, in an effort to restore the former power relationship. Their ceremonial consumption of rats and "medicines" placed the intruders in the dangerous category of polluting intruders. The sight of these new men had caused a general debilitation, and at Wanitabe people were afraid they might all sicken and die. By 1960, having adjusted to this structural change in the social order, Fore were quick to heed government edicts, an acknowledgment of their newly subservient position. The social dangers they now attempted to control lay within their own community, where the idea of pollution would have more effect.

In the 1960's, Wanitabe elders had little direct access to the consumer goods and new lingua franca (Pidgin) acquired by young men who were working for the missions or the government. During an epidemic of pig anthrax in 1963, the resentment of the seniors suddenly emerged. The older men said that the pig epidemic was caused by the football games the young men were playing, and by the hair oil they had purchased as a lure to young women. The "smell" of the football and hair oil was entering the pigs' noses, they said, bringing on respiratory difficulties and death. The seniors' oblique message was that the pigs were dying from the pollution of a challenge to their position. The epidemic, called *Satadei'ena biyei* ("Saturday hit them") was an unconsciously witty reference to the Seventh Day Adventist affiliation of several of the youths and to that denominations's prohibition of pork. By tabooing football and hair oil, both thought to be attractive to women but antipathetic to pigs, the elders were trying to weave a mesh of corrective ideology around a social group threatening to supplant traditional leadership. The message implied also that men of weight rank pigs above presumptuous youths, who themselves are superior to women.

Sorcery is a severe case of pollution. Both notions apply to opponents whose behavior is said to cause illness in their victims. Sorcery is the greater danger, since it represents the bid of a deprived person to offset a disadvantage that is neither permanent nor innate. The severity of the condition increases with the seriousness of the conflict. Thus, a wife pollutes by her uncontrollable physiology, and an act of defiance on her part causes symbolic male death. As the table of sorcery methods shows (Table 1, Nos. 11 and 12, p. 63), men believe menstrual blood to be used in the performance of sorcery. A wife who wished to eliminate her spouse can use this polluting substance as a poison. She may even give enemy sorcerers the semen she retrieves from her underskirts. In her adulterous moods, a discontented wife is almost as purposefully dangerous as a male rival. Cancellation of the danger depends on the sex of the evildoer. In response to bribes or intimidation, men perform counteracts to undo the damage they have caused. Women, on the other hand, free their victims solely through pity, a spontaneous, involuntary emotion said to be evoked only if the sorceress sees her victim.

Pollution, then, is attributed to categories of people—women and youths—whose behavior is curbed by a variety of other cultural modifiers. Women and youths belong to socially defamed groups, as do "rubbish people," the uninvestigated sorcerers of ill repute. Sorcery, on the other hand, is a kind of harmful power that operates through spells, rites, and

Young men playing football, which elders blamed for anthrax epidemic.

physical material. Involving a hidden act, it makes use of secret knowledge and components that may be discreetly purchased, and is performed by conscious choice. Sorcery thus stands in contrast to pollution, which is not hidden and requires no intermediate technology. Moreover, its source is known, predictable, and requires no divination. Thus, while sorcery is the achieved status of particular individuals, pollution is the ascribed attribute of social categories.

The Fore distinction between sorcery and pollution (to take the two ends of the continuum for purposes of the following discussion) thus parallels that described by Evans-Pritchard for Zande concepts of sorcery and witchcraft.[3] Among the Zande sorcery is a technique requiring no inherent qualities in the performer. It may be purchased and learned, and involves the treatment of the "leavings" of a victim with some intrinsically powerful substance that will cause illness or death. Witchcraft, by contrast is innate, and like pity may operate without the conscious intention of the witch. While witchcraft is reported infrequently in New Guinea, the preoccupations of New Guinea witches (like those of the Zande) resemble those of Fore polluters. Moreover, where witches occur in New Guinea they are frequently said to be women.[4] The power of Abelam witches, for instance, believed inactive before puberty, causes sickness and death among infants and pigs and the inexplicable breakage of domestic utensils—all female affairs over which a husband exercises little control.[5] Abelam witches and Fore polluters occupy the same social and psychological space.

Fore pollution, like witchcraft elsewhere in Melanesia, is a deplorable but involuntary condition. Those who harbor it are social inferiors on whom their superiors in some sense depend. Fore polluters are temporarily exiled and subjected to intermittent shame. As with rubbish people and upstart youths, their domestic responsibilities are conceived of as irrelevant to the masculine world of political influence. With proper management, their services contribute to community welfare. Their unacceptable conduct is not a crime, but a sin. (By 1970, as a result of mission usage, the Fore term for the "smell" of pollution had come to mean "sin.") "Rubbish people" and youths are adjuncts to Big Men, while women are, as Fore say, "our stores." The locus of prestige and authority here is in no serious dispute. It requires restatement merely to correct disobedience, discontent, and occasional insurrection.

The presence of witches in some New Guinea societies indicates variations on this theme of a challenge to the establishment. The bodies of witches are often said to harbor little creatures and substances. Abelam witches house the creature in the vagina, while the "thing" in the stomach of a Kuma witch resembles the fetus of a small animal.[6] Witches themselves become invisible, change their shape, and fly. More important, witches not only cause greater havoc than polluters, their activities specifically mirror the basis of their discontent. Witches feed on corpses. They kill to satisfy their inordinate craving for human flesh. Hewa witches, said to be women or weak old men (like Fore polluters and rubbish people) are those that society most consistently deprives of animal protein. Believed not only to consume other humans, they are also found characteristically standing outside houses staring in at people who are eating.[7] Kuma witches, too, have an appetite for pork and human flesh, and the accused are again those the society hopes to deprive of protein.

Witchcraft is more than a human attribute. As a supernatural force, it is more highly charged than pollution and thus indicates the threat of greater social opposition. Some communities, such as the Abelam, condone the presence of witches, and make no attempt at divination. Fore similarly cannot afford to dispense with polluters, and their objectionable behavior is merely decried. In some societies, however, witches are dispatched. In a period of two years, the Hewa, a population of 800, accused and killed some thirty female witches, while about 400 Etoro executed four alleged witches and forced sixteen others to leave the community. Etoro, who have an agricultural system of low intensity, regularly identify witches among co-resident though distant kin, and thus maintain small residential units averaging 35 members.[8] The graduated dangers of pollution, witchcraft, and sorcery appear to contribute to the resolution of particular demographic and productive problems. The persecution of witches, the branding of sorcerers, and the denunciation of agents of pollution affect the distribution of the fruits of agricultural production. The defamed may be killed, frightened off, defined as outside the boundaries of the community, or permitted to stay and share unequally in the resources of the environment. By elimination, dispersal, and partitioning of the population, the holders of power create a social hierarchy in which individuals have differing access to the resources of the local productive system.

THE POLITICS OF PROTEIN

Witches and polluters in several New Guinea societies compete with male establishments for similar resources. The contest between social strata is played out, to take one important example, by demonstrating access to the most favored form of protein. While all Fore have access to some domesticated pig (the protein of choice), women and children consume less of it than adult men. The women and children supplement their regimen with insects, small birds, rodents, and frogs (and, until the mid-1950's, human flesh). Meat (often serving as a metaphor for sex) is a topic of constant banter. A small boy who sees his mother's brother's daughter approaching, for instance, says to his male companions: "Here comes my insect now. Watch how I eat her," alluding to the sexual escapades that will later be permitted between them. Men's fables describe their encounters with old women who are catching and eating frogs. The women cry with delight at the delectability of these juicy morsels, which on closer inspection are revealed to be male testes. Men also call older women "frogs," a reference to the women's eating habits that simultaneously conveys the male view of the real hunger driving elderly women.

In the absence of clearly defined rules and the power to enforce them, the transmission of pork from hand to hand is an act requiring mystical coercion. While Fore do not invoke the notion of witches, they do regulate access to protein by the idea of pollution and by a variety of other intangible forces. Men have first access to pork obtained in exchanges with affines and maternal kin. A man is careful not to eat a pig from his own herd because, Fore say, it has consumed defiling matter given it by his own wife. Were he to eat the animal, he would catch cold, become weak, suffer the debilities of pollution. Not only does pollution endanger health, the idea is repulsive. Selfishness over domesticated pork, like intercourse between nuclear kin, is discouraged by aversion and fear for individual survival. Less random than supernatural power, pollution is a secure kind of disciplinary force, found regulating the most controlled fields of competition. Among Fore, it operates to distribute protein supplies among women and men.

Adult men assure prior right to domesticated pork by arguing that protein appropriate for women, children, and old men is unsuitable for them. Frogs, small game, insects, and wild pigs bring about wasting and respiratory disorders, classical pollution ailments. The introduction of chickens and human flesh into the Fore diet produced the same casuistic response: eating these foods would drain men of their fighting strength and the entire community would lose its protectors. The main social purpose served by the male pollution syndrome is the instruction of the audience. By their disciplined behavior and differential diet, women, children, and dependent old men acknowledge their protectors and contribute to the survival of their community.

Priority is conveyed by an above-below schema. Elevated things are superior to those at a lower level. Thus men, who are tall, are preferable to women, who are short. (To express admiration for a woman Fore say, "She was tall, like a man.") Female organs that surmount things bring about illness and death,[9] and a woman who steps over a man's meal renders it inedible. Men catch game in treetops, a more demanding and worthwhile pursuit than the production of food at ground level.[10] New fathers climb trees to rise above clouds of pollution. From their refined habitat in the sky, they look down on women who reproduce. And finally, things from below the ground (potatoes and yams) are not as "sweet" as things from above (pigs). It is a purity-pollution schema with a spatial dimension, from the sky above to the ground below. Sorcerers therefore bury their paraphernalia, and curers derive medicines from treebark. With consequences they could not foresee, the men's early rejection of meat that was interred protected them from kuru, while women defended their consumption of corpses by arguing that the dead were "too good to let the ground consume."

While the alimentary and political relations among these social groups are more or less resolved, the exchange of protein among affines requires special stimuli. The health of one's offspring is hostage to the payment of protein debts to affines. The grave illness of a newborn child indicates the father's delinquency in sending birth payments to his wife's brothers. The speedy gift of a pig or wild animal quells the anger of the child's mother's brothers, believed to be the force endangering its life.

Fore jokes, subversive comments on the social order, indicate other payments that are reluctantly met. A man was hunting in the forest, so the joke goes, and on returning to his hamlet, he handed his wife's mother a parcel of his own wrapped feces instead of the wild game she hungrily awaited. Wife's mother is apparently someone you would rather not supply with hard-won protein. General debility and weakness are said to follow from eating cassowary or wild pig when payments are owed to wife's kin. Here is the equalizing aspect of pollution: those in a position of weakness have discomforting powers of retaliation. Like the mystical threat of the inadequately recompensed mother's brother, the conceit stimulates good behavior among reluctant exchange partners, acting as a goad to conscience payments among affines. These apparently spontaneous responses cover a real battle for survival. Goods and services are produced and differentially distributed. The yielding to others of high-quality protein is the symbolic forfeiting of autonomous action, an act of deference. We are dealing here with a web of concrete imagery, allegory, and affect, which governs communication and control and has a real outcome for both physical and social status.

While Fore discriminate against certain groups of people (women and rubbish men), inferior status is not automatically passed to the next generation. That is, Fore do not have hereditary social classes.[11] Fore notions of sorcery, pollution, and the mystical power of mother's brothers nevertheless delineate a social universe marked by differential access to power and prestigious food. In another area of New Guinea, among southwestern Abelam in the East Sepik District (a region known as the Wosera), a class-stratified society based on distinctions similar to those recognized by the Fore appears to be emerging. The southwestern Abelam is reported to be an area with closed regional borders, dense populations, and severe land scarcity, conditions said to have led to this incipient stratification. In this seemingly egalitarian population of swidden horticulturalists, non-agnates and their wives and children differ in many respects from agnates in the same subclan. They are poorer, shorter, and thinner, and they suffer in greater numbers from a disfiguring skin disease, tinea imbricata. Tinea results from a ringworm infestation and is significantly related to nutritional status. Men with tinea have more trouble finding wives than do males without the disease, and the divorce rate among afflicted women is higher than among their healthy counterparts. Moreover, men with tinea are more likely to marry women with the disease, and to produce offspring with the same affliction, which is transmitted by body contact and also relates to nutritional stress. In sum, nutritionally deprived non-agnates with a disfiguring and socially disadvantageous skin disease constitute a relatively isolated reproductive population, which functions as a "class."[12]

The Fore do not have a similar degree of differentiation within the local community, yet the ghost of the system is already at work in Fore attitudes toward the physically impaired rubbish people, the somewhat disparaged late arrivals in the community, the youths, and the women. Neighboring parishoners appear to exhibit differences in rank (based on age, sex, and physical attributes, with their nutritional correlates), but no permanent stratification deriving from inherited status. The categories of rubbish people and late arrivals have not yet merged. Nor are relations among affines and matrikin, and the groups to which they belong, characterized by a permanent dominance of one side or the other. The exchanges between them (between lines, between sections, and between parish groups) give rise to relationships of alternating seniority. Fore say, "You give your sister to another group, then she has children, and soon they begin to outnumber you"—a measure of their uncertainty whether the brideprice or the woman is of greater value. Within district associations—Ibusa in the North Fore, Atigina in northern South Fore, and Pamousa to the south— there are no signs of permanent inequality. Surplus foods are distributed ceremonially among constituent units, and parish groups have similar access to women of the district, with their accumulated wealth circulating throughout the district at marriage and at death. Within the district, sorcery accusations between parishes are reciprocal, and sorcerers and their victims are of potentially equal status.

Between these large districts, however, there are signs of permanent differentiation. Here, populations have graded access to desirable foods, valuables, women, and the technology for advancement. Northerners feel superior to southerners, and fear the possibility of sorcery attacks from their less affluent relatives to the south, indicating an awareness that the southerners may overwhelm them. By focusing on the politics of protein, we can discern a cluster of ideas appropriate to a society based on partially intensive horticulture. Pig and human populations are small, and social power is limited. The Fore ideological system, with its concepts of sorcery, pollution, and other forms of mystical coercion, authorizes a differential pattern of resource use by age, sex, physical endowment, and, in a wider frame, by regional location. The resources include protein, women, valuables, goods, endowments of the environment, and technical information. The intervals between kibungs over the past thirty years suggest that South Fore have redefined these relationships of priority once a decade. Parish groups split and reassemble in different configurations, giving rise to regionally graduated local units.

In the same period, the pace of intruding phenomena has transformed the region. Fore are now aware of their own position in a north-south gradient. For thirty years, objects and ideas, individuals and diseases, have increasingly filtered in from what was once *terra incognita*, the process quickening with the absence of warfare. The intrusions have touched people unequally. Independent of their own community, youths acquire skills and wealth, and some men tend their coffee gardens more seriously than others. Kibungs, cargo cults, census-taking and the building of a public roadway have enlarged the regional audience, thus permitting the emergence of widely known cult leaders and curers of "international" reputation.

Stimulated by a desire for goods they cannot produce, individual Fore are now elevating themselves above others in ways not available to former generations. It remains to be seen if the benefits pass to their children. Certainly, these new men of stature find wives when others, because of kuru, cannot. Moreover, the new pattern of political expansion and status differentiation is occurring in the absence of a population increase or impacted boundaries, often considered necessary preconditions for such a development.[13] This suggests that the density of populations on the ground may not be the issue so much as the availability of an adequate audience. Fore and their neighbors now cross linguistic boundaries with greater freedom, in search of trade, wives, and curers. Sorcery accusations multiply, a sign of the intensified contest for status.

THE GEOGRAPHY OF FEAR

Just as the Kamano and Keiagana and other populations to the north view Fore with unease, people at Wanitabe fear dangers from areas farther south. The ingredients for sorcery paraphernalia exist in the "natural" forests of south and west, although the technology for using them may arrive by trade routes from the north, as it did in the case of kuru. Dangerous sorcerers and powerful curers are believed to inhabit areas lying just outside the Wanitabe region. The most acute sense of danger is inspired by active sorcerers in neighboring parishes. They are perceived as currently occupied with the grab for power. A less pressing and more general danger emanates from sorcerers such as the Nabu men who recently migrated to Abomotasa, a southern border settlement established only in the 1950's. The emigrants still visit particular kin in the north, but to residents of Wanitabe the life of these visitors from the south, whose vocabulary has begun to differ from their own, seems unfamiliar and difficult. Fore stories tell of men who enter an unknown terrain, only to have their bodies discovered later rotting in the bush—a comment on the biological hazards facing settlers on an untamed land, including new illnesses and shortage of food in newly gardened areas. Former co-residents and competitors, the men of Nabu now inhabit the perilous southland, whence they continue to radiate anger.

The direction from which sorcery emanates is a clue to regional ranking. Atigina, like the northern district of Ibusa and southern Pamousa, is more or less a single ecological zone, with relatively uniform population densities among people using similar agricultural technology. Within this zone, sorcery accusations are mutual. Weak groups disintegrate, amalgamate with one another locally, or get shunted to peripheral locations. Between districts, however, there are both permanent hierarchies and consistent patterns of fear. The capacity to harness energy from the environment rests to some degree on population size, new food crops, and agricultural techniques that permit intensive land use. Crops, goods, fashions, and technology filter down trade routes from north to south. Proceeding south from Ibusa, one finds diminishing population density, agricultural intensity, and elevation, along with appropriate changes in attitude toward residents of the other districts. Population density ranges from 54 persons per square mile in Ibusa to 27 in Pamousa. Changes in dialect underscore the differences.

Men from Ibusa duped their southern neighbors at Atigina with cargo cult technology they had found to be ineffective. Atigina Big Men subsequently extracted pigs from Pamousa. A period of virulent sorcery is said to have followed in the mid-1950's, when the disenchanted recipients of cult technology punished the sellers with a variety of mortal complaints. Backward southerners, it was said, were protesting the advantage taken of their gullibility. Wanitabe accounts of the period confirm the general pattern. Chastised by fellow residents for the failure of the cult, and suffering from the loss of wives and sisters, the Wanitabe Big Men were experiencing a distinct slip in prestige. They blamed their condition on former victims, inhabitants of the duped southland—the diagnosis of an elite explaining an incremental decline.

Similar perceptions of inferiority and danger among the North Fore occurred in 1952. Ronald and Catherine Berndt describe the flurry of sorcery attacks which hit the people of Kogu as the Berndts perpared to move southward to the settlements of Busarasa:

> The Kogu people could not understand why we wanted to
> leave, why we were taking some of our stores (which they
> viewed as their own) to an alien district, a potential enemy. We
> were their property, just as much as, for instance, their fertile
> gardens were; and there was no real comprehension of why we
> should "desert" friends for people regarded as vastly inferior.
> During this period there were nightly disturbances caused, we
> were told, by sorcerers now attacking their territory as we pre-
> pared to withdraw our "power" and patronage; running feet,

and clattering bows and arrows, as men raced in pursuit of
these sorcerers; a stretch of bush going up in flames one mid-
night as men and women hunted for intruders; armed guards
over ourselves and our house at night, to prevent, they said, attacks by stranger groups.[14]

Southern groups, then, are regarded with some anxiety and disdain.
Atigina residents joke about the Porakina, an eastern border region which,
as noted earlier, includes Fore groups at Ilesa, Awarosa, and Agakamatasa, as
well as some nearby Awa-speaking peoples. They are described as fat-bellied
simpletons who do no work to produce their food and just walk about
snatching at bananas and pulling up wild yams. Moreover, they eat so much
that they are forced to walk splayfoot to support their bulging torsos (the
tendency to regard one's inferiors as gluttons is apparently universal).[15] "But
don't tell them we said any of this," they add. "They would hammer us for
making such remarks." Fore feelings of superiority are confirmed when the
Awa invite selected Wanitabe men—usually tall men with light red-brown
skin—to participate in Awa rituals. The northern visitors receive food and
gifts in exchange for copulating with the assembled Awa women, thereby
endowing a desirable change in stature and skin color on the next generation (and complicating the issues for medical geneticists).

The trading and sampling of women's sexual services also conforms to
a regional pattern. The first North Fore visitors to arrive at Wanitabe speaking to one another in Melanesian Pidgin were greeted with alarm. With their
washed faces and cotton clothing, these intimidating northerners com-
manded the men and took the women. The government patrols that followed shortly afterward were showered with food, firewood, and offers of
females.

Sexual plunder may be a continuation of older patterns of regional
dominance. Wanitabe men tell of an artful forebear who provided technical
services for the Asagina, now a permanently dispersed Pamousa group,
whose subdialect is derisively mimicked. In return for wild game, Tokaso
performed nose-piercing ceremonies for Asagina initiates, bespitting their
food with barks, leaves, and stone that supposedly would speed their
growth. He is said also to have had intercourse with any Asagina woman
he desired, threatening the husbands who objected. For some time the
Asagina had resented such treatment by their northern neighbors, and had
fought with Purosa and Ivaki groups in an attempt to keep their women for
themselves. The event that caused their ultimate demise, however, had to
do with their singing style. During an Asagina festival, one performer told
some Purosa visitors: "While our singing is fine, that of Purosa is a pain to
endure. When you open your mouths," he unwisely continued, "shit falls
out." The shamed visitors returned home and reported the affront. Some
time later, Asagina men visited Purosa. Retiring to the men's house for the
night, they began to sing the songs of their region. The enraged listeners set

upon the entire group, burning the house and killing many of those who rushed from the flames. A few men survived to merge with one or another of the Pamousa groups, but this was the end of the Asagina as a separate entity. They had issued an insult in the wrong direction.

This discussion began by noting a geography of fear. The Fore reputation for powerful sorcery now extends to populations north and east. With peace and improved communications, Fore export their esoteric sorcery technology up to forty miles in exchange for new goods, women, and wealth, extending more recent patterns of trade.

As we have seen, Fore have social and trade relations with individually created networks, which themselves nest in larger, open systems. At one level, the zone of interaction is the district association; at another, all speakers of Fore belong to a community of social intercourse. The next level of abstraction might take the kuru region as the area of significant interchange: a population of some 40,000 people, belonging to nine language groups, defined by the presence of a socially transmitted infectious disease. Personnel, genetic material, food, technology, and goods flow across the region. At another remove, this boundary also fades, and Fore may be seen as belonging to a broader population aggregate for which the Chimbu provide the core. Population densities increase regularly across this larger region: from 27 per square mile among South Fore to 54 in the North, as already noted, to Kamano with 65, Benabena 82, Gahuku 83, Asaro 103, and Chimbu 200. The direction of mystical danger is a clue to the Fore position in the regional network: they are feared by populations of higher density and more intensive agriculture. In exchanges between systems differing in complexity of organization, the flow of material and energy is usually from the less to the more highly organized. Just as material and energy have a directional flow, so does the passage of spiritual force. The strong fear covert efforts to redress the balance on the part of those they exploit.

This pattern of intergroup experience occurs elsewhere in New Guinea. A general orientation of fear exists throughout the New Guinea Highlands: societies uphill fear the people below them. The pattern is reversed for societies on the coast.[16] In all cases, people of more complex organization fear the smaller, simpler societies on whom they depend and impinge.

The asymmetry of the exchanges between local communities can be seen in the articles traded. In one direction move lowland and coastal luxury items and objects that are largely collected, such as shells, feathers, furs, animals, ochres, oils, and other forest products. In return, highland groups export goods produced by intensive labor and superior technology—axes and pigs. Peripheral highlanders such as the Fore, who export forest products and import pigs and axes, are thus the recipients and consumers of goods from productive systems for which they have provided basic materials. Moreover, the items controlled by dominant highland groups (such as pigs and axes) may be used to acquire women, and thus have greater political currency.

Agricultural systems of high intensity, like those of the Chimbu and Enga, import luxuries to mark internal differences of status, a cornerstone of their productive systems. These affluent highlanders have an added relative advantage in the tendency of traders to travel uphill from peripheral regions. The energy cost of imports to downhill consumers is thereby increased, since they also bear the cost of transportation. With the cessation of warfare in their area in the 1930's and 1940's, the position of some highland groups became more commanding. Chimbu traders in search of forest products now visit the Karimui, a peripheral highland population about thirty miles to their south. Wagner reports that Chimbu return with convoys of Karimui carriers, who can be seen "toiling along with quantities of caged cassowaries, marsupials, and Pesquet's parrots."[17] By 1963 Chimbu feather traders had reached the South Fore.

Less organized groups are not without means of retaliation. A fearsome reputation, like the capacity to pollute, may be turned to the benefit of the weak. Thus, Chimbu are reported to fear the power of neighboring Gende sorcerers, a belief Gende use to assure safe passage in uphill trading trips. Sorcerers, like polluters, possess some item of enticing appeal or monopolistic control. The principal advantage held by Gende is their strategic location near the main pass into the Chimbu Valley, for through their hands must pass most of the shells from the north coast on their way to the huge populations of the Wahgi Valley. The affluent Chimbu show an uneasy dependence on Gende, who bring them the shell valuables and lowland luxury products they need to demonstrate status. Similarly, Gende are reported to fear the Ramu people in the valley below them.[18] The pattern of fear thus reflects a chain of dependent connections from the more highly organized societies of the highlands through the highland fringe to the lowland proper.

Seaboard groups reverse the direction of the highland patterns of dominance. Coastal and Mountain Arapesh, for example, fear the inland Plainsmen, whose reputation for sorcery permits them to walk haughtily, even arrogantly, through the mountain and beach country for the clam shells they so desire. Although the Plains Arapesh are cut off from the sea, they terrorize and even blackmail their mountain neighbors as they make their way on trading journeys to the coast. In addition, Plains Arapesh supply their other neighbors, the Abelam, with "activated" sorcerers' paint. The Plainsmen's power thus derives from their location at the intersection of two interdependent trade routes; yet a glance at the items traded shows that it is not they who dominate the network. Stone axes, bows and arrows, baskets, and shell ornaments, along with dances, songs, refinements of clothing, and hairstyles flow inland from the coast. The return flow of goods from mountain to coast consists of tobacco, feathers, shell rings, pots, and net bags, which the Mountain Arapesh acquire from the frightening Plainsmen. Although the Plainsmen themselves produce the shell ring currency from coastal clams, their position in the network is not commanding. Plainsmen in turn acquire their net bags, along with spears, cassowary daggers, building styles, masks, and all their dance paraphernalia, from the populous Abelam, whose return purchase of sorcery materials shows them to be the controlling partners.[19]

The four groups—Abelam, and Coastal, Mountain, and Plains Arapesh—are thus at this period of time, participants in a regional economic system. Their interchange is a competitive one between populations of unequal power and resources. By virtue of their particular skills, environmental endowment, and strategic location, some highland and coastal populations have drawn other groups into their domain. In the process, the core areas become internally diversified. When such regional differentiation occurs, it produces resistance. Some populations, such as the Gende and Plains Arapesh, translate their own small advantages of geography and environment into countermovements. Their reputation for sorcery suggests that they have the potential to reverse the order of dominance.

In other parts of the world, the presence of sorcerers and other dangerous beings reveals social hierarchies based on the direction of material and energy in systems of exchange. The Sharanahua Indians of eastern Peru consider the Culina, river dwellers like themselves, a backward group of less efficient fishermen. Sharanahua would like to take the Culina land and be rid of them. They regard the Culina with both contempt and fear, for the Culina are powerful sorcerers and Culina sorcery is beyond the reach of any Sharanahua shaman.[20] The pattern may also be present among the Jivaro and Canelos Indians of eastern Ecuador. Here, Jivaro appear to occupy the dominant position, as shamanistic power in diminishing intensity flows southward from Canelos.[21]

Local communities in New Guinea are open systems, all interconnected and aggregated into a wider system that can only be bound notionally at the edges of Melanesia.[22] Chains of linkage transmit fashions and foods, agricultural technology, illness, and genetic material in small increments across vast regions. The limits and the vitality of particular networks may be defined by a language, a slow virus, or attitudes and concepts. Polluters are those whose dependent position in the network is a matter of record. Sorcerers emerge in more enlarged political environments. More deadly than polluters, sorcerers have not conceded defeat. They have, instead, the potential for reversing the hierarchy.

With a sense of their own technical level, South Fore say, "We are men in the middle. Here, we only do a little *singsing* (incantation) to our pigs." Productive systems to the north, they know, depend on the commitment of greater technical skills, while those to the south are seen as lacking any human input. South Fore sorcerers reflect just this degree of technical accomplishment. They are men with access to new and secret knowledge. Uncurbed, they can cause the downfall of the presently constituted social order.

Fore sense the danger of new skills that run amok. As with Frankenstein's monster from the age of electricity, the Terminal Man created by a computer, and the recombinant DNA molecules of modern biology, the fear recurs that new technology is a social danger. It produces unnatural creatures who return to plague the community of inventors. Their insubordination is a threat to the human establishment. The remedy, Fore say, is to avoid monopolies of knowledge. Potential sorcerers and tyrants are defused when persuaded to work within socially imposed limits. The dangerous sorcerers are those autonomous beings who might willfully use their private technology to up-end the social order. Epidemics show the sorcerers threatening to take over, a political message conveyed in a medical idiom. For several decades kuru was the sorcerer's weapon of choice. But Fore sorcerers are known to have changed tactics before. In the 1950's, for instance, they lost interest in yaws. With their next choice, the Fore will be conveying information of political and epidemiological importance. The issue concerns the constitution of society and acceptable orders of dominance.

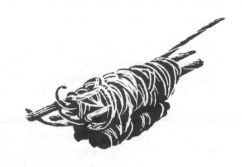

CONCLUSION 1979

11

I have tried in these pages to convey the resilience of a community facing apparent disaster. At the peak of the epidemic that was endangering their survival, the Fore spent many days debating how they might survive the holocaust. Kuru, they said, resulted from the jaundiced activities of sorcerers who would soon turn the Fore into a wasteland. They consulted diviners and curers who emerged to diagnose the problem, and when that failed, they turned within. In the mass meetings held throughout the region, Fore announced that sorcery was a corruption of human motivation, a form of competition gone amok. To save their women and themselves, they had to forgo this secret warfare. They should use other skills and build a future together.

If one looks at the whole period since Western contact, the events of the 1960's emerge as part of a series. In the past thirty years, similar oscillations have occurred between a quest for sorcerers and the pursuit of harmony, although each time the scale of the search has expanded. Both the forms of sorcery and their practitioners have increased in number within living memory. Social movements that induce temporary unity have also appealed to progressively larger audiences. While concerned with a local disease, Fore are responding at the same time to changes induced from outside their domain. Objects, information, and diseases arrive with increased frequency from neighboring populations, creating demographic and social imbalances between local Fore groups. Their encounter with a colonial government has stripped these communities of their sense of autonomy. At the same time, it has led to changes in the ground rules by which individual men acquire wealth and prestige. In conditions of a government-imposed peace, notable curers appeal to wider and wider publics. The Fore are increasingly preoccupied with matters of social inequality. In pursuing the sorcerers who strike at elevated status, they probe issues made urgent by the high incidence of kuru.

Sorcery, witchcraft, and pollution are concepts individuals with social power invoke to suggest that ill health and misfortune are caused by persons they wish to keep at a distance. Each category of social assault arises in an appropriate environmental and historical context, and creates a crescendo of conditions. Polluters nibble at establishment authority. Their little skirmishes cause minor troubles and ailments. Properly contained, the polluters are permitted to share in the resources of the community. Witches and sorcerers present a greater challenge. They emerge where incipient social hierarchies are not yet stabilized. Fore sorcerers contend for social rank on grounds other than sex, age, and physical condition. Like polluters and witches, however, sorcerers threaten to displace the establishment by using power their victims portray as unacceptable. To maintain their position, the powerful may attempt to stamp them out. While one aspect of social superiority is a claim to high-quality protein, the connection between poor health and social opposition is a real one. Since another aspect of status depends on female labor and fertility, women are the nub of the contest among competing Big Men.

Social power varies with the degree of control exercised over the environment. Fore environmental control is relatively modest. Direct control of others is limited, and there are many indirect avenues of psychic attack. Sorcery is an appropriately covert mechanism of coercion available to individuals with limited access to social power. It is associated with agricultural systems of low intensity in peripheral highland areas, rather than with regions of high population density and intensive agriculture, where issues are settled by more overt means, by physical violence, and by economic sanctions under the direction of men of great stature. Among Fore, the control of others rests more on the ability to influence public opinion than on mobilizing a predictable circle of genealogically related kin. The sorcery syndrome, like that of pollution, also serves to instruct the audience.

Gradations of fear in New Guinea coincide with particular hierarchies in local communities and across broad regions. The direction from which the danger emanates reveals the asymmetry of the social order; individuals fear the retaliation of those they dominate. Men fear women, and mature men sense danger from the youths who might dislodge them and from the weak and elderly whom they disenfranchise. Men of importance whose wives are ailing fear their already widowed rivals. Sorcerers exercise the most highly charged powers, since their secret behavior places them outside constitutional constraint, hinting at tyranny. Unlike polluters and witches, sorcerers may overturn the social order, and their ascendancy inspires both admiration and contempt.

A geography of fear tracks unequal relations between neighboring communities, from the dominating highland cores to their peripheries. The pattern is reversed among coastal groups, who regard unsophisticated inland people as the feared adversaries. A glance at the materials flowing between interacting groups reveals the imbalance of the exchange; dominant groups extract raw materials, labor and luxuries, and return a greater quantity of manufactured goods and items that have political impact. While the feared peoples monopolize some desired item, they also make a disproportionate contribution to the interchange.

In a masterly illusion projected by an egalitarian ethic, the dispossessed are characterized as a threat, a casuistic line of argument we share with the Fore. People in marginal positions are portrayed as a danger to the establishment. If kuru becomes the prototype for studies of slow virus infections, Fore beliefs about mystical danger may contribute to our understanding of the emergence of social inequality.

Neither biological nor social communities offer truly equal shares to all. A society stratified as little as the Fore shows individual men and women living in relationships of mutual aid and as parasite and host. Just as infectious disease results from inconclusive negotiations for symbiosis between humans and a few species of bacteria,[1] sorcery is portrayed as an overstepping of the line by one side or the other. In the absence of alternative methods of settling disputes, sorcery may serve to regulate relations between individuals who must cooperate and also compete. As has been postulated for immune reactions, sorcery seems designed not to interrupt but to modulate the process.[2] Disease symptoms, like sorcery accusations, signal a corrective response, an attempted reassertion of dominance by the protesting host. It is a paradox the Fore repeatedly face: how to dispose of the enemy on whom you also depend.

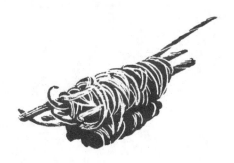

TELLING HISTORY

12

In June 1991, I returned to Wanitabe after an absence of some twenty years. For the next five weeks, I was a guest of the Open Bible Mission, an American evangelical ministry present in the South Fore since 1980.[1] Based on 160 hectares[2] of land leased from Wanitabe landowners, the mission had built an impressive campus of three houses, a trade store, a church, and a nearby clinic that would soon become a government health center. At dinner on the first night, the mission director spoke about the fighting between the clans of Amora and Wanitabe that had lasted for three months in 1989, as well as a general sense of disorder throughout the region, which he described as a ripple from the disturbances associated with the secessionist movement at Bougainville in North Solomons Province.[3] If they need to visit the towns of Kainantu or Goroka, the missionaries now leave the South Fore at 3 A.M. to avoid the *raskols* (Tok Pisin for criminals) who ambush travelers.

The next morning, I attended church in the capacious mission building with seating for the large congregation, more than half of them women and children. A Fore woman led the hymn singing, accompanied by a young man on guitar. During the singing, some women swayed back and forth, seemingly transported. At times, the Fore talk in tongues, a practice introduced by the mission as a kind of revelation. The Fore have added it to their repertoire of divination practices to identify sorcerers. A Fore pastor gave the sermon in Tok Pisin, which was translated into Fore for the benefit of older women and men.

The service ended and we spilled outside. One woman reminded me that I had contributed to her bridewealth, an act that still had resonance

See how many children we have!

three decades later. A man stepped forward, gestured at the crowd, and said, "See how many children we now have," an interesting shift in demographic thinking. In the 1960's, men said, "See how few pigs we have. Think of the number of women the sorcerers have killed."[4]

Inamba Kivita, my research assistant from the 1960's, now a Seventh Day Adventist, waited outside. He suggested that we spend the rest of the day visiting friends. Walking along the road, we passed the primary school, torn apart during the war with Amora and rebuilt with the help of the mission. Young men in team uniforms were playing soccer on the school grounds. We stopped to look at the remnants of a Wanitabe trade store, also destroyed during the battle with Amora. At the site of my old fieldhouse, Inamba indicated a place where he had once planted onions and sweet potatoes, now a graveyard shaded by casuarina trees. The hamlet is now called Batamiti, identified by a huge *bata* (avocado) tree planted by a local leader. The houses, no longer in the form of an open square or colonial "houseline," cascade downhill in a series of enclosed family compounds, each with its own small *mumu* hole for earth oven cooking. A small church has been built by Open Bible members to conduct their own weekly services. Seventh Day Adventists attend a church a short walk away.[5]

Some people, such as Inamba, have abandoned the old residential clusters, choosing to live near their coffee gardens on land they now consider to be individually owned, although customary clan ownership still prevails.

Fore look at photos of themselves.

He enjoys the quietness, he says, and the nighttime conversations between husband and wife tree possums. The *yentanama*, the small house once used by women from the hamlet during menstruation and childbirth, no longer exists. Women remain in their homes during menstruation and childbirth, and some give birth at the clinic.

Joined by Nantale Kaguya and Agame Abao, two other research assistants, we spent some time distributing photos taken in the 1970's, first to people returning from the morning church service and then to the soccer players who had been told they would find photos of themselves.

Fore look at photos of themselves.

Conversation turned to the Amora-Wanitabe war, which had begun with the death of a "half old" Amora woman, and accusations of Wanitabe responsibility. Three Amora men had been severely injured, provoking the Amoras to burn down the roadside store. The storytelling gained momentum as men pointed to scars on arms and legs, and described the corrugated iron roofing used as a shield to divert arrows. They agreed about the lineup of clans that had supported one side or the other, "but with some Amoras living inside Wanitabe and some Wanitabes inside Amora, we didn't fight to kill." As the sun went down and the temperature dropped, we set off for home. Leaving Batamiti, Nantale reminded me that he, too, had planted sweet potatoes next to my fieldhouse, and had looked after my chickens in an enclosure no longer visible. It seemed that we had all become historians.

This chapter looks at the many changes that have taken place in the South Fore in recent decades, with a focus on matters that most engaged people's attention. Following Independence in 1975, the government replaced Australian currency with the Papua New Guinea kina, the name for the precolonial shell money used in Coastal and Highland trade. By the 1990's, money was very much on peoples' minds:[6] why they needed it, how it could be acquired, how best to use it. The introduction of a local market and coffee as a cash crop, as well as an increase in wage labor, has provided opportunities for the Fore to integrate new forms of commerce into their own activities. The introduction of a state currency, however, has given rise to widespread anxiety throughout Melanesia about the impact of this new currency on the Melanesian exchange-based structuring of social relations.[7] Where commodity production has taken hold, the integration of rural communities with the market economy has resulted in a diversity of outcomes, as individuals participate in different social and spatial networks.[8] The Fore also view the new money with apprehension and desire, and have left their own cultural imprint on the way they acquire, think about, and deploy their wealth. While the account that follows draws attention to the market and to ceremonial exchange as money flows through new and old institutions, it describes simultaneous shifts in religious belief and practice, new forms of sociality, as well as the smaller changes that constitute the fabric of daily life.

THE MARKET

By 1991, the Fore population had indeed made a spectacular recovery. At the peak of the kuru epidemic in the 1960's, the population had been on the brink of a catastrophic decline. With the epidemic coming to an end, more women in their reproductive years had survived, mothers brought their children to the clinic for the treatment of fevers and diarrhea, and clinic nurses vaccinated infants for a wide spectrum of childhood diseases.[9] An informal survey of births and deaths at Akerakamuti (now Batamiti) in 1970 showed that in the preceding seven years, thirteen women had given birth to twenty five infants, ten dying in the first few months. In 1991, with greatly reduced

Nurse gives baby vaccine.

infant mortality, some families had seven or eight children. By 2008, Inamba would have eleven children and fourteen grandchildren. Many women had enrolled in the clinic's family planning program.

With large families to care for, women need money to pay school fees, which they see as their responsibility. They have increased the size of their gardens to sell vegetables in the local market, and consider market earnings to be their own. From their northern neighbors, the Fore have acquired many new vegetables,[10] which they cultivate on land they now expect to hand down to their children. In the past, the month of June was a time to prepare new gardens in advance of the rains. Crops once planted seasonally, however, are in constant production. "Once we thought about our mouths," they said. "Now we think about the market." On non-market days, some women sit by the roadside with small piles of bananas or peanuts, hoping to catch passersby.

The concept of a market as a place to buy and sell locally produced foods was a colonial introduction. Promoted by a local councilor to encourage development, market activities began at Wanitabe in the early 1980's. With no equivalent Fore word, people describe markets (a term they have adopted) as "gifts of food that in the past pulled in shells, now money." Some years earlier, following the arrival of cash, Eastern Highlanders had introduced an innovative practice called *singsing bisnis*, dance festivals that were also a kind of market, which David Boyd called a form of cultural resistance and renewal.[11] Patterned on the ceremonial slaughter and distribution of pigs, once the most sacred sequence of ritual events in the region, the dance festivals experimented with new ways of generating wealth and achieving leadership in performances that attracted crowds of people from around the region. As with the pig festivals, a well-organized event brought prestige to the sponsor and host group. Commodities, including beer, were sold, and some foods were given as gifts. Women kept profits from their food sales. Gate fees were collected from the male and female dancers entering the dance ground, and in this highly charged atmosphere, unmarried women sometimes danced up to men they wished to marry, a form of courting behavior that might induce their fathers to negotiate a marriage payment. Held on Saturday nights from the early 1970's to the early 1980's, the singsings ended at Wanitabe under mission pressure and from the shortage of pigs, because Adventists do not eat pork and also disapprove of alcohol.

The new market, called the Ivingoi market, had flourished, displacing the seasonal exchange of some surplus foods with other communities, and it soon had the complexity of rural markets found elsewhere in the world. Women now sell string bags of intricate design, as well as scones, donuts, tapioca, sweet corn, boiled eggs, and pieces of pork. They also offer new clothing purchased in town by their brothers, with whom they share the profits.

On Mondays and Fridays, large crowds stroll along the road that divides the marketplace, considering the cookware, padlocks, tools, and flashlights that men purchase in town at Lae and Port Moresby. The few men selling hardware sit with their wives in an arrangement of clan seating that was perhaps established when the market began. One man has a radio, turned on at full volume, drawing the attention of potential buyers. Women, however, are the main producers and sellers of market goods. Although profits are often small, they may be crucial for the reproduction of the household,[12] but there is more to the market than economics alone. Small groups of young women parade self-consciously back and forth, fashioning a new space for courtship. Unlike women in their fifties and sixties, still haunted by the fear of kuru, young people with little memory of the epidemic drop biscuit wrappings on the road, items a sorcerer might steal.

The market also offers a public space for people to air their grievances. Seventh Day Adventists from Purosa, five miles south, have adopted the large Friday market to broadcast their views about monogamy and the need for

The Friday market.

worship, as well as the dangers of alcohol, cigarettes, betelnut, and gambling (ignoring men playing the card game "Lucky," which their fire-and-brimstone sermons have not interrupted). A man from the neighboring Gimi people is selling indigenous medicines. In an adjacent field, young men display used clothing, called "Nixon clothes," a clue to their origin. The nearby mission

"Nixon" clothes.

store also influences consumer behavior, offering baby clothes; underwear; sanitary napkins; and a reliable supply of salt, soap, rice, tea, Pepsi, Fanta, tinned fish, spam, matches, cooking pots, pillows, and blankets.

Elected politicians view the crowds as a captive audience for discussing local issues. With Independence in 1975, the old kiap (government officer) was no more. Government-appointed lulais and tultuls were replaced by elected councilors and committee men, but the provincial government is not a strong presence. The sense of colonial oversight that overshadowed people's thoughts during the 1960's has been replaced by an awareness that a desirable future depends on gaining access to a distant political system. With little evidence of any services provided by the national government, the Fore are refusing to pay taxes.

Although the new market has captured most women's attention, a sprinkling of educated women are becoming teachers and nurses, and in 1991 some nurse graduates were working alongside a mission nurse in the nearby clinic. The Open Bible supports women's economic development, encouraging them to purchase sewing machines to make their own and their children's clothes, and to form work groups and savings clubs.[13] The mission also informs women about their rights in cases of rape, and how to take a child custody suit beyond the village to a higher court. Classes in literacy are provided for women too old to go to school, and some women have been given positions of responsibility in mission activities, recognizing perhaps the important role they had always played in interclan affairs. The long-festering hostilities and sorcery accusations between the communities at Waisa and Wanitabe, for example, were resolved in 1972 when two Waisa women, painted in the mud of mourning, led a peace delegation to Wanitabe, followed by their husbands and brothers carrying a gift of pigs. At Wanitabe, they met their two counterparts and a party of Wanitabe men with their reciprocal gift of peace-making pigs. A few years later, women helped to settle a dispute between Umasa and Ivaki-Intamatasa. Carrying tree branches recognized as peace signs, the women walked ahead, followed by truckloads of men who stepped forward to shake the hands of their adversaries. Describing the ceremony, one man said, "It is good to send women to speak first. Men dig up old graveyards and make things worse."

Husbands say that women's market participation has made them "smart." They now decide for themselves when to go to the gardens, and exercise some choice of a marriage partner, bypassing the cultural preference for cousins in favor of a man with wealth. Sex for money takes place close to the marketplace in the town of Goroka, and also near the South Fore markets at Wanitabe and Purosa. The market metaphor is included in the moral instructions given to young girls during initiation. "Don't sit in a way that reveals the upper thigh," say their older sisters. "Market open!" they warn, referring to the transactability of female sexuality[14] and an illustration of the market as a mental construct.

ACQUIRING MONEY

Although subsistence production for household consumption remains vibrant, in addition to school fees, people also need money for clothing; some foods; and travel to Goroka, Lae, Rabaul, or Port Moresby. A key to a different financial future was provided when the colonial government introduced coffee as a cash crop. The governments of Julius Chan and Paias Wingti (the second and third prime ministers of Papua New Guinea between 1980 and 1997) broadcast a capitalist message to the nation, encouraging people to do away with pigs and plant coffee trees: "Look after coffee and coffee will take care of you." Many people in the South Fore had planted their first trees in the 1970's, and by the 1990's coffee had become the main source of cash. ANGCO, the government coffee corporation, planted coffee trees on nine hundred hectares of land leased from local communities at Purosa and one hundred at Wanitabe. When the trees became productive, a surge of cash entered the local economy, reflected in inflated bridewealth and mortuary payments. In 1991, women and men earned a modest income picking coffee beans on ANGCO land (K22 each fortnight)[15] and by selling their own beans to ANGCO or to commercial buyers from Goroka.

In 1991, ANGCO had a Purosa workforce of 75 Fore carpenters and foremen, and 300 male and female bean pickers, a number of them from the Gimi region. At Wanitabe, twelve Fore pickers and an administrator were also on the payroll, as well as a small migrant group of Anga men (see map, p. 5). At the half-year mark, the corporation had distributed K90,000, and by the end of the year, K3million.

Employees pooled fortnightly wages, allowing single individuals to take turns investing the money pot, a practice found elsewhere in migrant labor camps. ANGCO had a factory at Purosa to process the beans, a trade store, a bank for workers to deposit some of their income, and an outdoor TV screen for a predominantly male audience passionate about national football. Some men at Wanitabe expected to receive K400 for their dried coffee beans; those with more trees were hoping for K1,000. At Purosa, where trees had been planted earlier, people expected K1,500 to K2,500 in a poor year, and K2,000 to K3,000 if the prices were higher. ANGCO was dismantled in 2001, and the land was returned to the original landowners, who now market their organic coffee through "Coffee Connections," a Fair Trade purchaser and distributor located in Goroka.[16]

The work week at Wanitabe in June 1991 had a new regularity. Monday, market day, women sell produce at the Ivingoi market, coffee buyers arrive from Goroka to purchase processed beans; Tuesday, maintenance of school grounds, garden work; Wednesday and Thursday, work in the gardens, pick coffee; Friday, market day, women sell produce locally, and some walk south to sell vegetables at the Purosa market; Saturday, a day of rest and church for Adventists; and Sunday, rest and church for members of the Open Bible. It was said that Adventist raskols, for whom Satan is their god, rest on Saturdays,

PMV in a ditch.

as do Evangelical raskols on Sunday. At 7 A.M. on weekday mornings, the clang of the school bell calls children to the new Community School.

In search of income and adventure, young men leave the South Fore to find work. During the 1960's, they cycled back and forth in short-term, low-level jobs in towns or on plantations. By the mid-1990's, a more educated male workforce found better-paid town work in Lae, Rabaul, Goroka, and Port Moresby, and wage labor became an important source of cash second only to coffee.

Dissatisfied with the poor rewards of wage labor, some men returned home to invest in small ventures such as a nursery for coffee seedlings, raising chickens, selling pups from a dog's litter, collecting butterflies for outside buyers, and importing used clothing.

Several wondered whether a tourist lodge or a museum to display ancestral bones and stone artifacts would attract visitors. The most successful Wanitabe coffee producer married a woman from Lae who arrived with two industrial-sized sewing machines to be powered by a generator. One man had a thriving business purchasing small amounts of local coffee, selling to ANGCO when prices rose, and a number of men opened trade stores. These ventures met with uneven success. By 1996, the coffee nursery, butterfly collecting, and the small dress factory had proved unprofitable. The coffee broker, accused of sorcery and faced with death threats, had left for Lae. Some trade stores had closed, but others had opened. An experiment trucking potatoes from Purosa to Lae, where a network of relatives loaded the

PMV heading toward Goroka.

produce onto ships for markets in Port Moresby, was also short-lived, even though the profits were considered encouraging. The hard work associated with bulky produce and the distance from towns has left local markets as the main outlet for the sale of garden produce.

The purchase of small trucks called PMVs (Public Motor Vehicles) by a group of brothers, or distributed by politicians to their supporters, was considered a better investment. The rusted skeletons of abandoned PMVs are a testament to the difficulties of vehicle maintenance and the poor state of the roads, but profits could be made by ferrying people around Port Moresby or carrying people and goods back and forth to Goroka or Lae.

Waiting to sell coffee.

Income from the sale of marijuana, said in the press to be second only to coffee as a cash crop in Papua New Guinea, is missing from this inventory of commercial activities. Marijuana, which some young men smoke, is said to leave Papua New Guinea through the ports at Daru or Lae, but no one acknowledges growing it in the South Fore.

The Fore are aware that coffee connects them to national and even international markets, but the distance from towns and the poor state of the roads has prevented them benefiting from the development they have seen or heard about elsewhere. They also know that if they could reach distant markets, they could participate in the inter-regional trade in fresh foods, as at Kesena, an Eastern Highlands village in the Asaro Valley, well situated on the Highlands Highway, with easy access to Goroka and Lae. Some Fore and Gimi migrants work at Kesena as wage-laborers.[17] As elsewhere in the Highlands, in the absence of opportunities to invest in more rewarding forms of economic activity, the Fore channel their wealth into maintaining and amplifying the circulation of cash and goods in ceremonial exchanges that strengthen political alliances.

CEREMONIAL EXCHANGE

The ceremonial exchange of wealth in Papua New Guinea is a topic of long standing in the ethnographic literature. Akin and Robbins, writing about state and local currencies, underscore the fact that the ceremonial exchange of local forms of wealth between certain categories of kin is the means by which social relations are structured. They also address the ways state money has proved destabilizing to Melanesian exchange systems. "What makes the new reign of money so threatening is that money can move against anything in any kind of exchange between people who stand in any kind of relationship to each other."[18] This is the problem that the Fore recognize as they try to harness the flow of money, confining it to the established channels of ceremonial exchange.

The following discussion of birth, initiation, marriage, and death leaves out much ethnographic detail, which can be found elsewhere.[19] I focus instead on the changes in the ceremonial exchange of wealth that have taken place from precolonial to postcolonial times, the imprint of the market on the practices and ideas that underpin ceremonial exchange, and the widespread concern with mounting costs. Since their first encounter with cash, the Fore have attempted to use it in ways that they see as compatible with their own social commitments and cultural identity.

An informal exchange called *arantana* existed in precolonial times, when women gave food and string bags to their brothers, receiving in return *giri* shells or *kinta* (*Cardiospermum halicacabum*), a seed grown locally and used in beads as a form of currency in a transaction women now describe as "our little market." In the 1960's, brothers gave sisters Australian shillings and then New Guinea kina following Independence in 1975. The practice continues today. Women who visit their wage-earning brothers bring gifts of food, and in return the brothers may send airline tickets and provide their sisters with pocket money. The brother-sister bond is complex and enduring. "Our sisters are our mouths," one man said. "We can't marry them. That would be like planting two yams in one hole. We receive pay for our sisters when they marry." This informal exchange of wealth and sentiment underlies the pattern of the more formal exchanges marking birth (*tiena*), initiation (*mabiena*), marriage (*wayena*), and death (*agoena*), which rest structurally on the fulcrum of the brother-sister relationship.

A sequential account of the exchange of ceremonial wealth would begin with marriage, when a man marries his mother's brother's daughter,[20] resulting in a recurrent debt to his wife's maternal kin (the mother's brothers and cross-cousins). The payment of bridewealth transfers some rights in the woman to the husband's group, but does not cancel the affiliation with her father and other paternal kin. Dawn Glass suggests that the obligatory payments made to his wife's agnatic clan for her life-giving substance (her blood) are seen as "her clan's inalienable possession," which, even though transacted, are paradoxically "kept-while-given."[21] I begin by describing the birth ceremony, the tiena, during which the child is named, leaving until later the initiation, marriage, and more spectacular mortuary distributions involving the wealth exchanges that are uppermost in people's minds.

BIRTH

When a child is born, the child's father, assisted by his brothers, gives a gift of food to his wife and an obligatory payment to his wife's paternal relatives, the mother's brothers and cross-cousins (called the *kandere* in Tok Pisin), although it is the mother's brothers who are the father's main concern. The wife's brothers respond with a reciprocal gift of food and a small amount of money. The tiena, known as "the payday for the child," also called the "head pay," begins to induct the child into the father's lineage. Head payments are also a kind of insurance, because the anger of a mother's brother denied payment is thought to endanger the child's health. The father's gift compensates the mother's brothers for the loss of their clan's blood, their agnatic bodily substance, a loss recognized each time the woman bears a child. In the 1960's, the "head pay" included possums, replaced now by chickens and imported lamb.[22]

The women who join the mother in the birth house (yentanama) include her brothers' wives who assist with the delivery, bring food and firewood, and provide the first breast milk, indicating that the constitution of the new person is still defined by bodily substance from the mother's paternal clan, an index of a continued claim of ownership. Together the women eat sugarcane and *ebia*, leafy greens.[23] Gillian Gillison suggests that among the nearby Gimi, the mother's brothers' wives are present at a woman's confinement as suspicious overseers to ensure that the mother does not kill the child.[24] In the past, Fore women who gave birth to twins did kill one of them, concerned that they would be unable to feed both. The birth house, seen by men as polluted space and beyond their view and control, gave women considerable freedom.

Following a week or so in seclusion, the mother and child make their exit. The cost of hosting a tiena is modest, and in some recent cases the father gave a small payment when the first child was born, promising the full amount following the birth of two or three children. Men with little wealth and no brothers to help them say they have given a mumu for their wives but will not hold a tiena. The new mothers receive a variety of "female" goods from mothers' brothers' wives and fathers' sisters: nappies, baby blankets, soap, and oil (in place of pig fat) to protect the baby's skin. Women say the tiena is also "our little market," and is tied to another form of good business: the exchange of wealth to celebrate the initiation of youths.

INITIATION

During the 1960's, male initiation ended in most of the South Fore. With Independence in 1975 and a revived sense of cultural identity, initiations began again.[25] Gone were the painful nose piercings to purge the mother's blood; cane-swallowing to eject female-delivered foods; sleep deprivation; hoaxes; lessons about warfare, hunting, and the value of shell money; and the long seclusion. By the 1990's, the initiates remained secluded for a shorter period of time and were drilled now about the value of education, church attendance, growing coffee, and making money to look after the "family," not the "line" (lineage), as would have been said earlier. The initiates were now about eighteen years of age, unlike those in the 1960's who were initiated at age nine or ten. In the past, women's noses were also pierced, and a modified celebration for the first menstruation is still observed.[26] The youths who exit the seclusion hut are called *mabis*, confirming their elevated status in the paternal clan, no longer the young *masis* who belonged more to the world of women.

The new initiates sit side by side. Their initiators, the mothers' brothers as in the past, are called to receive their share of taro, yam, chicken, freezer meat, and pig (unless they are Seventh Day Adventists), the payment that secures the recruitment of sons into the father's clan. When he decides to host an initiation, the father sends word to the boy's mother's brothers and cross-cousins, telling them to begin assembling the money expected in the return gift. (Men say that "the line of my mother's brothers, they are my market. The line of my father's sisters, we are their market"). Initiation is more costly than tiena, so the ceremony is usually held during the coffee season when everyone can afford such affairs, and the provision of food is generous. The parents hosting an initiation in 1993 estimated that they had spent K2,000 on food, but considered it a good investment. The fathers and fathers' brothers who contributed to the initiation fund also expect the

Coffee buyers.

young men to remember them when they find work. "We live in the bush here, and it is hard work making money, so we will hold fast to this custom."

These were brave words. The initiations held in 1991 and 1993 were the last to take place at Wanitabe. Farther south, the ceremonies continued for a few more years. Holding fast to the custom appears to be the desire of an older generation with access to fewer resources and a desire to retain their authority. Schoolboys are no longer initiated. The transmission of culturally valued modern knowledge has shifted in part to the school, and

1991 initiates.
Sister gives her
brother a gift.

1996 Christian baptism.

baptism effects a change in status at the expense of old cosmologies. At an Open Bible baptism in 1993, the sisters, who gave towels to their brothers instead of the string bags they would have given in the past, acknowledged the resemblance to mabiena.

The mantle of male adulthood has been acquired also by young men leaving home to work in town, a rite of passage in which they gain knowledge about the market economy and a wider social universe but also acquire a sense of tension about their commitment to town life and their obligations to kin.

In the eyes of the older generation of men, the end of initiation has changed the constitution of male bodies. They tell their children that they lack the ability to fight and to carry out heavy work because they still contain their mother's "weak blood," which nose-bleeding and forced vomiting once expelled. They are, in sum, different kinds of men. Because they also live in the same house with women, they can expect a shorter life span.[27] It remains to be seen if a new generation, inspired by an appreciation for old cultural values, will reintroduce some form of the ceremonies that once created men and allowed a father to call his sons his own.

MARRIAGE AND MORTUARY CEREMONIES

When people speak of the exchange of wealth during tiena or mabiena as a kind of market, they are not saying that it is the same as a marketplace transaction. Paternal and maternal kin exchange the material wealth and the bodily substances that define the nature of their relationship, provide social continuity, and mold the constitution of the person. The "head pay" given to the mother's brothers during the birth and initiation ceremonies marks the importance of the brother-sister sibling set, those who share the same maternal substance. The loss of this blood, the maternal agnatic substance, is the driving force underlying the cycle of "head payments."[28] Ceremonial wealth is infused with sentiment and symbolic value. In Rupert Stasch's felicitous phrase,[29] "Gifts are thoughts and feelings in a knowable, material form."

While the birth and initiation ceremonies are described as markets, those associated with marriage and death, which involve a much greater assemblage and distribution of wealth, are not. They are not markets because "they don't pull in money," and their mounting costs are considered extremely onerous. The shortage of cash makes it difficult to fulfill ceremonial obligations. Many key items, such as frozen lamb, chickens, and sometimes pigs, are now purchased, and costs are rising. The New Guinea kina, devalued by 12 percent in September 1994, was subsequently floated, resulting in a further 10 percent devaluation,[30] and the currency has continued to lose value. By 2010, 1 U.S. dollar was worth 2.4 kina.

People at Wanitabe could recall discussing the burdens of bridewealth in the 1980's, when they received the alarming news that payments at Yagusa, a community a few miles north, had reached K1,000. At that time, they had notified the police of their decision to limit costs, but two Wanitabe men had quickly broken this "law."

At the height of the kuru epidemic in the 1960's, when people were exhausted emotionally and financially by frequent funerals, bridewealth negotiations often began with the groom declaring that the payment now offered should be accepted, and no mortuary payment would follow if the wife soon died.

In spite of a history of complaint, however, Fore bride payments have become more expensive. In the 1960's, Purosa marriage payments had consisted of shells, small amounts of colonial shillings, bark cloaks, string bags, sugarcane, and a small number of pigs. By 1991, K1,500 would be given for an uneducated bride or a poor worker, K3,000 for a rare high school teacher. By 2011, the Kamano, the Fore's northern neighbors, were regularly giving bride payments of 2,000 to 3,000 kina, the higher price for a first marriage and the lower sum for remarriage after divorce, a new category. In the same year, bride payments among the Gimi, the Fore's western neighbors, had also reached K3,000, with less for a second marriage or if the wife is seen as promiscuous.[31]

Why then do the Fore say that marriage is not a market because it fails to pull in money? Bridewealth recipients are, in fact, obliged to make a reciprocal payment. One South Fore man said that the money he receives in marriage payments "slips out between my fingers," a statement that conveys his sense of dismay, unable to hold onto money as he might in a more market-like transaction. A recent study by Dawn Glass of North Fore marriage[32] provides the ethnographic context that explains his predicament.

North Fore marriage occurs in three stages. First, the brideprice[33] negotiation includes the "decorating of the fertile body," a ceremony in which the bride is dressed by women of her natal clan, creating a "new body," the transformation of the young woman into a wife. She is encouraged to forget her adolescent self and embrace her new role. The payment of brideprice payment (wayena) by the husband's clan is the second and core event, followed by the *ibaena*, the "dressing, loading, and farewelling." During the ibaena the new wife's natal clan dress her, load her with household items to ensure a productive marriage, and accompany her as she leaves home to live with her new affines. (See the photo taken in 1962 on page 41. The bride, supported here by her brothers, wears skirts and beads to distribute to her female affines, as well as shell currency, a symbol of the fertility and wealth she brings to her husband's clan. As she entered her husband's hamlet, her brothers momentarily loaded her with string bags containing cooked pork, an additional component of the return gift.) The goods given at the North Fore ibaena are now mostly purchased and sometimes cost more than those received in her brideprice. In 2007, a brother gave his sister a sewing machine to help her to provide for her new family and estimated that his clan had spent well over K4,700.

The brideprice received by the women's relatives is also widely distributed, shared among three recipient groups. The recipients of the largest component then redistribute the cash, food, and goods to others who can claim kinship or significant acts of nurture performed for the bride before her marriage. Moreover, all brideprice recipients are expected to donate as much as they have received toward the hosting of the ibaena. Patterson Kassam,[34] the son of my friend Kassam Uvinda, confirms that the wealth contributed to South Fore brideprice is also returned during the ibaena. If K2,000 in cash and another K2,000 is spent on frozen meat, for example, the same amount would be spent, "kina for kina," on utensils, tools, bedding, clothes, and food for the bride to take when she leaves home to live with her husband.

In the past, the bridewealth in both the North and South Fore was used to procure a bride for another clan member, but today this is rare. With consent of clan members, the North Fore say that the major recipient can claim the bulk of the money to start a business or buy a block of land in Goroka. Having lived with the Fore for extended periods of time beginning in 2000, and as a recipient of brideprice herself, Dawn Glass notes that in her experience this has never happened, an index of the tension that exists between using money for "development" and the continued flow of wealth into the spheres of exchange that structure social lives.

Fore bride payments seem modest when compared to their cost elsewhere in the Highlands, which may amount to tens of thousands of kina. As among the Fore, however, the wealth amassed through gift exchange and commercial activities is not often put into productive investment, but is distributed along local networks that allow others to flourish, which supports Big Men's quest for leadership in local, regional, and national politics.[35]

DEATH PAYMENTS

Mortuary distributions are now the most expensive and spectacular ceremonial events taking place in the North and South Fore.[36] The cost of mortuary payments during recent decades rose more than those for marriage. The funeral held in 1991 for one of the Waisa peace emissaries was more expensive than anyone could remember. The woman's husband, a well-respected leader, and an Open Bible member, had purchased 85 boxes of frozen lamb, as well as clothing, blankets, and a coffin. Local items consisted of 42 pigs, twelve chickens, sugarcane, and vegetables. One wage-earning son, like many in his generation, was a reluctant contributor.

Small sticks marked the food piles to be given to the houselines attending. Nabu (a Wanitabe houseline) was called first, recognizing the role of the Wanitabe women in the 1972 peace ceremony. After the visitors were fed, food was given to twelve kandere lines (the woman's maternal kin), first to the biological mothers' brothers, and then to more distant mothers' brothers and agemates. As the coffin was lowered into the grave, and women cried out in despair, the casket was covered with several blankets. With a large pile of blankets remaining, one of the hosts intervened. "We should keep these for the woman's children," he said. The host's brother, a retired medical orderly, and a person of some status, rose to speak. "In the past we had a lot of kuru here. My wife died of kuru, but we are now living in good times. We celebrate the presence of the school, the mission, and business, and we sit down together making *patis*" (Tok Pisin for ceremonies—pronounced "parties"). A man from Purosa objected: "We are making patis for the wrong people, for those who die of kuru, or those killed by tokabu [payback killings]. We should stop doing this. We should bury these people without patis. Sorcerers are killing them, so they should be buried without ceremony. People who die in car accidents, or those who fall from trees, or who perhaps die of some sickness, these are the people we can hold patis for." This was a reference to the 1980 government law on compensation payments, designed to accommodate customary practices that allow compensation in disputes concerning the exchange of wealth—as well as for death, injury, or property damage except when they result from tribal warfare, payback killings, or injuries. People seemed to agree with the speaker and said that another bad practice should also be ruled out: divination to identify the sorcerer who had caused the death, an unsettling accompaniment of mortuary ceremonies.

The next day, back at Wanitabe, some Seventh Day Adventists said they no longer attended patis for the dead, but if as close kin they were obliged to do so, they would not eat. "If I ate, I would get sick." Another added, "I went to the Waisa ceremony yesterday but I didn't contribute" (visitors can also bring food to fulfill a debt), "and I also didn't eat any meat, just taro from the vegetable mumu," another allusion to the prohibition on pork, as well as to Seventh Day Adventists' attitudes toward the appropriate use of resources. The well-organized Adventists, in contact with national and international directives, say their reluctance to participate in mortuary ceremonies began in 1988 when a speaker at an Adventist rally announced the "new law" to end the waste of money on bridewealth and mortuary payments. Although they found it hard to resist the temptation to give large payments for educated brides, money once used for mortuary payments would now be used to buy medicines for sick people. The Open Bible members who withheld blankets from the grave at Waisa were responding to the same financial pressures: the need to pay school fees and other expected and unexpected claims.[37]

Among the latter were compensation payments for death or injury, the issue discussed at Waisa. In the past, the Fore had given compensation to injured allies, but the law now provided an opening for the inflated claims seen as hindering development. One hundred thousand kina had been demanded recently by the kin of a man from Ivaki, injured while playing soccer at Purosa. The ANGCO coffee corporation had helped Purosa pay the claim, a debt they were still repaying.

The Open Bible Mission viewed compensation claims and the ceremonial distribution of wealth at funerals as a false economy, one based on death and disability. People at Wanitabe, Waisa, Amora, and elsewhere were described as so involved in death payments that no productive work was being done. Money should be invested to make money, not distributed and consumed in patis. The Christian message was to give freely and not to expect a return. Free gifts were gifts to the Lord. Most Fore agreed with the mission that something should be done about the excessive costs, a position they had debated for many years.

Addressing the crowded Friday market in 1996, a local councilor declared once again that bride payments and mortuary distributions were too high. "This is the coffee season and we are throwing money away on patis. Women help us with work and give us children, so we can perhaps retain some small marriage payments, but dead men don't help us. We should just meet for one day of mourning, cook a small amount of food, bury the person, and go back home." Everyone should discuss this with their families, and at next Monday's market they could all clap hands as a sign of agreement. By the following Monday, no decision had been made. There was a sense that the mortuary payment could be reduced, and the lengthy patis held to mourn the deceased might be limited to one day, which they thought had been the custom in the past.[38] The discussion to limit the mourning period was related to a mortuary ceremony I had attended several days earlier.

In recent years, a new element has entered into mortuary observances. The ceremonies now last for several weeks, and participants come from a great distance. With warfare at an end, and with less fear of kuru, men now bring their wives. Temporary shelters called *haus krai* (Tok Pisin: mourning houses) or *pasindia* (the house for "passengers," meaning visitors) are constructed to shelter the guests who are described as attending "in the thousands." At Wanitabe the new fashion was said to have come from the north, from the Kamano people around the town of Kainantu, and had been

1996 Mortuary food distribution. Haus Krai in background.

introduced by policemen and other government employees with the means
to host such events. I first noticed a haus krai at Wanitabe in 1996, built
to shelter the crowds who had been awake all night singing the ancestral
songs that help put an end to sorrow and shepherd the dead person's spirit
as it joins those of its clan in the land of the ancestors.

So much food had been provided by the family of the deceased man
that the recipients had arrived in trucks to carry uncooked food back home.
Ribbons of smoke could be seen on the following day from the mumus held
in distant villages.[39]

Since 1996, Fore mortuary ceremonies have continued to expand. A
North Fore ceremony held in 2004 for the death of a young girl, observed
by Dawn Glass, was attended by crowds from the surrounding region and
proved expensive for the family obliged to provide a substantial "head payment." Following the day of burial, the close kin assembled for two weeks,
eating together and expressing their grief in mourning songs that helped to
relocate the spirit of the dead person to a place in the forest where it joined
its ancestors. The concluding feast to farewell the mother's brothers included
lamb, pigs, and chickens, but significantly no money was permitted. Money
collected for the "head pay" was converted into the food and blankets that
were buried with the coffin. In some recent North Fore ceremonies, the coffin
was lowered onto a mattress, a glass plate in the casket allowing mourners

to view the head of the deceased person. "We look after our dead better than we look after our living," they said.[40]

A South Fore mortuary ceremony at Purosa in 2011 set a record for attendance and expense. The deceased man, Kassam Uvinda, was an important person. As a youth in the 1950's, he had accompanied a policeman exploring distant parts of the Highlands and was later appointed tultul by a colonial administration that governed through local leaders. In his late twenties, already a tultul, he was one of the first research assistants to work with Robert Glasse and me. Retiring to Purosa, he became the elected Ward Committee Member as well as a member of the Purosa Community School Board. He was an advocate for peace and harmony, and people came to him for advice about family history and clan boundaries. He had ensured that his five sons and two daughters were well educated, and at the time of his death his eldest son held a senior position in the national government and he and his son were studying political science at the University of Papua New Guinea.

When the first son arrived from Port Moresby three days after his father's death, he found the clan collecting money to distribute on the following day.[41] Asked by the elders for his contribution, he called a halt to the proceedings, demanding a return to "the old style of mourning," to the way it was done in his father's day. Money should not be distributed, but should be used instead to buy food. The elders agreed, and with 66,000 kina they purchased 27 pigs (most from the Markham Valley in Morobe Province), 100 cartons of frozen meat (trucked in from Goroka), a locally domesticated cassowary (K1,000), and 400 live chickens (purchased from communities along the Highlands Highway).

The ceremony was not exactly as it was in the old days. In the past, two ceremonies were held months apart. The *isosoena,* a distribution of food for the women who had consumed the body of the dead person, was usually held on the first day. The agoena, the head pay given to the mother's brothers, was then held later when the hosts had accumulated sufficient pigs. In addition, leaves from the isosoena earth oven were placed on the ground for women to tread as they left the widow's house, the steam from the leaves purifying their bodies.[42] With the end of cannibalism, the isosoena is now considered to be the feast to feed and then disperse distant cousins, mother's relatives, agemates, and visitors who are invited to return some weeks later for the agoena, the main event. In 2011, Kassam Uvinda's death occurred during the coffee season, when people had plenty of money, so the ceremonies took place in a shorter sequence of events. As in the North Fore ceremonies held in 2004, until the visitors returned, close relatives remained singing ancestral songs each night to accompany the spirit on its journey to its final place of rest in the land of the ancestors.

At Purosa, the hosts constructed sixteen temporary shelters (haus krai) for the "two thousand people" who came from surrounding areas, each shelter designated for the local groups who attended: the Wanitabes, the Kamilas, the Agakamatasas, and so on. A headstone, said to have been requested by Kassam, was the first to be seen in the region.[43] The son and organizer contributed K17,000, the largest individual cash contribution, and expected it would take him many months to pay for the additional costs of dismantling shelters; for erecting the headstone; and for the coffee, tea, sugar, and utensils distributed to people in the haus krai. He noted, however, that the party was hailed as the largest ever held in the Okapa region, and that people had praised him and his family for an event that matched the person in whose memory it had been held.

Those who attended came from throughout the region and included many prominent people. The National Member of Parliament for Okapa and the District Administrator sent their representatives. An invitation was extended also to the foreman and workers upgrading the road between Okapa and Purosa. Friends and close relatives living and working in Port Moresby, Lae, Goroka, and other parts of the country brought their families and also contributed to the funeral costs.

The Purosa ceremonies revived earlier forms of work activity, in which kin groups exchanged labor free of charge, in contrast to the recent trend that free labor is no longer given even for customary obligations. Faced with an immensity of tasks, the son called on close and distant relatives as well as agemates to volunteer their labor, and thus affirm their respect for old customs. The son's temporary house, located at the center of the sixteen haus krai, provided a coordinating point for the decisions made by the collectivity. He divided his male and female workforce into separate committees responsible for public relations; pigs; frozen meat; chicken; and the firewood, leaves, stones, and water used in the mumus. A general committee was named to integrate the activities. Three more committees involved elders who selected young people to distribute food to the general public and to monitor the separate distributions for women visitors who could not eat with men. In all, the committees distributed more than 100 heaps of food.

On a cold evening when the work plans were still being considered, an elderly man crept into the central shelter and suggested that they recall the sacred flutes, once sounded at singsings and the ceremonial exchange of pigs. The flutes had conveyed a message of truce among feuding villages, so it was appropriate to hear them again to honor the man who had promoted peace in what was once known as "the bloody valley." Just before dawn the next morning, the cry of the flutes caught everyone by surprise. At first, there was silence. Then a few old men gathered on the common ground in disbelief, tears rolling down their cheeks. Elderly women were soon heard crying inside the makeshift shelters. From their hilltop location, out of the reach of women and children, the flutes were heard for the duration of the mourning period, when a ceremonial mumu was held to ask them to return to their pandanus-grove home in the forest.

Kassam had been a firm believer of the Christian faith, and before he died he had called for the local pastor to pray for him. A prayer service was thus conducted for the large congregation that gathered for the burial on the fourth day. Abandoning earlier practices, his children, agemates, and members of his mother's line did not rub themselves with mud and ashes, and his widow did not cover her head with old string bags. Instead, the immediate family wore black-and-white clothing brought from Port Moresby, the men's T-shirts bearing the message "Goodbye Papa Kassam." Energetic and continuous crying over the body was discouraged.

Kassam Uvinda's son acknowledged that Christianity discourages funeral parties of this magnitude, and some of the faithful at Purosa, anxious about disregarding this religious prescription, initially resisted. Arguing instead for retaining a hold on beliefs and practices that he sees as fast dying out, his father's funeral was, in his view, the beginning of a future in which he intends to broadcast the message that religion should not discourage respect for good traditions and customs. At Purosa, no divination ritual was performed to determine the cause of Kassam's death, although immediate family members and some distant relatives suspected tokabu (vengeance) because Kassam had appeared to be in good health when he died suddenly.

Kassam's son observed that his father had in him enormous wealth, an essence contained in the person. He was a great warrior and famous hunter, his gardens were plentiful, his pigs were fat, he relished sharing food with others, and he also played a leading role in brideprice and funeral parties. Following his funeral, people were heard saying that this son had indeed inherited the position of his father. His son said later, "I will have to show by example whether I have this wealth hidden in me."

Many echoes of earlier events seem present in the organizational feat carried out by the first son: the prestige acquired by the sponsors of ceremonial pig exchange and singsing bisnis, as well the attendance of relatives and visitors from other villages and districts, an index of the organizer's "sphere of political influence."[44] Pig exchange ceremonies had similarly provided great quantities of food to ensure harmonious interaction among potential enemies, and flutes were also played each day and at night when men entered the ceremonial ground while women remained behind closed doors.

As ritual objects, the flutes were a symbol of male dominance. Fore myths say that men stole the flutes from women, their first owners, but men also say that their haunting sound is the voice of a "wild bush woman," a clue to their androgynous identity and appeal. When first shown the flutes, initiates were warned not to reveal their nature to women. Each man once possessed a named flute, which was a part of himself, his spirit and physical strength. At death, his flute was broken and buried with him. His physical strength having disappeared, his spirit joined those of the ancestors. Since the last pig exchange took place at Wanitabe in 1969, and at Purosa possibly in the same year, the wondrous sound of the flutes some forty years later seems to have effected a spiritual awakening.

The venerated place of the sacred flutes in the Eastern Highlands has been described by a number of ethnographers.[45] When Lutheran missionaries forced men to show the flutes to women and children in communities just north of the Fore in 1952, the rituals and ceremonies associated with them were discarded. In an attempt to denigrate the more conspicuous forms of pagan belief and practice, Lutherans are said to have burned the sacred flutes of the Gahuku,[46] (Eastern Highlanders not far from the town of Goroka), as did the first missionary to visit the Gimi region.[47] Native evangelists condemned almost all traditional belief and activity as uncongenial to Christianity or to their version of Christianity, which Ronald Berndt notes were not necessarily the same behaviors singled out by the European missionaries of their parental church.[48] With little supervision, and accompanied by native police, the evangelists encouraged haircutting and wearing clothing, but discouraged or prohibited the use of pig fat to oil hair and anoint newborn babies. The seclusion of women during menstruation was also proscribed, as well as separate eating and sleeping quarters for women and men, and the performance of sacred rituals and ceremonies.

The elders at Waisa remember the first missionaries telling them to cast off old ways, and to stop performing magic and sorcery. People sold their shields, weapons, and working tools, and turned away from old customs, including initiation.[49] As Berndt noted, however, the pig exchanges may have disappeared, but the dominant values of the belief system still remained, a prescient observation that Kassam's funeral so movingly confirmed.

HISTORY-TELLING

The history of these decades can be told in many ways. One brief account would say that in 1975 Papua New Guinea became an independent nation, warfare ended, the kuru epidemic waned, and the population revived. Most people now consider themselves to be Christians; at the same time, they honor their own beliefs. The encounter with capitalism has left in its wake a huge concern about acquiring money and using it in culturally appropriate ways. The desires of young people for commodities, new forms of romance, as well as new forms of sociality and sexual experience are emerging in the context of state and marketplace interventions that elicit and shape new behaviors and desires.[50]

This chapter suggests that the same history is contained in events of different magnitude, in the apparently less-significant shifts in day-to-day practice, as well as in the striking changes in bridewealth ceremonies and mortuary rituals.[51] The shift from shells and *kinta* to Australian shillings and then kina, for example, provides a quick summary of the currencies that underwrite and reconfigure changing social and commercial transactions from precolonial to postcolonial times. Changes in burial practice record the transformation of spiritual life taking place in the same years. In the past, some deceased kin were consumed, and some were buried in the person's sugar gardens, which were then abandoned. Ghosts of the dead were considered to be a potential danger to living relatives. Missionaries said that the dead were not to be feared, and bodies should be buried in tree-shaded cemeteries. Retaining a hold on older beliefs, Fore agemates were buried together so their spirits could travel as companions to the place of the ancestors. Following further mission instruction, families buried their dead next to their houses, where they could look after them. The South Fore now say, without a sense of conflict, that they live with two religions. Ancestral songs at funerals are sung with heads bowed toward the earth, the ground from which the original Creative Beings emerged. Church hymns are sung with heads raised toward heaven, where dead souls are said to find a resting place with Jesus. The Fore also have their own forms of history-telling in narratives about the bush spirit Nokoti, a surrogate self, whose adventures describe the sense of lost autonomy during colonial times and the rebirth of national pride following Independence.[52]

The investment of time and wealth in ceremonial exchange may be the most visible index of change. The Fore are not alone in their concern about the use of cash in bridewealth ceremonies. As cash entered into bride payments in the Western Highlands in 1959, people at Mount Hagen similarly attempted to limit its use, as did the Sina Local Government Council in 1965, but in both places the payments have continued to rise.[53] The Fore have similarly been unable to contain the size of cash in bridewealth transactions, and as elsewhere in the Highlands, they distribute it conspicuously in a ceremonial enterprise associated with prestige.

The Fore say that restricting the use of cash in mortuary payments was first proposed by the government interpreter in the 1950's, shortly after the government began to pay wages in cash, not shells. By converting kina into older forms of wealth, the rituals described here reanimate precapitalist concepts of productive work, as well as the "wealth" that resides in persons. The momentous return of the flutes and the ritual attention given to spirits of the dead endow on wealth a measure of cosmological meaning that is missing in bridewealth transactions. In addition, the funerals have a wider sociopolitical reach in their ability to pull in a larger audience of both kin and visitors, infusing new life into old forms of leadership, suggesting that the rituals are activating networks of support for the organizers to perform on a regional, even national, stage, a new sociopolitical form in the making.

In some parts of the North Fore, the increasing cost of meat is said to have persuaded donors to give mortuary payments in cash, not food,[54] as the elders at Purosa were about to do. Nevertheless, as with singsing bisnis, most of the Fore appear to have found a way, for the moment, to reconcile the demands of an increasingly commoditized economy in a ritual language that speaks to this condition and offers a means of self-possession.

THE END OF KURU

13

Chapter 12 provided an account of how the Fore gave cultural meaning to introduced concepts of wealth, work, and religion. This chapter brings into focus their accommodation with the concepts and practices of biomedicine.[1] As noted earlier, when the epidemic was at its height, the Fore had faced a demographic emergency, the dimensions of which they grasped clearly. They turned to a variety of desperate remedies, consulted curers in distant locations, and took ambulant victims on healing pilgrimages. At home, they held public meetings to persuade sorcerers to stop killing the women who gave birth to the next generation. Much has changed since that time. As the incidence of kuru declined, the question that preoccupied the Fore was no longer how to identify sorcerers in order to save the victims, but whether kuru was a form of sorcery or sickness—the latter a designation they knew to be held by medical investigators, the government, and missionaries.[2] The sorcery-sickness debate arose first during the 1962 kibungs when the speakers had little doubt that sorcerers caused kuru, and were concerned that the colonial authorities would hold them, not the sorcerers, responsible. Following decades of close contact with people who do not share their views about diagnosis and therapy, the presumed causes of illness and death seemed more complex.

Biomedical diagnoses are now accepted for some forms of sickness, and many reasons are given for the disappearance of kuru and kuru sorcerers, but the belief in sorcery for fatal and some non-fatal conditions remains intact. The old kuru curers have given way to local practitioners who treat new infectious diseases that biomedical practitioners also treat, and that neither considers to be caused by sorcery. The challenge now is to demonstrate to an international audience that their own remedies for these conditions are effective.

Three sets of actors take part in this complex interchange: medical investigators, the Fore, and anthropologists, each with their own ideas about disease causation, remedies, methods of inquiry, and ways of putting knowledge into practice. Given the complexity of presenting different styles of reasoning, research, and conduct, it is necessary at times to tease them apart. I hope to show, however, that the thoughts and activities of all three were part of a larger single conversation.

As outlined in Chapter 2, some observers first thought that kuru was a psychosomatic phenomenon. Berndt, an anthropologist working in the North Fore region in the 1950's, thought that patient deaths were associated with a particularly malignant form of sorcery, reflecting a widely held view that death often occurred in people who believed themselves to be bewitched, a position not unlike an early medical diagnosis of a case observed in 1955 as acute hysteria in an otherwise healthy woman. Well-documented medical reports of kuru in 1957 and 1959 provided a clinical description of the disease and its patterns of occurrence for a medical audience and a colonial administration concerned with the health of the population.[3] Kuru was said to be an almost invariably fatal, acute, progressive, degenerative disease of the central nervous system, restricted to members of the Fore cultural and linguistic group and their immediate neighbors with whom they intermarried. The victims were predominantly women and adolescents of both sexes. Adult men were rarely victims, and no cases had been found in children under four or five years of age. Cases removed from the Fore environment did not recover. Because of its familial pattern, a genetic basis for the disease was soon proposed.

Supported by a grant from Adelaide University Department of Genetics, Robert Glasse and I arrived in Papua New Guinea in 1961 with a charge to study Fore kinship, which, it was thought, would provide data confirming the genetic hypothesis. We set about learning Fore kin terms, drew genealogical charts, observed kinship in action, and began to learn something of Fore domestic and political affairs. We had been asked to document Fore "pedigrees," a clue perhaps to the problem that lay ahead. It soon became apparent that Fore kinship was flexible, and that some kuru victims were not closely related biologically, as the term pedigree implies, but were considered by the Fore to be kin in what we would call a social sense. Nestled within political units, immigrants from nearby or distant communities were welcomed as long as they demonstrated loyalty and observed their new social obligations. In time, immigrants were said to possess "one blood" and to stem from a common ancestor, conveying the idea that those who reside and act together, and eat food grown on the same land, share bodily substance. Fore permitted the adoption of children "orphaned" by the kuru deaths of their mothers, and kinship could be created by the ceremonial consumption of food. Fore genealogies, it seemed, were not pedigrees, but social documents that gave legitimacy to culturally defined notions of kinship. They provided a guide for living, but were not reliable statements of genetic proximity.

Our genealogical information included causes of death: warfare, deaths during the dysentery epidemic, and a variety of deaths caused by sorcery. People remembered seeing the first cases of kuru and could provide the gender, age, and names of the victims. That the epidemic was so recent came as a surprise, so with two research assistants we walked through the South and the North Fore and into the territory of the neighboring Keiagana people, collecting information about first sightings in each location. This historical narrative indicated that kuru had spread through Fore villages within the remembered past, entering their territory from the north around the turn of the century (see Map 4). The genetic theory held at that time, which implied that kuru must have been of remote origin, no longer seemed plausible. Genetics, however, re-enters the story later, based on non-Mendelian, protein-based theories of inheritance.

CANNIBALISM

The historical narratives we collected indicated that deceased kuru victims had been consumed by close relatives. Although we had not come to the Fore to focus attention on cannibalism, we collected detailed information about the practice. In 1962 and 1963, we sent reports of our fieldwork to John Gunther, the director of Public Health for Papua New Guinea,[4] which provided evidence that kuru was of recent origin, information about the rights of certain kin to consume deceased relatives, and description of the effects of high female mortality on gender relations and family life. My diary entries indicate that we continued to gather ethnographic accounts about cannibalism in 1962, motivated by a perception that those who were dying of kuru had participated in the consumption of a relative who had died of the disease, and speculated about possible biological explanations.

As Chapter 2 also notes, all body parts were eaten, except the gall bladder, which was considered too bitter. Significantly, not all Fore were cannibals. Some elderly men rarely ate human flesh, and small children residing with their mothers ate what their mothers gave them. Initiated youths, at approximately age ten, moved to the men's house, away from their mothers, where they began to observe the cultural practices and dietary taboos that define masculinity. Consuming the dead was appropriate for adult women but not men, who feared the pollution and physical depletion associated with eating a corpse. The early medical reports, indicating that kuru occurred among women, children of both sexes, and a few elderly men, thus matched Fore rules of cannibal consumption.

We spoke about our findings to a variety of medical audiences, including a kuru workshop held at the University of Adelaide in 1962, which Gajdusek attended, and to a group of visiting scientists who visited us in the

South Fore in 1963. The visitors included Michael Alpers, who would soon make his own important mark on the epidemiology of kuru, and MacFarlane Burnet, a virologist awarded the Nobel Prize in 1960 for his contributions to immunology. Addressing our cannibalism hypothesis later, Burnet observed that "some, like the present writer, initially found the suggestion incredible but must confess now to at least an open mind on the matter."[5] Unknown to us, Burnet had been losing faith in the genetic theory and was secretly receptive to the idea that cannibalism might be implicated.[6]

Meanwhile, in 1959, William Hadlow had made the seminal connection between the neuropathological features of kuru and scrapie, a disease in sheep. Moreover, he said that scrapie was transmissible by inoculation. Hadlow's observation inspired Gajdusek and his co-workers to test the transmissibility of kuru on chimpanzees, which was successfully carried out in 1966. Kuru, like scrapie, was now considered to be an infectious disease, caused by a "slow virus" of very long incubation.

The transmissibility of kuru provided a major medical piece of the puzzle. John Mathews, who as a medical student had heard Burnet talk about kuru, arrived in Papua New Guinea in 1964 to begin his own research. Based on quantitative analysis of our Fore genealogies, Mathews published papers in 1965 and 1967 that confirmed that kuru was of limited time depth and that the average age of kuru cases was rising each year, evidence hard to accommodate with the original genetic theory, but consistent with the cannibalism hypothesis.[7] In 1967 Robert Glasse presented the case for cannibalism as the mode of transmission to the Division of Anthropology at the New York Academy of Sciences,[8] and in 1968, Robert and I joined Mathews in a publication that would reach a wider audience.[9] Our paper showed that the cannibalism theory was supported by a wealth of epidemiological and ethnographic data, and was consistent with stories about named individuals who had taken part in mortuary feasts and who had themselves died from kuru. In 1968, Alpers' analysis of a comprehensive body of epidemiological data also concluded that cannibalism was the mode of transmission.[10]

Some still doubted the cannibalism hypothesis. Perhaps the most surprising resistance came from Gajdusek, who proposed an alternative route of disease transmission. The mechanism, he said, lay in the contamination of highly infective tissues through cuts and scrapes on the hands of mourners, as well as from brain tissue purposely rubbed on the body during mortuary ceremonies, a practice the Fore have denied.[11] While the handling of infectious body parts could possibly be a means of occasional self-inoculation, Gajdusek had begun to overstate the case. His resistance to the idea of oral ingestion as the route of disease transmission has elicited speculation from many who knew him. He and his colleagues were said to have found it difficult to imagine how social and cultural studies could be rendered commensurate with contemporary biological research and pathological findings. The ecological mantle Gajdusek had adopted on first encountering the disease had shifted to a narrower focus on microbe hunting.[12] The sensitivity of the topic may also explain some unwillingness to accept the role of cannibalism. In recent years, many well-documented accounts of cannibalism have been published by anthropologists who once thought the topic was too delicate to discuss, given the image of the cannibal as an icon of primitivism.[13] It is also the case that Gajdusek's data on cannibalism were inaccurate. His published letters and field notes[14] indicate that, based on information provided by men, he thought the human brain was not consumed.[15]

Gajdusek did not doubt that the Fore consumed deceased relatives, although skepticism about the practice has a long history in Western thought.[16] The notion that cannibalism as a socially approved custom did not exist, however, was finding a receptive audience among some anthropologists,[17] a position that is no longer accepted. In addition, it was asserted that this purported custom would never stand up in a court of law and would be too flimsy to merit a news report, but such accounts were readily available. An episode of cannibalism reported in Australian newspapers, for example, noted that the essential facts of the case were undisputed since the remaining body parts had been produced as evidence. The judge said he was bound to convict the three accused men, despite acknowledging that they saw nothing wrong in what they did and were ignorant of the introduced law outlawing cannibalism.[18]

In the 1980's and 1990's, a general shift in the human sciences, glossed as "postmodernism," gave close attention to metaphor and representation, providing new life for the idea that cannibalism was nothing more than a colonizing trope and stratagem, a calumny used by colonizers to justify their predatory behavior. Postcolonial studies proposed that the "figure of the cannibal was created to support the cultural cannibalism of colonialism through the projection of Western appetites onto the cultures they consumed."[19] A common factor in the history of cannibal allegations is the combination of its denial among ourselves, and its attribution to those we wish to defame, conquer, and civilize. In an atmosphere of postcolonial guilt, denial about cannibalism was extended to denial on behalf of those we wished to rehabilitate and acknowledge as our equals.[20]

Unfortunately, cannibal denial and the debate it engendered diverted attention from a deeper analysis of collective ideas of prejudice. The assumption of the cannibalistic nature of others is one instance of a broader ideology that attempts to discredit political rivals and unfriendly neighboring communities, and belongs to a category of disparaging allegations about the malevolence of others, such as ethnic groups to which the accuser does not belong, who from time to time in human history have been identified as witches, Satanists, and heretics. We have here a manifestation of racism, a topic that has received recent attention, allowing us to return to the issue of cannibalism in a more serious and sensitive way.

The figure of the cannibal, long used to construct racial boundaries, can now be called upon in projects to deconstruct them. The stigma is best countered when we look to our own behavior as well as the behavior of others.[21] We may then be in a position to dislodge the savage-civilized dualism once essential to the formation of modern Western identity and Western forms of knowledge. We know, for example, that medicinal ingestion involving human flesh, blood, heart, skull, bone marrow, and other body parts was practiced widely throughout Europe from the sixteenth to the eighteenth centuries, and placentophagia, in which the mother eats her newborn baby's placenta (as was the case among the Fore), became popular in the United States with the spread of the home birth movement in the 1970's.[22] And as discussed in detail later, recent genetic studies' probing questions of human history and evolution provide evidence of our own distant cannibal past. Although the topic of cannibalism still elicits a compulsion by some to joke about the practice, and has nourished salacious accounts of Fore behavior, we are now better armed to respond to the call[23] for philosophical housecleaning around the complexities of getting to know cannibals.

Jerome Whitfield, an anthropologist who joined the MRC kuru project in 1996, began long-term research with a team of twelve young Fore men who interviewed their elderly family members. This has resulted in a rich account of the mortuary ceremonies and the cosmological foundations of the practice of cannibalism. In the 1960's, much ceremonial life had been suppressed in the encounter with colonial officers and missionaries bent on putting an end to the consumption of deceased relatives and the rituals and ideas associated with the practice. Decades later, in the context of self-government, a sense that the kuru years were behind them, and assertions of cultural renewal, the elders spoke about beliefs and behaviors that had not been passed on to the younger generation.

Fore myths depict an original being (bagina) creating the land as well as the guardian spirits (amani), whose descendants make up the clans found on the land today. Just as the bagina created the founding amani, it was the duty of humans to ensure that the dead were transformed into living ancestors. By eating the dead, the female affines of the deceased person confined the dangerous ghost inside themselves, thus protecting the family from ghostly attack and the pollution from a decomposing body. The final mortuary ritual enabled the ghost to depart to the land of the ancestors, the deceased person finally being reborn as an ancestor.[24] Dawn Glass, writing from an insider's perspective as well, also emphasizes the ceremonies' mythological foundations, and notes that by mixing and eating the deceased person's ground bones and blood with wild greens, North Fore women ensured the regeneration of ancestral substances through bodily consumption.[25]

INFECTIOUS PROTEINS AND MOLECULAR GENETICS

In 1976, Carleton Gajdusek received the Nobel Prize for the successful transmission of kuru to laboratory primates. Stanley Prusiner, a neurologist from California, then entered the kuru story with a visit to the Fore in 1978.

In 1982, he described the elusive infectious agent as a "prion," until that time called a "slow virus" by Gajdusek and others. Prions, Prusiner said, consisted of malformed proteins and nothing else. Moreover, prions might be inherited, transmitted through infection, or occur spontaneously. This sensational hypothesis, sometimes called "the protein-only hypothesis" is now accepted, although at the time Prusiner took his lumps.[26] In 1997, Prusiner was awarded the Nobel Prize for his finding that normally innocuous cellular proteins can convert their structures into pernicious conformations that damage nerve cells. At his Nobel banquet speech, Prusiner noted that some scientists and the press had difficulty grasping the concept. His contribution, nevertheless, gave conceptual unity to a spectrum of prion diseases in humans and animals: Creutzfeldt-Jakob disease (CJD), kuru, Gerstmann-Sträussler-Sheinker syndrome (GSS), and fatal familial insomnia in humans, and in animals, scrapie, bovine spongiform encephalopathy (BSE, popularly known as mad cow disease), chronic wasting disease in deer, and transmissible mink encephalopathy. BSE caused the death of domestic cats in Europe, as well as the death of exotic ruminants in English zoos. Bison, nyala, gemsbok, orynx, greater kudu, and eland have all been shown to die from BSE, as did Major, a popular lion, despite treatment with conventional medicines, a magnetic collar, and faith healing.[27]

With the appearance of BSE in the United Kingdom in 1986, and the identification of variant Creutzfeldt-Jakob disease (called *variant* because, compared to classical, sporadic CJD, it has a distinctive clinical presentation and neuropathology), the kuru epidemic acquired new global relevance. John Collinge, the director of the Prion research group, turned his attention to kuru, concerned that BSE prions might infect humans. Kuru provided the example of an epidemic thought to have resulted from consumption of an individual dying of sporadic CJD, followed by the recycling of the infectious agent within the community as others developed the disease and were themselves consumed.[28] Recent molecular analysis of kuru prion isolates supports this view.[29] Kuru could perhaps provide important lessons in understanding a human epidemic resulting from BSE exposure. The recognition of vCJD in 1996, and Collinge's demonstration that it bore the molecular signature of BSE, gave this project increased impetus.[30]

The current view about the origin of the BSE epidemic is that the disease was derived not from sheep infected with conventional scrapie but from feeding cattle the recycled remains of cattle infected with BSE itself (that is, cannibalism). And as with kuru, the first case may have originated [in a cow in this case] as a consequence of a gene mutation. The spread of BSE was thus a result of the unforeseen dangers associated with industrialized farming, as well as the ineptitude of a government bureaucracy and the collusion of government agencies charged with monitoring the beef industry.

By the end of the 1960's, a framework for future clinical and epidemiological research on kuru had already been established. Building on more than two decades of surveillance of the epidemic by the Institute of Medical Research, Jerome Whitfield and his Prion Unit team documented all cases of kuru from 1996 to the last case in 2009. It is now apparent that the clinical features and duration of the disease have remained unchanged, averaging about twelve months from onset to death.[31]

In 2003, the London group reported that kuru had apparently exerted a strong selection pressure on the human prion gene in the context of kuru-like epidemics in the past, when cannibalism was thought to have been widespread.[32] The majority of elderly Fore women known to have consumed deceased kin, but who had not developed kuru, were shown to have a distinct genetic type of prion protein gene (129MV), which provided relative protection when exposed to the prion infectious agent. Global patterns of diversity in the same gene suggest that European populations show similar, but older, evidence of selection resulting in survival advantage conferred by genetic variation of the prion protein gene during episodes of endocannibalism and prion-related epidemics in ancient human populations. The archaeologist Tim White's proposition[33] that we had all once been cannibals now seems less provocative than it did in 2001.

Subsequent study of genetic, clinical, and genealogical data from a larger sample of Fore and neighboring groups (3,000 Eastern Highlanders, including 700 who had participated in mortuary consumption of the dead and 152 who subsequently died of kuru) has located a novel variant of the prion protein gene (127V) at the epicenter of the epidemic in the Purosa Valley. Variant 127V is also an acquired prion-disease resistance factor, selected in this case during the kuru epidemic.

Variant 129MV is a globally distributed polymorphism, found at particularly high frequencies throughout the Eastern Highlands, that provided relative protection from kuru wherever it occurred. In the Purosa Valley, most of the kuru survivors were 129MV, and some had the additional protection of 127V. One person with 127V was located at Wanitabe, outside the Purosa Valley, the northern edge of where this variant was observed. In sum, variant 129MV is said to demonstrate a population genetic response to an earlier epidemic of prion disease, and 127V, a powerful episode of recent selection in response to the kuru epidemic.[34] The development of a blood test in 2011 to detect the abnormal prion protein associated with variant Creutzfeldt-Jakob disease in living persons could lead to the large-scale screening and detection of asymptomatic individuals who pose a risk to others via blood transfusion.[35] With advances in early diagnosis, the challenge now is to find effective treatment for neurodegenerative disease.

THE FORE VIEW OF THE EPIDEMIC

For many decades, the Fore confronted a multitude of new objects and technologies, introduced by a regime of power whose personnel held different conceptions of life and death. A particular challenge for the Fore has been how to explain the disappearance of the disease that once endangered their survival. Most people said that kuru had disappeared with the arrival of the mission, the school, and the market—a set of coherences that seemed causal. Some said that sorcerers had turned to more profitable kinds of business, and most agreed that kuru would end when the last of the generation of old men had died, taking with them their special knowledge of kuru sorcery. Their sons, most of whom had not been initiated, declared that this knowledge had not been passed on to them.

Women were considered to be the victims of sorcery, not sorcerers themselves, and they were often unsure about how to explain the epidemic's end. Their memories of the kuru years are filled with a sense of sadness and anxiety. One woman, Aninta, said:

> When our mothers and fathers got this sickness and died, we asked ourselves what it was all about. Why were they dying and leaving us behind? People were dying all around us, and we thought we would be finished. We wondered if men were making poison and causing the sickness that was killing us. We wondered if any good women would survive, and we felt very sad. They died and we buried all of them.... I sometimes think that kuru will come and touch me. But maybe I will live to an old age and die without getting it. I often wonder about this.

In response to my question about cannibalism, she added:

> I am not so old. You remember how small I was when you first came here. In my mother and father's time, maybe they ate people, but I didn't see it.

Another woman, Atiya, joined the conversation.

> In the past, we had a lot of kuru here. Then I was born and grew up, and I saw a few cases. But I had the same confusion. Did men cause it, kill people, or what? Now the gospel has come to us. We go to church and live in good times and there are plenty of young people and we have no kuru. But when I was small I also saw women with kuru, and inside me I still think about it and am afraid. It was here before so maybe it will come back again and attack me.

Men found the question just as challenging. Four men holding different views also based their arguments on life's experiences. Kabaiya's sorcery beliefs were intact; Negimba thought that Fore and Western medicines could cure diseases caused by sorcerers; and Obeta said he thought, but mostly hoped, that kuru was a form of sickness. Daniel offered a convincing way to test whether kuru was or was not the result of sorcery.

Kabaiya, a local councilor, considered himself to be a leader and facilitator of the new political and commercial order. Like the colonial administrators of yesteryear, he had the authority to conduct local court hearings and to expect compliance. Telling his story in heroic mode, he said:

> I told people I had outlawed kuru sorcery. I spoke strongly about this. I was instrumental also in introducing the market here. And I announced that if people had any problems, they should come to us, the councilors and committee men. People listened to me and they stopped making sorcery. And as you see, there are now plenty of men and women here.

In 1963, Negimba had signed on as an assistant to medical investigators, observing medical examinations, assisting in the collection of blood and urine, and gaining family permission for autopsies that he attended. His association with kuru research lasted until 1977. Between 1964 and 1967, he accompanied the government medical patrols that gave people "two injections to kill the germs that came in the blood," injections he thought were responsible for eliminating kuru. Negimba was describing the medical patrols that gave BCG vaccine to prevent tuberculosis and benzathine penicillin injections for yaws.[36] Like Kabaiya, Negimba drew on singular work experience not shared by many of his generation, and the authoritative knowledge acquired working with medical teams. He still thought kuru was caused by sorcerers but, like all Fore, that medicines could cure it. His classificatory brother, Patali, was a curer who he said had successfully treated many kuru cases using indigenous medicines, but the patients died because they failed to follow dietary or behavioral rules, or because sorcerers poisoned them a second time. In his view, kuru had joined a list of ailments, such as yaws, now eradicated by biomedicine.

Obeta, a few years younger than Kabaiya and Negimba, had completed primary school. Often present when the others spoke about the epidemic, he provided a more poignant personal account.

> My strongest thoughts are that it is not men who are doing this, because if men did it they could transfer this knowledge to their brothers and children. These people could then train the Amoras [an adjacent community] and then another houseline and another, and it would spread across the Eastern Highlands and on to other provinces. But it stops inside our district, so I think it is a sickness that comes along from time to time. It arrived when people died of kuru and people ate them.
>
> My mother and father both died of kuru, so I thought I would get it too. But I didn't, and I have six children and none of them are getting this sickness.... So I think I am lucky that white men came at this time and gave injections, otherwise I would have had kuru and died. [Negimba had just given his account of the curative medical patrols.] I have a strong hope that it was the injections that conquered it.

Obeta said he changed his thoughts about kuru following a conversation we had in 1991. I had given him a photograph of his mother when she was pregnant with him. I knew his mother well, and this was a bond in our long friendship.

> You told me that my mother had died of kuru. I don't remember her. You also told me that kuru was transmitted by people eating people who had died of the disease. My father died of kuru, so I am a child of two people with kuru in the blood. [Information about the transmission of the disease has resulted in the Fore calling kuru "a disease of the blood," and young men who have not been initiated say that they live in fear because their bodies still contain their mother's blood.] At first, I thought my father had sick malaria, but then his body began to shake and he had to walk about with a stick, and there came a time when he fell down and couldn't walk any more, and he just stopped in the house.... I looked after him when I was a small boy. My mother and father had died of kuru and I was very confused.

I asked if he ever thought that a sorcerer had killed his father, and he said:

> No, it came from eating people. Here's an example. I eat plenty of green vegetables and good *abus* [Tok Pisin for meat], and this good food produces blood. So this first man ate someone, and this produced the sickness inside the blood, and then he sleeps with his wife, and his semen goes into the mother, and she gives birth to the child, and the sickness goes into the baby. This is what I think—my father's father ate someone and he gave it to my father, and he gave it to my mother, and I thought I would get it too.

Obeta's analysis is a sophisticated composite of personal experience, local biological concepts, and biomedical ideas about disease transmission. It also reflects the influence of others, as well as the searing experience of caring for his dying father. The story begins with a first man, not a woman, eating someone, followed by a sequence of events compatible with Fore ideas of patrilineal inheritance of body traits and substances. (Biomedicine does not support the notion of vertical transmission of the disease in humans, but vertical transmission is possible for prion diseases in some other species, such as sheep and cows.) In Obeta's story, his mother acquires the sickness from his father (not from eating a deceased person), and he and his children have been protected by the intervention of medical investigators (which is not the case). Although a Seventh Day Adventist, he said that the church had not influenced his thinking. "They tell us that the gospel says we can't kill people, steal women, or speak untruths. What I have told you about kuru, these are my thoughts."

Daniel presented his case that kuru was indeed a form of sorcery. Daniel held no political office and had no schooling, but he had worked for many years in a variety of jobs in Port Moresby and Goroka. A forceful person, he moves back and forth between home and Port Moresby, where he has the ear of senior politicians and lobbied for the new Wanitabe high school. Many people in his family died of kuru, including his mother. In 2008, he saw that the epidemic was coming to an end but, like the epidemiologists, he said he would wait until 2012 to see if that was really the case. Meanwhile, he held two thoughts about kuru:

> In the past, we Fore all said that kuru was a poison caused by sorcerers. Then whites came and told us it was a sickness that arrived when our ancestors ate people, and some of them said that people in England who ate cows have the same sickness. [This widely shared piece of information has resulted in the Fore calling mad cow disease in humans "English Kuru," and some now say they will not eat beef.] But if there is no more kuru by 2012, it will be clear that sorcerers were the cause. The old generation of men who had this knowledge will have died, taking their knowledge with them.
>
> Furthermore, if kuru was sickness as whites say, they would have found a medicine, but they have failed to do so. Malaria is caused by mosquitoes and for this there is medicine. For TB also there is medicine. Kuru was caused by men who poisoned women who went to the seclusion hut [the yentanama, called the "house blood" in Tok Pisin] when "the moon kills them" [menstruation], or when they gave birth to children. Now there are no seclusion huts, so the sorcerers can't steal scraps of clothing or traces of blood. And this is why kuru is disappearing. When I met John Collinge I promised him that if I get kuru he could operate on my body. I would do this to help the community.

Collinge's account of the same encounter says that Daniel suggested a research project using actual and mock sorcery bundles with Daniel as the subject, a proposal that was not conceptually different from a placebo-controlled trial.[37]

Whatever their views, most Fore share the modernist mantra that the end of the epidemic can be attributed to a break with the past brought about by Christianity, the markets, and the school. A few may speak with uncertainty about kuru as a form of sickness (as did Obeta and the two women), but they have not changed their views about sorcery in general. Nor do the Fore assume, as many scholars have supposed, that all belief in sorcery and witchcraft will disappear with "modernization" and modern science. This has not been the case in Papua New Guinea or elsewhere in the world.[38] Sorcery still provides an explanation for deadly ailments and misfortune, a belief inscribed in the Sorcery Act of 1971, now part of the Revised Laws of the Independent State of Papua New Guinea, which defines acts of sorcery to be illegal. The Fore are correct, however, in assuming that "modernity" had a place in ridding them of kuru. As a result of their encounters with those early messengers of modernity, the missionaries and colonial administrators who spoke out against cannibalism, which they considered to be a perversion and a legal offense, the Fore gradually gave up the practice. At that time, the Fore, the missionaries, and government officers saw no relationship between kuru and consumption of deceased relatives, but all three had unwittingly impeded disease transmission.

NEW DISEASES: NEW PRACTITIONERS

With occasional cases of kuru occurring in the 1990's, the old kuru curers, called *yanda yagalas* (bush medicine men), continued to collect medicinal barks and leaves, their efficacy derived from the power of the spirit people, the amani, who inhabit (and in some sense *are*) the trees in the undomesticated forest. The amani identified specific plants, revealed to the curers in dreams, a source of unquestioned knowledge, and often a potent red in color. The elders at Waisa said recently that medicine from forest plants must be cooked with "protein" containing blood, the only medicine for making peace with the spirits.[39] (See page 56 for a discussion of spirit-caused ailments and cures in 1962. The amani here are called *masalai,* the Tok Pisin term.) Combined with wild ginger, they caused patients to sweat, cleansing the body of "poisons." The first test was always carried out on a close female relative, usually the wife of a fellow lineage member. With news of this initial success, the yanda yagalas extended their practice to patients living within a two- or three-mile range. Bush medicine men, however, were not seen as having the special knowledge needed to cure the diseases the Fore now encountered.

Local practitioners, now called *yavandagaria*, a term conveying higher status, were beginning to treat people with a number of diseases not thought to be caused by sorcery: gonorrhea, syphilis, chlamydia, cancer, and AIDS, which they said their medicines could cure. The yavandagaria, as well as many Fore, are knowledgeable about AIDS, which they call "Sik AIDS," indicating its status as a disease not caused by sorcery. (This may change as a wave of witchcraft accusations and murder of women thought to be spreading AIDS has arrived in the Eastern Highlands.) They are aware that AIDS has caused the deaths of many people elsewhere in the world and is present in Papua New Guinea. They know also that American scientists can prolong the life of people with AIDS, but as yet have no cure.

From time to time during the 1990's, my research assistants spoke about the work of the new practitioners, and some practitioners visited me to discuss their cures. No longer working alone, the new groups consist of educated young men, accompanied sometimes by an older relative. They continue to use forest medicines, which are revealed now not in dreams but in visions sent by God, often to the older man. One group tested their medicines first

Patali and his medicine tree.

on a dog said to have a sexually transmitted disease, and with visible proof of a cure, they gave the medicine to a person with gonorrhea. In another case, the practitioners treated a woman who had first tested positive for HIV, but whose second hospital test indicated that she was negative. In the interim, she had received their medicine. All the practitioners took their medicines to be tested by technicians in hospitals or scientific institutes in Papua New Guinea. Some saw proof of their medicine's efficacy when a laboratory test showed that HIV-infected blood became clear when it was mixed with their medicine. Others, told that their samples were too small for the machines to test, were planning to send new samples, this time to Australia.

A biomedical assessment would perhaps say that a conjunction of circumstances had provided reasonable evidence that their medicines were effective: the gonorrhea sores that disappeared (a clinical feature of the disease), the hospital patient who had first received a false positive HIV report, changes in the color of the blood in the test tube. The practitioners, and the

Kuru coffins for sale in Goroka.

Fore in general, do not view biomedical procedures and local therapies as opposed, and most people who receive the care of practitioners also seek health care at the clinic. This does not mean that they are in some sense equal: practitioners borrow procedures and diagnoses from biomedicine, but the reverse does not occur. However, the practitioners' certainty that their medicines are effective does not depend on the validation of a laboratory test. Belief in their own cures derives also from the foundations of Fore knowledge: visible proof, the power of spirit beings, and the authority of a Christian God.

ON VISUAL PROOF AND TRUTH-TELLING

The significance of visual evidence is a recurrent theme in Fore accounts of veracity. To see is to know. Something has to be observed for it to have happened. Aninta was reluctant to say that her parents had eaten people because she hadn't seen it, and in response to my questions about recent events people often said, "I didn't see this myself and I don't want to tell you something that isn't true. I will ask someone who saw it and let you know." The Fore have long had their own techniques and procedures for providing visual evidence. Autopsies could determine the cause of death, and divinations could identify the person responsible. (The body was said to discharge fluids as the guilty party approached the corpse.) The Fore thus found compelling the many visual technologies introduced by kuru investigators. In 1957, Gajdusek had carried a microscope, which he used to show the Fore the "insects in the blood."[40] As indicated in Chapter 6, increased contact with the investigators had persuaded the Fore that photographs would reveal sorcerers holding kuru bundles in their raised right hands, and the ophthalmoscope, an instrument for viewing the interior of the eye, could reveal hidden thoughts.[41] When scientists said later that kuru was a sickness, like malaria, caused by a worm or an insect in the blood,[42] the Fore readily accepted the explanation, but the image remained lodged in Fore theories of disease causation.

In addition to visual evidence, the Fore have accepted the concept of verbal truth-telling as the mark of Christian identity. Practitioners often pray before administering their medicines and profess no interest in payment, saying that their reward will come from God, although one practitioner had a sliding scale for payment: a smaller fee for people aged 30 to 48 years, who are "getting old already," and larger for those between twelve and 30, who have a long time left to live. In their search for validation, the therapy groups often consult scientists from their own religious denomination, fellow Christians who fear God, whom they believe they can trust.

As the cases just described indicate, the practitioners consult scientists in a variety of town and city institutes, giving them their medicines to test. They are reluctant to identify the ingredients because, as they said in 1999, other people, not the Fore, profit from their knowledge. This view was not new. During a discussion with different groups some years earlier, one man said, "We think white men came, took photos and plants, went back home, made medicine, and returned to give the medicine to us. So kuru disappeared. The doctors also took women with kuru to Okapa, sawed off their heads and took their brains. I think white men took the barks and leaves and the brains, and then came back with the medicine, which we ate, and now this sickness has ended." Biomedical procedures and technologies in American laboratories had apparently harnessed the spirit power in bush medicines. Another man said he thought kuru investigators had received millions of dollars for their medicine, a comment I thought might have been prompted by news that the Institute of Medical Research had just been awarded a large research grant. It also reflects the all-too-apparent differences in wealth between themselves and the investigators.

The topic of the theft of local resources and intellectual property rights has recently acquired a more critical edge. As a result, in 2008, the new therapists said they would not reveal the identity of their medicines to anyone until they had secured a patent. Local high school teachers, familiar with the work of the practitioners, said that bush medicines found only in

Papua New Guinea could cure AIDS. This would result in a big income for their country and perhaps a Nobel Prize.[43]

MEDICAL KNOWLEDGE AND MEDICAL PRACTICE

While the old curers and new practitioners were treating people with their own medications, the local clinic was providing health care based on different assumptions about medical knowledge and practice. The most dramatic effect appears to have been in the survival of infants. Clinic records, which began in 1983 under the guidance of an Open Bible nurse, indicate that 27 infants were delivered safely that year. In 1990 and 1991, the 58 infants born at the clinic included six sets of twins. The impact of the clinic can be measured by the fact that between January and December 1983, clinic nurses treated 9,227 outpatients and 155 inpatients, most of them children. Dental care began in 1983 with a new school dental program, and 2,490 vaccinations were given for childhood illnesses. The Open Bible mission also began to transfer difficult cases by road to the hospital at Goroka or called for a government helicopter.

The acceptance of clinic care was enhanced by its Christian image. A category of Spiritual Comments entered the clinic register in 1985. In that year, following prayer, a patient with a severe head injury had recovered "within minutes," and a patient diagnosed with meningitis had also

The clinic.

Nantale in his AIDS awareness shirt.

recovered quickly due to prayer. In 1988, a female patient "gave her heart to Christ," and in 1989, a patient with psychosis was recorded as "demon-possessed." In addition, the clinic's reputation for providing good health care was recognized when the first group of student nurses arrived from Goroka to join the resident team of three South Fore nurses. The local clinic and the hospital in Goroka were both providing treatment for diseases new to the Eastern Highlands: typhoid, asthma, TB, and sexually transmitted diseases (STDs). Public health messages about these conditions were broadcast widely, and the local clinic had posters providing visual information. In 1999, clinic nurses were regularly treating gonorrhea and syphilis. The yavandagaria were also providing medicine for STDs.

As this account of medical care indicates, the Fore have access to two forms of medicine: one based on their own understandings of the natural world, the anatomical self, and the world of social and spiritual relations,[44] and the other based on biomedical ideas and practices, which are not seen as incompatible. Ethnographic accounts of health and illness elsewhere in Papua New Guinea, and elsewhere in the world, provide similar reports of the integration of biomedical and indigenous modes of therapy, sometimes called "medical pluralism."[45]

Charles Rosenberg, a historian of science and medicine, has observed that by the end of the nineteenth century the increasing dependence on tools and techniques derived from the laboratory resulted in a vocabulary of named disease pictures that were an unquestioned component of modern medicine, and a definition of disease in increasingly objective terms.[46] The Fore have also been captivated by introduced technologies and laboratory procedures, and adopt them for their own purposes. The therapists test their medicines on animals, mix their medicinal powders with liquids to give to patients, and ask scientists to test their medicines to gain the authoritative stamp of a dominant medical form.

They also accept a vocabulary of named disease categories introduced by biomedicine, as well as some biomedical concepts of causation, such as the role of mosquitoes for malaria and of bacteria and sexual behavior for STDs. Their STD treatments include a period of abstinence for both husband and wife. The resilience of indigenous concepts is still present, however, in the continued use of forest medicines identified by revelation, and in some cases the application of one medicine for several diseases, a feature of the earlier use of forest products by the yanda yagalas who treated sorcery-caused ailments.[47] With changes in social life, however, the use of forest medicines has narrowed. Plants once used to promote the growth of male initiates have been replaced by imported foods, and Western medicine has eradicated some sorcery-caused ailments such as yaws and leprosy, once treated locally. New medical conditions, however, keep the concept of sorcery alive. In 2007, the Fore said that *tauwa*, a form of sorcery transmitted in a handshake, resulting in sudden death, had arrived from the Gimi region. Clinic nurses suggested that it was a form of stroke.

This account of the activities of the new practitioners may suggest that the Fore are following a script foretold in the history of biomedicine, that diseases once thought to be caused by mystical entities reach an endpoint in laboratory-based understandings of illness defined in increasingly objective terms. Writing about the history of biomedicine, Rosenberg cautions against adopting this assumption, advising instead that "we should think of science as well as medicine as a set of generation- and place-specific practices, and not accumulations of knowledge advancing ineluctably, if sometimes erratically, toward a deeper understanding of nature."[48] Rosenberg's framework can be applied also to the history of indigenous medicine. Just as modernization has not eliminated sorcery beliefs and practices, indigenous medical practices have not disappeared, and may even have flourished, enlivened by the nationalist sentiments of a generation of young people.

The charge to place ideas and practices in specific historical and generational settings allows us to appreciate the changes taking place in Fore therapeutic practice, as well as the commonalities that exist with other changing cultural beliefs and behaviors. Contemporary forms of ceremonial exchange have been adapted to incorporate certain concepts and practices of capitalism, spiritual life finds a place for a form of Christian religion, and Fore health behaviors bear the stamp of the creative appropriation of aspects of biomedical ideas and practices that are compatible with their own concepts of local biology and cultural heritage.

EPILOGUE

THE KURU LEGACY

The kuru epidemic may have come to an end, but it has left its mark on the minds of many Fore who are concerned that the disease may yet return. These fears are harbored by older people who remember the loss of family members, when victims of the disease lay sick in every hamlet and funerals were accompanied by impassioned appeals to sorcerers to relinquish their dangerous work. Young people have heard about the epidemic, but, like the clinic nurses, say they have not seen a case of kuru. As time passes, however, the epidemic will still leave an imprint.

Kuru introduced generations of the Fore to the work of scientists. Since 1957, their most frequent contact with scientific practice has been as patients, subject to physical examination, photography, and blood tests, or as a relative of patients who provided autopsy material. Some have had long-term relationships with the medical surveillance team, or with anthropologists, where the reciprocal flow of knowledge is communicated in more subtle ways, in the memories of what was said and done in shared work over long periods of time.

A younger generation of the Fore now study science in high school. A few have advanced to institutes of higher learning in Goroka, Lae, and Port Moresby, and some are employed in a variety of capacities at the Institute of Medical Research. A small number of women are nurses, and some women and men may go to medical school, where the history of the disease will no doubt be part of the curriculum, as it now is in medical schools throughout the world. The physician who carried out the last kuru autopsy in 2003 was an Eastern Highlander, though not from the Fore region, who said he heard about kuru while studying medicine.[1]

It is here that they will learn about not only the genotypic change that resulted from their encounter with kuru but also an older genetic marker, the legacy of an earlier encounter with a prion-related disease, as well as a history of past cannibalism that they are said to share with other Eastern Highlanders and Europeans. Students of history and anthropology may read about the social effect of the epidemic, about grandparents or great-grandparents growing up without the care, or memory, of their biological mothers.

Local practitioners, heirs to older forms of indigenous therapy, are creating a postepidemic form of medical practice, influenced by their perception of scientific research during the kuru years. Biomedical practices and Christian beliefs are folded into their experiments with culturally based concepts of health care. For them all, their participation will be professional and personal as they live and write the next chapter in the history of the epidemic.

Fore at End of Kuru Conference, London 2007.

NOTES

CHAPTER 1

1. See the Ethnobotanical List in S. Glasse 1963.

2. Wurm 1962, 1964.

3. Wiesenfeld and Gajdusek 1976.

4. Brody and Gibbs 1976.

5. Michael Alpers, personal communication.

6. Scott 1963.

CHAPTER 2

1. J. McArthur 1954.

2. My task in bringing together this history of kuru research has been greatly facilitated by an earlier summary by John Mathews. For a fuller account, see Mathews 1971.

3. Gajdusek 1973:378.

4. R. Berndt 1958:22.

5. J. McArthur 1955. A different diagnosis might perhaps have been given for a disease largely affecting men.

6. Quoted in R. Berndt 1958:22–23. Ronald and Catherine Berndt carried out anthropological research between 1951 and 1953 among the Kamano, Usurufa, Jate, and North Fore. See the Bibliography for their publications.

7. Gajdusek and Zigas 1957.

8. Hornabrook and Moir 1970.

9. Bennett, Rhodes, and Robson 1958, 1959.

10. Mathews 1971:13–14. Certain hereditary diseases are either fatal or markedly compromise the ability of individuals to reproduce. Therefore, one would expect these diseases to eventually disappear in the population groups afflicted by them. To explain their persistence, geneticists have introduced the concept of *balanced polymorphism.* This implies that along with the unfavorable disease state, some characteristic favorable to survival is simultaneously inherited. An example is the gene for sickle cell anemia in African Blacks. People who have inherited two genes for this disorder usually die in childhood or early life of the disease sickle cell anemia. People who have inherited a single gene for this disorder, which is a much more common situation, have a benign disorder known as sickle cell trait, and have a survival advantage over the general population because the sickle cell trait protects them against malaria, a common cause of illness and death in Africa.

11. The Fore distinction between sickness and sorcery is discussed in Chapter 5.

12. Mathews 1971:99, 109, indicates a possible change in the clinical features of kuru.

13. R. Glasse 1962a, 1962b, 1963; S. Glasse 1964; Hornabrook and Moir 1970:1175, 1178; Mathews 1971:3,4; Sorenson 1964:42.

14. R. Berndt 1962:272–73.

15. Mathews 1971: Mathews, Glasse, and Lindenbaum 1968.

16. Mathews 1971.

17. As chapter 13 notes, Jerome Whitfield's recent research with Fore elders describes ritual consumption of the dead, information that had not been revealed to their children who were Whitfield's research assistants.

18. Watson 1971.

19. J. Diamond, 1966.

20. Dornstreich and Morren 1974.

21. R. Berndt 1962:271.

22. Mathews 1965; Alpers and Gajdusek 1965.

23. Hadlow 1959.

24. Gajdusek, Gibbs, and Alpers 1966.

25. Mathews, Glasse, and Lindenbaum 1968.

26. Hornabrook and Moir 1970.

27. King 1975.

28. Gajdusek, Zigas, and Baker 1961.

29. Mathews 1971:14.

30. Weiner, Johnson, and Herndon 1973; Brody and Gibbs 1976. Multiple sclerosis is a chronic, often episodic central nervous system disorder, in which there is patchy loss of the myelin covering of nerves and of nervous system function. Because of the patchy distribution of the lesions, the symptoms are quite variable and unpredictable. In many but not all patients, there is eventually a long downhill course.

31. Peterson *et al.* 1973–74. Creutzfeldt-Jakob disease has also recently been transmitted to another laboratory host, the hamster (Manuelidis *et al.* 1977).

32. Herzberg *et al.* 1974. The danger of accidental person-to-person transmission of Creutzfeldt-Jakob disease by surgery has been noted (Bernouilli *et al.* 1977).

33. Weiner 1973. SSPE is a fatal disease of children and young adults, characterized by the insidious onset of intellectual deterioration, followed by increasing rigidity of the extremities and sometimes blindness. The pathology of the brain shows loss of nerve cells as well as the myelin covering of the nervous tissue (demyelination). PML is a fatal disorder of adults characterized by rapidly advancing intellectual deterioration and, variably, by impairment in use of the extremities, speech, and vision. Demyelination of the brain is extensive.

34. Amyotrophic lateral sclerosis is a disease of middle age, more common in men, which is usually fatal within three to five years. The typical feature is progressive loss of motor function. Loss of myelin and nerve fibers from the cerebrospinal tract of the nervous system results in progressive weakness, muscle atrophy and irritability, and twitching of muscles. Alzheimer's disease is a disorder characterized by premature senility, most commonly occurring in middle-aged women and lasting two to five years. There is early loss of memory, later followed by confusion and complete dementia. Degenerative changes of nerve cells and their blood supply are found in the brain. A familial variant of the disorder has been described. Two cases of the familial form of Alzheimer's disease have been transmitted to subhuman primates (Gajdusek and Gibbs 1975).

It has recently been postulated that slow virus infections may be responsible for diseases in other organs. Endemic nephropathy, also known as Balkan nephropathy, occurs only in adjacent areas of three Balkan countries, Yugoslavia, Bulgaria, and Rumania, where there are currently an estimated 20,000 cases. It is endemic in some villages and has a familial incidence. Immigrants into the endemic areas contract the disease, as well as emigrants from these areas, after a latent period of some years. In one village in which the disease was endemic, the population of 24,000 was 50 percent Muslim and 50 percent Christian, but only one of 54 victims of the disease was a Muslim. Muslims avoid pigs. The victims of the disease are peasants practicing pig-husbandry and living in close contact with their animals. Coronaviruses have been isolated from pigs, leading to the suggestion that a slow coronavirus infection causes endemic nephropathy in humans (Apostolov, Spasic, and Bojanic 1975).

35. Gajdusek 1973.

36. Traub, Gajdusek, and Gibbs 1976. The unconventional characteristics of these viral agents have led to speculation that they are small pieces of genetically active nucleic acid, tightly bound to fragments of plasma membrane, with just enough codons to code for themselves, such information forming an integral part of the genetics of the host cells.

37. Gajdusek and Gibbs 1975.

38. Gajdusek, quoted in Brody and Gibbs 1976. For more recent implications, see Gajdusek *et al.* 1977, and Manuelidis *et al.* 1978.

39. Fenner 1976.

40. R. Berndt 1953:134.

41. Colman 1955.

42. Allen 1961.

43. Colman 1955.

44. *New Guinea Post Courier*, Nov. 26, 1969.

45. *Australian Age*, Apr. 7, 1973.

46. N. McArthur 1964:348–49.

CHAPTER 3

1. Mathews 1971:70; Alpers 1968.

2. Mathews 1971:74–75; Alpers and Gajdusek 1965:859.

3. Hornabrook 1972, personal communication, 1976.

4. M. Alpers, personal communication, 1977.

5. Hornabrook 1972.

6. Murrell 1966.

7. Lawrence and Walker 1976.

8. Alpers and Gajdusek 1965.

9. Pharoah and Hornabrook 1974. See also Hetzel and Pharoah 1971.

10. Hornabrook 1976.

11. Van de Kaa 1967; Mathews 1971:72.

12. Mathews 1971:72–73. and Knodel 1977.

13. See Ridley, 1965:159–60.

CHAPTER 4

1. Meggitt 1965a.

2. Patrol Officer Colman's 1955 report indicates similar use of a word by people at Henganofi and Kainantu, and of the term Bomai used by the Chimbu.

3. Glasse and Lindenbaum 1969. These data were collected in 1962.

4. An elderly member of Line 1 of Yagareba section of Wanitabe parish, for instance, married his matrilateral cross-cousin, (the daughter of his mother's brother), who belongs to a line in the parish of Takai, and it is Takai who will collect the major payment at the elderly man's death. Yet he characterizes his own Line 1 as wife-givers to Line 3 of Yagareba section of Wanitabe parish, and as wife-receivers to Line 1 of another section of Wanitabe parish. Moreover, the wife-giving and wife-receiving relationships are said apply to pairs of Lines. That is, Lines 1 and 2 join to give women to Lines 3 and 4; thus Lines 1 and 2 are the mother's brothers, while 3 and 4 are the sister's sons. See also Glasse and Lindenbaum 1976.

5. These massive fortress-like enclosures were dismantled in 1957 at the Australian government's request. The most dramatic account is McArthur's description of Orie, 1953: "Built on a slight rise, Orie is at the moment surrounded by 5 concentric palisades, about 16 feet in height, pickets of which are firmly lashed together with cane rope and round the whole is a great outer palisade which runs for half a mile and encloses some gardens. . . . One may walk through a long laneway, pass through another door, and then after passing through 3 to 5 close and concentric palisades, suddenly find oneself in a hamlet. Exit is made through another complicated system, and one can go on like this to further hamlets and all the time be walking within

palisades. Complete exit from Orie is not made until the great outer palisade is passed through." (McArthur patrol to the Gimi, July/Aug. 1953.)

6. Meggitt 1977.

7. Village endogamy among the neighboring Awa, for instance, increased from 70 percent in 1965 to 85 percent in 1972, a finding Boyd 1975 interprets to reflect the increased value of women.

8. In 1970, eleven youths of one section of Wanitabe parish were employed in wage labor outside the community.

9. Wiesenfeld and Gajdusek 1976.

10. Malcolm 1966. See also Knodel 1977.

11. Strathern 1973.

12. Lindenbaum and Glasse 1969. Women do have some choice in the matter. Contesting suitors gather around the hut where the widow secludes, poking sticks of sugarcane through the bamboo walls (in present times, a cigarette). The widow eats (or smokes) the offering of the man she prefers.

13. An indication of where Fore expect hostilities to occur, and the speed with which the affront might theoretically fade.

14. Lindenbaum 1976.

15. While a man may marry his father's sister's daughter in the North Fore, this is not the case among South Fore, although the distinction is not recognized terminologically.

16. Scott 1975.

17. The morpheme *no* (breast) in *nanonempa* (my mother) appears also in *nono* (breastmilk) and *nononta*, a prolific and widely cultivated species of the staple sweet potato.

CHAPTER 5

1. An earlier version of this analysis may be found in Lindenbaum 1971, 1976b.

2. Clarke 1976:252.

3. Knowles 1977.

4. Offenses within a certain range may be ignored. One Wanitabe man lost his soap while washing clothes at a spring on Wanitabe land. Two parish section members were with him at the time. He explained his loss by saying that a spirit had seized the soap bar while his head was turned.

5. R. Berndt 1962:220.

6. Western diagnoses were suggested by two physicians, John Mathews and John Lindenbaum.

7. Tokabu is sometimes regarded by a Western audience as largely fanciful. The *New Guinea Post Courier*, Nov. 26, 1969, however, reports the prosecution of five men from Okapa, hired as assassins to kill a village councillor they believed to be a sorcerer. All pleaded guilty to a charge of willful murder. The councillor was found with his Adam's apple broken, and a 3-inch nail driven into his skull. The *Post Courier* also reports the assemblyman representing the Eastern Highlands District as saying that sorcerers practicing "Afa" (i.e., tokabu) use razor blades to rip off the

victim's internal organs while he lies senseless. Modern sorcerers, he said, are "still practising their foul ways," but by adopting "knives, razor blades, batteries and other poisonous chemicals" are "improving their rotten technology."

8. Yanda, Tokabu, and Imusa are said to be the oldest forms of assault.

9. Sorceries Nos. 1, 3, 11, 12, and 15 all suggest liver disease. Liver disease caused by ingestion of wild plants containing toxic alkaloids has been reported from Jamaica, Northwest Afghanistan, and Central India (Mohabbat *et al.* 1976 and Tandon *et al.* 1976. It has recently been suggested that liver disease in Papua New Guinea might be caused by groundnuts contaminated by aflatoxin, a fast-acting toxic agent produced by a mould. Collins *et al.* 1975.)

10. See R. Berndt 1959, 1962, for similar spells.

11. Douglas 1970b:114. Douglas suggests that soul sucking and poisoning should be practiced by the witch within the local community, weapon throwing by the far-off witch. Note that she uses the term witch to cover both witches and sorcerers.

12. Sinnett and Whyte 1973:270.

13. Reay 1959:192.

14. Hogbin 1970.

15. R. Glasse 1970:211.

16. Brookfield and Hart 1971:113.

17. Meggitt 1965b.

18. The importance of dual categories is frequently cited in the Melanesian literature. The distinction between hot/cold, dry/wet, hard/soft, male/female, domestic/wild, occur in various permutations in different societies. The merging or separation of these paired oppositions communicates important information about significant objects and categories, and the necessary human behavior toward them.

19. Fore chew several kinds of bark which contain a variety of alkaloids known to be hallucinogenic. For example: *Galbulimima belgraveana* and several *Psychotria* (family Rubiaceae).

20. Lewis 1975.

21. Meggitt 1977:39–40.

CHAPTER 6

1. R. Berndt 1962:214.

2. Julius 1957.

3. Souter 1963 documents the interest in the interior of New Guinea that began in the 1920's with news of the first big gold strikes on a tributary of the Bulolo River. Dredging equipment was flown by prospectors from neighboring Australia, and the value of New Guinea gold exports in the 1920's soon amounted to more than a million and a quarter pounds. For the 1930's the figure would rise to 15 million. In the early 1930's, small parties of Australians searching for gold thus began to explore the Eastern Highlands of New Guinea.

4. R. Berndt 1952:23, 1, 50; also 23, 3, 202.

5. Several years later, others followed the same path, and a South Fore boy was given to the Kamano in return for lodging rights en route to Kainantu.

6. Three parties of Fore encountered the wreck of this Japanese military plane, which was scouting the area during World War II. The first two parties from Ilesa and Abomotasa were killed when they tried to hack axe blades from the casing of an unexploded bomb. The third party, traveling from Purosa, directed the two Japanese survivors of the crash back toward Kainantu, where Fore lost trace of them. They were possibly taken prisoner by the Australian government forces stationed at Kainantu.

7. See Chapter 10 for a discussion of this point.

8. C. Berndt 1953:117.

9. Ibid., 118.

10. On liver disease, see Chap. 5, n. 9.

11. Sorenson and Kenmore 1974. The north-south axis of gene frequencies shows Fore associations with Kamano-Gimi-Keiagana populations in the northwest, and Awa-Auyana-Gadsup-Tairora in the southeast (Wiesenfeld and Gajdusek 1976).

12. In a sample of 151 sisters, just over one-third married toward the north, and less than one-fourth toward the south. Of 281 wives, one-third moved north, one-quarter moved south.

13. R. Berndt 1952, 1954.

14. Many people were still of the opinion in 1963 that whites simply sent written messages for the goods they desired, and the cargo subsequently arrived, with no hint that labor or the exchange of currency was required.

CHAPTER 7

1. Gajdusek and Gibbs 1975:116.

2. A typical pollution effect.

3. Their Gimi names are *Haniyei, Raso, and Ruma. Raso,* the only bark I have been able to identify, is *Podocarpus amarus.*

4. Medical orderlies trained at Okapa hospital learn about Western hygiene and the use of a limited number of Western medicines. They receive a small monthly salary for treating patients at their local medical aid posts.

5. The Fore names are *Poiya* (unidentified), *Taso* (*Podocarpus amarus,* see n. 3 above), and *Agigilei* (*Vitaceae, Leea*)

6. Evans-Pritchard 1936:194.

7. House of Assembly Debates, Territory Papua New Guinea, vol. 11, no. 12, pp. 3677–79.

CHAPTER 8

1. Fore are aware that whites believe kuru to be a form of sickness, not sorcery. This places kuru in the same category as dysentery, which in its epidemic nature it resembles. Fore, however, have not changed their minds on the matter.

2. Turner 1957:126.

3. C. Berndt 1953.

4. For a fuller account of the eclipse, see R. Glasse and Lindenbaum 1967.

5. Brown 1972:90.

6. Clarke 1971:43.

7. July and August are the driest months.

8. A government report from Okapa for the period July-Sept. 1962 notes: "Fairly acute shortage of native foods . . . insufficient gardens were planted." Mathews notes a significant negative correlation from 1962–67 between heavy rainfall and the supply of sweet potato about six months later. This was what happened in 1961–62 (Mathews 1971: App. 2, 4). It should also be noted that the 1961 planting season was disrupted by the mid-year exodus to Uvai, and the interruptions caused by other kuru tests and trials.

9. Fore have recently begun to hold pig festivals, which like those of other Highland groups occur about once a decade. While both kibung gatherings and pig festivals preclude open aggression among participants and distribute information over a wide region, the Fore pig festivities differ in that they advertise group strength. Parishes give pigs to one another in boisterous, competitive ceremonies, in which the predominant theme is self-aggrandizement and the embarrassment of recipients. They communicate dominance and distribute wealth. Both the pig festivals and the kibungs, which bring together large numbers of people, are forces of political amalgamation.

10. Alland 1970:128, 187. See also Horton 1970:139.

CHAPTER 9

1. The analysis in this chapter rests mostly on incidents said to have occurred in the three decades before 1963. Here, a sorcerer acts on his own behalf, meting out punishment for personal grievances. This depicts a struggle for leadership, with incipient ranking but no chiefs. As Chapter 2 notes, however, Fore also perform sorcery on behalf of others. I take this to be a recent trend, involving greater specialisation and greater rewards.

In some societies, such as the Mekeo and the Trobriands, sorcerers appear to hold high office and are represented as henchmen or even competitors of the chiefs. Reigning groups thus project different degrees of lawful command. Where chiefs have henchmen, sorcerers add a potent but capricious force to the office; where sorcerers oppose a chief, the system of ranking is presumably still unstable.

CHAPTER 10

1. Sinnett and Whyte 1973.

2. Faithorn 1976.

3. Evans-Pritchard 1937:21–26.

4. Patterson 1974:145.

5. Forge 1970.

6. Reay 1976:2. See also n. 12 below.

7. Steadman 1975.

8. Kelly 1976.

9. Menstruating women are said to squat over a male item in order to inflict sorcery. The improper inversion presumably has a sexual reference.

10. In order to prevent the navel-rope from detaching inside the body while men climb trees, the umbilical cords of male infants are cut inches longer than those of females, a practice that may contribute to higher female infant mortality from tetanus.

11. In a sense, women constitute a permanent social class, but they may have sons who do not share this class status.

12. Gorlin 1977; see also Serjeantson and Lawrence 1977. Gorlin does not report on the ideology of southwestern Abelam. Hints from other reports, however, indicate that there is little concern here with female pollution, and that the division between the sexes is less emphasized. The major area of conflict occurs instead within the male community, where there are both male sorcerers and witches. Since witchcraft is a lesser, inherent kind of mystical power, it would be interesting to know if sorcery accusations (representing more equal bids for status) occur against fellow agnates, while witchcraft allegations define the relations between agnates and non-agnates. A similar situation occurs among Kuma of the Central Highlands, where female pollution is similarly unimportant. Kuma sorcerers are men of standing, but witches, who are usually males, are rubbish men or men of little account in their own community (Reay 1976).

13. Fried 1967.

14. R. Berndt 1962:xi.

15. Maquet 1960 documents the same idiom used to express the hierarchical relations of three Central African groups. The Tutsi boast of never eating solid food at any time, the Hutu are represented as greedy, and the Twa are considered more gluttonous still. An attitude of contempt applies also to each group's food staple, suggesting again the reaction of Fore men to the food of women and juveniles.

16. Hughes 1973.

17. Wagner 1971:28.

18. Hughes 1973:101–10.

19. Mead 1935. This analysis of intergroup relations applies to data reported more than forty years ago. Patterns of dominance in the region may have changed since that time.

20. Janet Siskind, personal communication.

21. Harner 1973. The situation is complicated here by the presence of missions among the Canelos, but the proposition appears to be worth pursuing since sorcery moves in a counterdirection to the flow of trade goods. The direction of witchcraft fears and patterns of dominance among trading groups in the Trobriands might also be investigated (Malinowski 1961).

22. Brookfield and Hart 1971:77.

CHAPTER 11

1. Thomas 1974.

2. Ibid.

CHAPTER 12

1. The Open Bible Mission had a continuous presence in the South Fore from 1980 to 2001. From 2001 to 2007, the South Fore station was administered by representatives in Goroka. In 2007, an official ceremony was held in Goroka turning over all mission work to national pastors. My thanks to Debby Brandt for this information. Personal communication, May 20, 2012.

2. One hectare=roughly 2.47 acres.

3. Conflict between Bougainville landowners and Bougainville Copper Ltd., one of the world's largest open pit mines, led to the emergence of a secessionist movement in the late 1960's. Following further disturbances, the mine closed in 1989 as the result of sabotage by the Bougainville Revolutionary Army and others seeking secession from PNG. A referendum on whether Bougainville should secede is expected to be held between 2015 and 2020. With copper reserves currently estimated at $50 billion, the rewards could be substantial. The mine remains closed, and the exodus of workers from the mine area across the province has devastated the provincial and national economies. The landowners campaign has provoked renewed demands by landowners in the Ok Tedi area, Western Province, and concern in Enga Province where gold mining is under development.

4. See page 115.

5. Most Fore now consider themselves to be Christians. Lutheran missionaries, the first to arrive in the Eastern Highlands in 1926, were followed by Seventh Day Adventists in 1933. John James, the first missionary in the South Fore, settled at Purosa in the late 1950's, representing World Missions, Inc. Two American missionaries joined him in 1961 and 1962. In 1975, following a visit to the United States, James returned, but left permanently in 1979. During the 1980's, the Open Bible expanded, and by 1991 had 27 churches administered by local pastors. Seventh Day Adventists are also well established in the South Fore, along with a scattering of smaller missions that include Salvation Army, Evangelical Brethren Church (Swiss Mission), Jehovah's Witnesses, Highland Christian Mission, and Assembly of God.

6. An observation made also by Jorgensen in his detailed account of the changes taking place among the Telefomin people of the Sepik Headwaters, 1993:59.

7. Akin and Robbins 1999:5-7

8. Benediktsson 2002:51, in his excellent study of an Eastern Highland community making the transition from subsistence to a market economy.

9. Diptheria, tetanus, polio, hepatitis, measles, and TB.

10. The infusion of new vegetables and new varieties of old cultivars include sweet potatoes, winged bean, *kumu* (leafy greens), taro, green beans, *pitpit* (*Setaria palmifolia*), pumpkin, and banana. New cash crops include cardamom, red chili peppers, and peanuts. The Fore names often indicate place of origin, price, or qualities of growth.

11. This information comes from David Boyd's elegant account of singsing bisnis. See Boyd 1985.

12. Hide 1993.

13. Men also help others to build houses, the work team receiving K10 and a meal at the end of the day. Similar groups, with or without church affiliation, are reported elsewhere in the Eastern Highlands. See Benediktsson 2002:253.

14. Glass 2011:80.

15. In 1991, one US$=1.0498 kina.

16. Thanks to Paige West for this update on the marketing of coffee. See West 2012 for a comprehensive account of the place of New Guinea producers in the global coffee industry.

17. Benediktsson 2002:112–13.

18. Akin and Robbins 1999:12. This is but one quote from Akin and Robbins's illuminating discussion of the impact of money in Melanesia.

19. Berndt 1962; Glass 2011; Whitfield 2011.

20. The preferential marriage choice for a man is still the mother's brother's daughter, but the expansion of social networks results in increased flexibility in the choice of marriage partners.

21. Glass 2011:116. Dawn Glass, carried out anthropological fieldwork in Moke village, North Fore, from 2003 to 2004.

22. See Gewertz and Errington 2010 for an account of the trade in inexpensive fatty cuts of lamb, called "lamb flaps," from New Zealand and Australia to markets in the Pacific.

23. Rungia klossi, a ritual food, eaten with meat, thought to replenish the mother's blood. See Glass 2011:187.

24. Gillison 1993:240.

25. David Boyd 2001:261 notes that the Awa Irakians revived initiation in 1993.

26. Berndt 1962; Glass 2011.

27. Wandagi Pako, personal communication, 2012. Interview with his father, Mr. Pako Ombeya.

28. Glass 2011:242.

29. Stasch 2009:259. The many meanings of money arose in exchanges with my research assistants, confusing the boundaries between relationships based on commerce and kinship. Agame, the most business-oriented of the group, often brought food from his gardens, saying, "You are my market." (I kept a weekly debt record along with the tally of fortnightly wages.) On the other hand, discussing compensation payments in the case of accident, the group decided that since I apparently had no mother's brothers, they would have been the recipients had I died in a car accident that had occurred some weeks earlier.

30. This useful information is in Benediktsson 2002:21.

31. Thanks to Katayo Sagata for the Kanite information and Enoch Kale for the Gimi.

32. Glass 2011.

33. I use *bridewealth* and *brideprice* to describe marriage payments, following Glass (2011:155–56), who notes that although in Tok Pisin the Fore speak of *baim meri* (buying women), they do not speak of selling them. The Fore terms for the brideprice payment, *waya ena maema nauna*, which means "woman's body-thing we get and eat it," focuses on consumption, not sale. Whether or not women are viewed as commodities in particular contexts is a topic to be further explored, given the huge brideprice payments in some parts of Melanesia. The return of brideprice, as in Fore transactions, may be a significant variable.

34. Personal communication, 2012.

35. Zimmer-Tamakoshi 1997; Benediktsson 2002:3.

36. Marilyn Strathern said that they are also the most prominent and frequent events held now in Mount Hagen in the Western Highlands. Personal communication, 2012.

37. School fees for students in grade five, K60 each year; grades six to eight, K100; day students at the new high school, K750; and boarders, K950. Open Bible Mission pastors receive an annual salary of K350, augmented by tithes from congregants.

38. Jerome Whitfield noted that Big Men often make such statements to gauge the level of public support before committing themselves to a path of action. Personal communication, 2012.

39. Note that the 1991 Waisa ceremony was hosted by the dead woman's husband, who is obliged to give food to her matrikin. By contrast, the 1996 Wanitabe ceremony was for a dead man, so his patrikin were responsible for the payment to maternal kin.

40. See Glass 2011:220 for the North Fore.

41. This account of the funeral was provided by his son, Patterson Kassam. Personal communication, 2011.

42. Whitfield 2011:pp.279, 293.

43. His son thinks that Kassam Uvinda may have seen headstones when he visited the Lae War Memorial Cemetery. Silverman (unpublished ms.) suggests that cement graves and some objects associated with the departed person represent a shift in the memorializing of individuals, whose spirits may no longer dissolve fully into the river of collective representation.

44. Berndt 1962:64.

45. Read 1952; Berndt 1962; Salisbury 1965; Langness 1967; Herdt 1981; Godelier 1986; Gillison 1993.

46. Read 1952:96.

47. Gillison 1993:5.

48. Berndt 1962:382.

49. Wandagi Pako. Personal communication, 2012. Interview with his father, Mr. Pako Ombeya, who is describing a time during the 1960's when several independent missionaries were in the South Fore before the arrival of the Open Bible Mission.

50. See *Making Sense of AIDS: Culture, Sexuality, and Power in Melanesia*, Butt and Eves 2008.

51. My thanks to Silverman, Carucci, and Dalton for their unpublished manuscripts on changing mortuary rites in the Pacific; and also to Bainton, Ballard, and Gillespie for their jointly authored essay. All reveal the insightful ways in which mortuary rites are a sensitive register of regional and global shifts in political and economic circumstance, as well as in spiritual life.

52. Nokoti appears in Chapter 6. An account of Nokoti narratives from pre- to post-colonial times shows the capricious bush spirit, who once helped and sometimes hindered hunters, becoming less benign as he enters village space where his small thefts cause bewilderment. Now called a wild man, he begins the life of a raskol, stealing from trade stores and a government office. Captured by the colonial police and jailed in Australia, he reemerges following Independence as a unifying figure for the Eastern Highlands, appearing on the provincial flag, in public monuments, and in the productions of a national theatre. This lovable trickster of yesteryear continues to live in the South Fore, though in hiding (see Lindenbaum 2002).

53. Thanks to Robin Hide, fellow scholar and generous provider of information for all who work in Melanesia.

54. I thank Katayo Sagata for this information. Personal communication, April 17, 2012.

CHAPTER 13

1. Anthropologists have refined the terms they use for indigenous medicine (once called *folk* or *ethnomedicine*) and biomedicine (formerly *Western medicine*). As a product of Western culture, biomedicine, like all forms of medical knowledge and practice, takes form in a particular social and cultural context, its assumed universalism now questioned. An excellent account of the issues can be found in the Introduction and Chapter 1 of *Biomedicine Examined*, Lock and Gordon 1988.

2. As Jerome Whitfield commented (personal communication, 2012), the colonial government thought kuru was a disease, but it is not clear that the indigenous government thinks so.

3. Anthony Radford, a doctor who worked in the Eastern Highlands of Papua New Guinea, notes that Zigas and Gajdusek were not the first to describe kuru, as had been thought. The disease was reported earlier by several patrol officers: Arthur Cary in 1950, Bill Brown and John McArthur in 1954, and John Colman in 1955, as well as a medical officer, Frank Earl, also in 1955. See Radford 2012:241.

4. See bibliography entries for Robert Glasse (1962a, 1962b, 1963) and Shirley Glasse (1963).

5. Burnet 1972.

6. Anderson 2008:168.

7. See Mathews 2008 for his personal account of kuru research.

8. Glasse 1967

9. Mathews, Glasse, and Lindenbaum 1968.

10. Alpers 1968.

11. Whitfield et al. 2008.

12. Anderson 2008; 2010:251–67.

13. Lindenbaum 2004.

14. Farquhar 1981:260.

15. John Gunther, the director of Public Health, describes a 1979 meeting with Jack Baker, the patrol officer who had accompanied Gajdusek.. Baker said that the information about cannibalism came from interviews with men who "gave their oath that the brain was not eaten," and that he and Gajdusek "kick themselves for not following up cannibalism better than they did." Gunther letter to Lindenbaum, May 22, 1979. Women, the main consumers of the dead, were apparently not interviewed.

16. See Avramescu 2003:254–262.

17. Arens 1993; Steadman and Merbs 1982.

18. *The Age*, September 1, 1978.

19. Kilgour 1990.

20. Rawson 1997.

21. Alpers (2007:3710) has suggested using the word *transumption* to avoid the derogatory connotations associated with endocannibalism.

22. Lindenbaum 2004.

23. Brady 1982.

24. Whitfield: 2011:152–82.

25. Glass 2011: 212, 241.

26. Prusiner 1982. The concept of the prion as a disease-causing agent was particularly challenging because it was not bacterial, fungal, or viral, and contained no genetic material.

27. Lindenbaum 2004.

28. Alpers and Rail 1971.

29. Wadsworth et al. 2008.

30. Collinge et al. 1996.

31. Alpers 2008.

32. Mead et al. 2003.

33. White 2001.

34. Mead et al. 2009.

35. Collinge 2008. See Edgeworth et al. 2011.

36. Thanks to Michael Alpers for identifying the treatment provided by the medical patrols.

37. Collinge 2008:3693.

38. Geschiere 1997.

39. Thanks again to Wandagi Pako for this information.

40. Gajdusek, personal communication, 2007.

41. Both photography and the ophthalmoscope were thought to offer nineteenth-century scientists objective images, eliminating subjective bias and speculation introduced into visual representations of the body by artists and engravers. See Daston and Galison 2007:174–75.

42. See Beasley 2006:195.

43. Kuru investigators have been sensitive to the reciprocities expected by people in the communities where research has been conducted. Investigators with long-term personal relationships have supported the community school and preschool at Wanitabe, and have contributed to an education Trust Fund to pay school fees. Instead of paying cash for information or for blood, the medical teams purchased materials for community projects and provided community services, such as treatment to control malaria in low-lying areas and assistance to the local clinic with medicines, diagnostics, and casualty evacuation by car and helicopter. The help of NGOs was elicited to establish a Visiting Nurse Service, and the British High Commission for clean water to be piped to the school and the marketplace. The Institute of Medical Research provides employment for children of field staff, and the MRC Prion Unit has raised funds to support three new schools, and the cost of education for their teachers. All the above contributed to a fund for the fifteen Papua New Guineans (twelve from the Fore region) who attended the "End of Kuru Conference" at the Royal Society in

London in 2007. Kuru research since 1996 has been approved by the PNG Medical Research Advisory Committee and ethics committees of the National Hospital for Neurology and Neurosurgery in London with respect to the work of the MRC Prion Unit. Plans have been made for continued support as kuru research ends.

44. See Knauft 1989:255.

45. Frankel and Lewis 1989.

46. Rosenberg 2002:247.

47. Araliaceae Macklinaya was given for kuru as well as for three other ailments. S. Glasse (Lindenbaum) 1963.

48. Rosenberg 1992:5.

EPILOGUE

1. Boone 2008:3639.

GLOSSARY

acute   (disease) of rapid onset and generally short duration, as opposed to
chronic.

affines   persons related by marriage

agnatic   kinship traced through male links only

ami-kina   a Fore term denoting two co-resident lines, whose members live
in harmony and share legal and economic responsibilities

ataxia   failure to coordinate the muscular actions involved in performing
movement

autosome   chromosome concerned with body characteristics other than
sex

balanced polymorphism   the simultaneous inheritance of an unfavorable
disease state and of some characteristic that is favorable to survival

cargo cult   a millenial movement characteristic of Melanesia, based on the
expectation that Western material goods will be received by supernatural means

cerebellar dysfunction   poor functioning due to damage to the cerebellum,
that part of the brain concerned with reflex adjustment of voluntary
movements, muscle tone, and balance

chronic   (disease) of long duration, often of gradual onset. *See* acute.

classificatory kinship   a system of classifying relatives in which collateral
kin are terminologically equated with lineal kin. For example, Fa Bro
= Fa, Mo Sis = Mo

dysarthria   impaired speech

dysphagia   difficulty in swallowing, a symptom of blockage or muscle spasm in the throat or gullet

endemic   (disease) always present in a given population or region (in contrast to epidemic disease, which arrives, spreads, and disappears)

endocannibalism   the eating of human beings defined as members of one's own group, in contrast to exocannibalism

epiphyte   a plant that grows nonparasitically on another, deriving its nutrients and water from rain, air, dust, etc.

etiology   the study of the causes of disease; the cause or origin of a disease

exocannibalism   the eating of human beings defined as outsiders. *See* endocannibalism.

habus   (sometimes *abus*) Melanesian pidgin term meaning a food delicacy, especially meat

homeopathic   the principle that similar things influence one another; in therapy, the idea that like cures like

kiap   Melanesian pidgin term for a government officer or official possibly derived from the English "captain"

laplap   Melanesian pidgin term for a cloth skirt worn usually by men

lounei   a Fore word meaning "line," denoting a group of people united by one principle, as through relationship to a common male ancestor

luluai   a local or village chief appointed by the government

matrilateral   relatives on the mother's side, whether kinsfolk or affines

montane   a zone of vegetation with characteristic plant communities, occuring in New Guinea at altitudes of about 1,000 m. and above

morphological   deriving from the form and structure of an organism

pathogenesis   the process by which a disease develops

Ples Masalai   a Melanesian pidgin term for a spirit place, a scared grove

scabies   a skin disease caused by the itch-mite *Sarcoptes scabei*

serological   pertaining to the study of serum, especially of the reactions of serum with microbes

subacute   between acute and chronic (*q.v.*)

subcutaneous   under the skin

strabismus   squint

tetegina   the Fore word for whites; literally "red people"

titubation   the action of staggering, reeling; unsteadiness of gait

tultul   member of a local group chosen by government officers to assist the local luluai (*q.v.*)

BIBLIOGRAPHY

Akin, David, and Joel Robbins. 1999. *Money and Modernity: State and Local Currencies in Melanesia*. Pittsburgh: University of Pittsburgh Press.

Allen, Mason. 1961. *Okapa Patrol Report*.

Alpers, Michael. 1968. *Kuru: Implications of Its Transmissibility for the Interpretation of Its Changing Epidemiological Pattern*. International Academy of Pathology Monograph No. 9. Baltimore: Williams and Wilkins.

———. 2007. "A History of Kuru." *Papua New Guinea Medical Journal* 50: 10–19.

———. 2008. "The Epidemiology of Kuru: Monitoring the Epidemic from its Peak to Its End." *Philosophical Transactions of the Royal Society B* 363: 3707–13.

Alpers, Michael, and D. C. Gajdusek. 1963. "Changing Patterns of Kuru: Epidemiological Changes in the Period of Increasing Contact of the Fore People with Western Civilization." *American Journal of Tropical Medicine and Hygiene* 14:5: 852.

Alpers, Michael, and L. Rail. 1971. "Kuru and Creutzfeldt-Jakob Disease: Clinical and Aetiological Aspects." *Proceedings of the Australian Association of Neurologists* 8: 7–15.

Anderson, Warwick. 2008. *The Collectors of Lost Souls: Turning Kuru Scientists into Whitemen*. Baltimore: Johns Hopkins University Press.

Apostolov, D., P. Spasic, and N. Bojanic. 1975. "Evidence of a Viral Aetiology in Endemic (Balkan) Nephropathy." *The Lancet* 2: 1271.

Arens, William. 1993. *The Man-Eating Myth: Anthropology and Anthropophagy*. New York: Oxford University Press.

Avramescu, Catalin. 2003. *An Intellectual History of Cannibalism*. Princeton, NJ: Princeton University Press.

Bainton, Nicholas A., Chris Ballard, and Kirsy Gillespie. n.d. *The End of the Beginning? Mining, Sacred Geographies, Memory and Performance in Lihir.*

Beasley, Annette. 2006. "The Promised Medicine: Fore Reflections on the Scientific Investigation of Kuru." *Oceania* 76: 186–202.

Benediktsson, Karl. 2002. *Harvesting Development: The Construction of Fresh Food Markets in Papua New Guinea.* Ann Arbor: University of Michigan Press.

Bennett, J. H. 1962. "Population Studies in the Kuru Region of New Guinea." *Oceania* 33: 24.

Bennett, J. H., F. A. Rhodes, and H. N. Robson. 1958. "Observations on Kuru: A Possible Genetic Basis." *Australian Annals of Medicine* 7: 269.

———. 1959. "A Possible Genetic Basis for Kuru." *American Journal of Human Genetics* 11: 169.

Berndt, Catherine H. 1953. "Socio-Cultural Change in the Eastern Central Highlands of New Guinea." *Southwestern Journal of Anthropology* 9:1: 112.

Berndt, Ronald M. 1952. "A Cargo Movement in the Central Eastern Highlands of New Guinea." *Oceania* 23:1: 40, 23:2: 137.

———. 1954. "Reaction to Contact in the Eastern Central Highlands of New Guinea." *Oceania* 24:3: 190, 24:4: 255.

———.1958. "Devastating Disease Syndrome: Kuru Sorcery in the Eastern Central Highlands of New Guinea." *Sociologus* 8: 4.

———.1962. *Excess and Restraint: Social Control among a New Guinea Mountain People.* Chicago: University of Chicago Press.

———.1965. "The Kamano, Usurufa, Jate and Fore of the Eastern Highlands." In *Gods, Ghosts and Men in Melanesia,* edited by P. Lawrence and M. J. Meggitt, 78–104. Melbourne: Oxford University Press.

Bernoulli, C., J. Siegfried, G. Baumgarter, F. Regli, T. Rabinowicz, D. C. Gajdusek, and C. J. Gibbs Jr. 1977. "Danger of Accidental Person-to-Person Transmission of Creutzfeldt-Jakob Disease by Surgery." *The Lancet* 1: 478.

Boone, Ken. 2008. "An Account of the Last Autopsy Carried Out on a Kuru Patient." *Philosophical Transactions of the Royal Society B* 363: 3630.

Boyd, David. 1975. "Crops, Kiaps and Currency: Flexible Behavioral Strategies among the Ilakia Awa of Papua New Guinea." PhD diss., UCLA.

———.1985. "The Commercialization of Ritual in the Eastern Highlands of Papua New Guinea," *Man* (N.S.) 20: 325–40.

Brady, R. 1982. "The Myth-Eating Man." *American Anthropologist* 84: 595–610.

Brody, Jacob A., and J. Gibbs Jr. 1976."Chronic Neurological Diseases," "Subacute Sclerosing Panencephalitis," "Progressive Multifocal Leukoenaphaloathy," "Kuru," "Creutzfeldt-Jakob Disease." In *Viral Infections of Humans,* edited by Alfred S. Evans. New York: Plenum.

Brookfield, H. C., and Doreen Hart. 1971. *Melanesia: A Geographical Interpretation of an Island World.* London: Methuen.

Brown, Paula. 1972. *The Chimbu: A Study of Change in the New Guinea Highlands.* Cambridge, MA: Schenkman.

Brown, Paula, and Georgeda Buchbinder, eds. 1976a. *Man and Woman in the New Guinea Highlands.* American Anthropology Association, Special Publication No. 8.

———. 1976b. "Maintenance of Agriculture and Human Habitats within the Tropical Forest Ecosystem." *Human Ecology* 4:3: 247.

Burnet, F. MacFarlane. 1972. "Kuru." In *Encyclopaedia of Papua and New Guinea Vol.1,* edited by Peter Ryan, 568–88. Melbourne: Melbourne University Press.

Butt, Leslie, and Richard Eves, eds. 2008. *Making Sense of AIDS: Culture, Sexuality and Power in Melanesia.* Honolulu: University of Hawaii Press.

Carucci, Laurence Marshall. n.d.. "Dying to Live: Continuities in Death and the Marshall Islands Diaspora."

Clarke, William C. 1971. *Place and People: An Ecology of a New Guinea Community.* Berkeley: University of California Press.

———. 1976. "Maintenance of Agriculture and Human Habitats within the Tropical Forest Ecosystem." *Human Ecology* 4:3: 247.

Collinge, John. 2008. "Lessons from Kuru Research: Background to Recent Studies with Some Personal Reflections." *Philosophical Transactions of the Royal Society B* 363: 3689–96.

Collinge, J., K. C. L. Sidle, J. Meads, J. Ironside, and A. F. Hill. 1996. "Molecular Analysis of Prion Strain Variation and the Aetiology of 'New Variant' CJD." *Nature* 383: 685–90.

Colman, J. 1955. *Okapa Patrol Report.*

Dalton, Doug. n.d. "Death and Experience in Rawa Mortuary Rites."

Daston, Lorraine, and Peter Galison. 2007. *Objectivity.* New York: Zone Books.

Diamond, J. 1966. "Zoological Classification System of a Primitive People." *Science* 151: 1102.

Dornstreich, Mark D., and George E. B. Morren. 1974. "Does New Guinea Cannibalism Have Nutritional Value?" *Human Ecology* 2: 1.1.

Douglas, Mary. 1966. *Purity and Danger: An Analysis of Concepts of Pollution and Taboo.* New York: Praeger.

———.1970a. "Introduction: Thirty Years after Witchcraft, Oracles and Magic." In *Witchcraft Confessions and Accusations,* edited by Mary Douglas. London: Tavistock.

———.1970b. *Natural Symbols: Explorations in Cosmology.* New York: Random House.

Edgeworth, Julie Ann, Michael Farmer, Anita Sicilia, Paul Tavares, Jonathan Beck, Tracy Campbell, Jessica Lowe, Simon Mead, Peter Rudge, John Collinge, and Graham S. Jackson. 2011. "Detection of Prion Infection in Variant Creutzfeld-Jakob Disease: A Blood Assay." *The Lancet* (February 3): 1–7.

Evans-Pritchard, E. E. 1936. *Witchcraft, Oracles and Magic among the Azande.* Oxford: Clarendon.

Faithorn, Elizabeth. 1976. "The Concept of Pollution among the Kafe of the Papua New Guinea Highlands." In *Toward an Anthropology of Women,* edited by Rayna R. Reiter. New York: Monthly Review Press.

Forge, Anthony. 1970. "Prestige, Influence and Sorcery: A New Guinea Example." In *Witchcraft Confessions and Accusations,* edited by Mary Douglas. London: Tavistock.

Fortune, R. F. 1932 (1963). *Sorcerers of Dobu.* New York: Dutton.

Frankel, Stephen, and Gilbert Lewis, eds. 1989. *A Continuing Trial of Treatment: Medical Pluralism in Papua New Guinea.* Dordrecht, Holland: Kluwer.

Gajdusek, D. C. 1963. "Kuru." *Transactions of the Royal Society of Tropical Medicine and Hygiene* 57:3: 151.

———. 1973. "Kuru in the New Guinea Highlands." In *Tropical Neurology,* edited by John Spillane. New York: Oxford University Press.

Gajdusek, D. C., and Michael Alpers. 1975. "Recent Data on the Properties of the Viruses of Kuru and Transmissible Virus Dementias." *Papua New Guinea Medical Journal* 18:4: 207.

Gajdusek, D. C., and C. J. Gibbs Jr. 1972. "Transmission of Kuru from Man to Rhesus Monkey (Macaca Mulatta) Eight and a Half Years after Inoculation." *Nature* 240:5380: 351.

———. 1973. "Slow Virus Infections of the Nervous System and the Laboratories of Slow Latent and Temperate Virus Infections." In *The Nervous System. Vol. 2: The Clinical Neurosciences,* edited by Donald R. Tower. New York: Raven.

Gajdusek, D. C., C. J. Gibbs Jr., and Michael Alpers. 1966. "Experimental Transmission of a Kuru-like Syndrome to Chimpanzees." *Nature* 209: 794.

Gajdusek, D. C., and V. Zigas. 1957. "Degenerative Diseases of the Central Nervous System in New Guinea: The Endemic Occurrence of 'Kuru' in the Native Population." *New England Journal of Medicine* 257: 974.

Gajdusek, D. C., V. Zigas, and J. Baker. 1961. "Studies on Kuru 3: Patterns of Kuru Incidence. Demographic and Geographic Epidemiological Analysis." *American Journal of Tropical Medicine and Hygiene* 10: 599.

Gajdusek, D. C., C. J. Gibbs Jr., David Asher, Paul Brown, Arwin Diwanb, Paul Hoffman, George Nemo, Robert Rohwer, and Lon White. 1977. "Precautions in Medical Care of, and in Handling Materials from, Patients with Transmissible Virus Dementias (Creutzfeldt-Jakob Disease)." *New England Journal of Medicine* 297: 1253.

Garner, M. F., and R. W. Hornabrook. 1970. "1968 Survey of Treponematosis in the Eastern Highlands of New Guinea." *British Journal of Venereal Diseases* 46: 13.

Geschiere, P. 1997. *The Modernity of Witchcraft: Politics and the Occult in Postcolonial Africa.* Charlottesville: University of Virginia Press.

Gewertz, Deborah, and Frederick Errington. 2010. *Cheap Meat: Flap Food Nations in the Pacific Islands.* Berkeley: University of California Press.

Gillison, Gillian. 1993. *Between Culture and Fantasy: A New Guinea Highlands Mythology.* Chicago: University of Chicago Press.

Glass, Rosalind Dawn. 2011. "'It's All about the Blood': Eating the Head Food. The Cultural Indebtedness of the North Fore." PhD diss., James Cook University, Cairns, Australia.

Glasse, Robert. 1962a. "South Fore Cannibalism and Kuru." Territory Papua New Guinea: Department of Public Health. Mimeo reprinted by the National Institutes of Health.

——. 1962b. "The Spread of Kuru among the Fore." Territory Papua New Guinea: Department of Public Health. Mimeo reprinted by the National Institutes of Health.

——. 1963. "Cannibalism in the Kuru Region." Territory Papua New Guinea: Department of Public Health. Mimeo reprinted by the National Institutes of Health.

——. 1967. "Cannibalism in the Kuru Region of New Guinea." Transactions of the New York Academy of Sciences. Series 11, Volume 29, No.6: 748–54.

——. 1969. "Marriage in South Fore." In *Pigs, Pearlshells and Women,* edited by R. M. Glasse and M. J. Meggitt, 16–37. Englewood Cliffs, NJ: Prentice Hall.

——. 1970. "Some Recent Observations on Kuru." *Oceania* 40: 210.

Glasse, Robert, and Shirley Lindenbaum. 1967. "How New Guinea Natives Reacted to a Total Eclipse." *Trans-action* 5:2: 46.

——. 1976. "Kuru at Wanitabe." In *Essays on Kuru,* edited by R. W. Hornabrook, 38–52. Faringdon, UK: E. W. Classey.

Glasse, Shirley. 1963. "A Note on Fore Medicine and Sorcery with an Ethnobotanical List." Territory Papua New Guinea: Department of Public Health. Mimeo reprinted by the National Institutes of Health.

——. 1964. "The Social Effects of Kuru." *Papua New Guinea Medical Journal* 7: 36.

Glick, L. 1963. "Foundations of a Primitive Medical System: The Gimi of New Guinea." PhD diss., University of Pennsylvania.

Godelier, Maurice. 1986. *The Making of Great Men: Male Dominance and Power among the Baruya.* Cambridge: Cambridge University Press.

Gorlin, Peter. 1977. "The Interrelationship of Disease and Culture in a Primitive New Guinea Community." *Human Ecology* 5:1: 37.

Hadlow, W. J. 1959. "Scrapie and Kuru." *The Lancet* 2: 289.

Hayano, David M. 1973. "Sorcery, Death, Proximity and Perception of Out-Groups: The Tauna Awa of New Guinea." *Ethnology* 12:2:179.

Herdt, Gilbert H. 1981. *Guardians of the Flutes.* New York: McGraw-Hill.

Herzberg L., N. Herzberg, C. J. Gibbs Jr., W. Sullivan, H. Amyx, and D. C. Gajdusek. 1974. "Creutzfeldt-Jakob Disease: Hypothesis for High Incidence in Libyan Jews in Israel." *Science* 186: 848.

Hetzel, Basil S., and Peter O. D. Pharoah, eds. 1971. *Endemic Cretinism.* Monograph No. 2. Papua New Guinea: Institute of Human Biology.

Hide, Robin. 1993. "Women and Market Trade." Unpublished manuscript.

Hogbin, Ian. 1970. *The Island of Menstruating Men: Religion in Wogeo, New Guinea.* Scranton, PA: Chandler.

Hornabrook, R. W. 1972. "Syphilis." In *Encyclopaedia of Papua and New Guinea,* edited by Peter Ryan. Melbourne: Melbourne University Press.

——, ed. 1976. *Essays on Kuru.* Faringdon, UK: E. W. Classey.

Hornabrook, R. W., and D. J. Moir. 1970. "Kuru: Epidemiological Trends." *The Lancet* 2: 1175.

Hornabrook, R. W., and J. T. Nagurney. 1976. "Essential Tremor in Papua New Guinea. *Brain* 99: 659.

House of Assembly Debates, Papua New Guinea. 11:12: 3677.

Hudson, E. H. 1963. "Treponematosis and Anthropology." *Annals of Internal Medicine* 58: 1037.

Hughes, Ian. 1973. "Stone-Age Trade in the New Guinea Inland: Historical Geography without History." In *The Pacific in Transition.*, edited by Harold Brookfield. New York: St. Martin's Press.

Jorgensen, Dan. 1993. "Money and Marriage in Telefomin: From Sister Exchange to Daughter and Trade Store." In *The Business of Marriage: Transformations in Oceanic Matrimony,* edited by R. Marksbury, 57–83. Pittsburgh: University of Pittsburgh Press.

Julius, C. 1957. "Sorcery among the South Fore with Special Mention of Kuru." Report to the Director of Public Health, Papua New Guinea.

Kelly, Raymond. 1976. "Witchcraft and Sexual Relations: An Exploration in the Social and Semantic Relations of the Structure of Belief." In *Man and Woman in the New Guinea Highlands,* edited by Paula Brown and Georgeda Buchbinder, 36–53. American Anthropology Association, Special Publication No. 8.

Kilgour, M. 1990. *From Communion to Cannibalism. An Anatomy of Metaphors of Incorporation.* Princeton, NJ: Princeton University Press.

King, H. O. M. 1975. "Kuru: Epidemiological Developments." *The Lancet* 2: 761.

Knauft, Bruce M. 1989: *Bodily Images in Melanesia: Cultural Substance and Natural Metaphors.* New York: Zone.

Langness, L. L. 1967. "Sexual Antagonism in the New Guinea Highlands: A Bena Bena Example." *Oceania* 37: 161–77.

Lewis, Gilbert. 1975. *Knowledge of Illness in a Sepik Society.* Atlantic Highlands, NJ: Humanities Press.

Lindenbaum, Shirley. 1971. "Sorcery and Structure in Fore Society." *Oceania* 41:4: 277.

———. 1975. "Sorcery and Danger." *Oceania* 46:1: 68.

———. 1976a. "A Wife Is the Hand of Man." In *Man and Woman in the New Guinea Highlands,* edited by Paula Brown and Georgeda Buchbinder, 54–62. American Anthropology Association, Special Publication No. 8.

———. 1976b. "Kuru Sorcery." In *Essays on Kuru,* edited by R. W. Hornabrook, 28–37. Faringdon, UK: E. W. Classey.

———. 2001. "Kuru, Prions, and Human Affairs." *Annual Review of Anthropology* 30: 363–85.

———. 2002. "Fore Narratives through Time: How a Bush Spirit Became a Robber, Was Sent to Jail, Emerged as a Symbol of Eastern Highlands Province, and Never Left Home." *Current Anthropology* 43. Supplement (August–October): S63–S73.

————. 2004. "Thinking About Cannibalism." *Annual Review of Anthropology* 32: 475–98.

Lindenbaum, Shirley, and Robert Glasse. 1969. "Fore Age Mates." *Oceania.* 39:3: 165.

Lock, M., and D. Gordon, eds. 1988. *Biomedicine Examined.* Dordrecht, Holland: Kluwer.

Malcolm, L. A. 1970. "Growth and Development of the Bundi Child in the New Guinea Highlands." *Human Biology* 42:2: 293.

Manuelidis, Elias E., Edward J. Gorgzca, and Laura Manuelidis. 1977. "Transmission of Creutzfeldt-Jakob Disease with Scapie-like Syndrome to Mice." *Nature* 271: 778.

Mathews, J. D. 1965. "The Changing Face of Kuru: An Analysis of Pedigrees Collected by R. M. Glasse and Shirley Glasse and of Recent Census Data." *The Lancet* 1: 1138.

————. 1967. "A Transmission Model for Kuru." *The Lancet,* 285: 821–25.

————. 1971. "Kuru. A Puzzle in Culture and Environmental Medicine." PhD diss., University of Melbourne.

————. 1976. "Kuru as an Epidemic Disease." In *Essays on Kuru,* edited by R. W. Hornabrook, 83–104. Faringdon, UK: E. W. Classey.

Mathews, J. D., Robert Glasse, and Shirley Lindenbaum. 1968. "Kuru and Cannibalism." *The Lancet* 2: 449.

————. 2008. "The Changing Face of Kuru: A Personal Perspective." *Philosophical Transactions of the Royal Society B* 363: 3679–84.

McArthur, J. 1954. *Okapa Patrol Report.*

————.1955. *Okapa Patrol Report.*

McArthur, N. 1964. "The Age Incidence of Kuru." *Annals of Human Genetics* 27: 341.

Mead, Simon, Michael P. H. Stumpf, Jerome Whitfield, Jonathan A. Beck, Mark Poulter, Tracy Campbell, James B. Upbill, David Goldstein, Michael Alpers, Elizabeth Fisher, and John Collinge. 2003. "Balancing Selection at the Prion Protein Gene Consistent with Prehistoric Kurulike Epidemics." *Science* 300: 640–43.

Mead, Simon, J. Whitfield, Mark Poulter, Paresh Shah, James Uphill, Tracy Campbell, Huda Al-Dujaily, Holger Hummerich, J. Beck, Charles A. Meib, Claudio Verzilli, John Whittaker, Michael Alpers, and John Collinge. 2009. "A Novel Protective Prion Protein Variant That Colocalizes with Kuru Exposure." *New England Journal of Medicine* 361:21: 2056–65.

Meggitt, M. J. 1965a. *The Lineage System of the Mae Enga of New Guinea.* New York: Barnes.

————.1965b. "The Mae Enga of the Western Highlands." In *Gods, Ghosts and Men in Melanesia,* edited by P. Lawrence and M. J. Meggitt, 105–31. Melbourne: Oxford University Press.

————. 1974. "Change, Violence and Sorcery among the Mae Enga of the New Guinea Highlands." Paper presented at the Symposium on Sorcery,

Witchcraft and Magic in the New Guinea Highlands for the American Anthropology Association, Mexico City.

Murrell, T. C. G. 1966. "Some Epidemiological Features of Pig-Bel." *Papua New Guinea Medical Journal* 9: 2–39.

Patterson, David A., Lauren G. Wolfe, Friedrich Deinhardt, D. C. Gajdusek, and C. J. Gibbs Jr. 1973–74. "Transmission of Kuru and Creutzfeldt-Jakob Disease to Marmoset Monkeys." *Intervirology* 2: 14.

Patterson, Mary. 1974. "Sorcery and Witchcraft in Melanesia." *Oceania* 45:2: 32, 45:3: 212.

Pharoah, P. O. D., and R. W. Hornabrook. 1974. "Endemic Cretinism of Recent Onset in New Guinea." *The Lancet* 2:1038.

Prusiner, S. B. 1982. "Novel Proteinaceous Infectious Particles Cause Scrapie." *Science* 216: 136–44.

Radford, Anthony. 2012. *Singsings, Sutures and Sorcery. A 50 Year Experience in Papua New Guinea.* Preston, Victoria: Mosaic Press.

Rappaport, Roy A. 1967. *Pigs for Ancestors.* New Haven, CT: Yale University Press.

Rawson, C. 1997. "The Horror, the Holy Horror." *Times Literary Supplement* (October 31): 3–5.

Read, Kenneth E. 1952: "Nama Cult of the Central Highlands." *Oceania* 23: 1–25.

Reay, Marie. 1959. *The Kuma.* Melbourne: Melbourne University Press.

———. 1976. "The Politics of a Witch-killing." *Oceania* 47: 1.

Rosenberg, Charles E. 1992. *Explaining Epidemics and Other Studies in the History of Medicine.* Cambridge, Cambridge University Press.

———. 2002. "The Tyranny of Diagnosis: Specific Entities and Individual Experience." *Milbank Quarterly* 80:2: 237–59.

———. 2007. *Our Present Complaint: American Medicine, Then and Now.* Baltimore: Johns Hopkins University Press.

Salisbury, Richard F. 1965. "The Siane of the Eastern Highlands," In *Gods, Ghosts and Men in Melanesia,* edited by P. Lawrence and M. J. Meggitt, 50–77. Melbourne: Oxford University Press.

Scott, G. K. 1963. "The Dialects of Fore." *Oceania* 33:4: 280.

———. 1975. "Linguistic Aspects of Fore Kinship" Unpublished manuscript.

Silverman, Eric Kline. n.d. "Funerary Failures: Traditional Uncertainties and Modern Families in the Sepik River."

Simmons, R. J., J. J. Graydon, Michael Alpers, and R. W. Hornabrook. 1972. "Genetic Studies in Relation to Kuru." No. 2. *American Journal of Human Genetics* 23, supplement: S39–S71.

Sinnett, P., and H. M. Whyte. 1973. "Epidemiological Studies in a Highland Population of New Guinea: Environment, Culture and Health Status." *Human Ecology* 1:3: 270.

Sorenson, E. Richard. 1965. "Expedition to the Kuru Region, 1963–1964." Unpublished journal.

———. 1976. *The Edge of the Forest: Land, Childhood, and Change in a New Guinea Protoagricultural Society.* Washington, DC: Smithsonian Institution Press.

Sorenson, E. Richard, and Peter E. Kenmore. 1974. "Proto-Agricultural Movement in the Eastern Highlands of New Guinea." *Current Anthropology* 15:1: 67.

Stasch, Rupert. 2009. *Society of Others: Kinship and Mourning in a West Papuan Place.* Berkeley: University of California Press.

Steadman, Lyle. 1975. "Cannibal Witches in the Hewa." *Oceania* 46:2: 114.

Steadman, L. B., and C. F. Merbs. 1982. "Kuru and Cannibalism?" *American Anthropologist* 84: 611-27.

The Age. 1978. September 1.

Thomas, Lewis. 1974. *The Lives of a Cell: Notes of a Biology Watcher.* New York: Viking.

Traub, R. D., D. C. Gajdusek, and C. J. Gibbs Jr., 1976. "Precautions in Autopsies on Creutzfeldt-Jakob Disease." *American Journal Clinical Pathology* 64: 417.

Turner, V. W. 1957. *Schism and Continuity in an African Society: A Study of Ndembu Village Life.* Manchester: Manchester University Press.

Van de Kaa, D. 1967. "Medical Work and Changes in Infant Mortality in Western New Guinea." *Papua New Guinea Medical Journal* 10: 89.

Waddell, Eric. 1973. *The Mound Builders.* Seattle: University of Washington Press.

Wadsworth, J. D. F., S. Joiner, J. M. Linehan, E. A. Astante, S. Brandner, and John Collinge. 2008. *Philosophical Transactions of the Royal Society B* 363: 3747-54.

Watson, James B. 1971. "Tairora: The Politics of Despotism in a Small Society." In *Politics in New Guinea,* edited by M. Berndt and Peter Lawrence. Nedlands: University of Western Australia Press.

Weiner, L. P., R. T. Johnson, and R. M. Herndon. 1973. "Viral Infections and Demyelinating Diseases." *New England Journal of Medicine* 2: 1278.

West, Paige. 2012. *From Modern Production to Imagined Primitive: The Social Life of Coffee from Papua New Guinea.* Durham, NC: Duke University Press.

White, T. D. 2001. "Once We Were Cannibals." *Scientific American* 285: 58-65.

Whitfield, J. T., W. H. Pako, John Collinge, and Michael Alpers. 2008. "Mortuary Rites of the South Fore and Kuru." *Philosophical Transactions of the Royal Society B* 363: 3721-24.

Wiesenfeld, Stephen L., and D. C. Gajdusek. 1976. "Genetic Structure and Heterozygosity in the Kuru Region, Eastern Highlands of New Guinea." *American Journal of Physical Anthropology,* 45:2: 177.

Wurm, S. A. 1962. "The Languages of the Eastern, Western and Southern Highlands: Territory of Papua and New Guinea." In *A Linguistic Survey of the South-Western Pacific,* edited by A. Capell. Technical Paper No. 136. Noumea, New Caledonia: South Pacific Commission.

————. 1964. "Australian New Guinea Highlands Language and the Distribution of Their Typological Features." *American Anthropologist* 66:4(2): 77.

Zigas, V., and D. C. Gajdusek. 1957. "Kuru: Clinical Study of a New Syndrome Resembling Paralysis Agitans in Natives of the Eastern Highlands of Australian New Guinea." *Medical Journal of Australia* 2: 745.

Zimmer-Tamakoshi, L. 1997. "The Last Big Man: Development and Men's Discontents in the Papua New Guinea Highlands." *Oceania* 68:2: 107–22.

INDEX

118, 120, 122; categories of, 114; as
cause of death, 59, 64–65, 121*t*; as
cause of kuru, 9, 14, 16, 19, 28–30,
56, 61, 65–67, 74, 100–101, 103, 144,
174, 184; changes in techniques
of, 87–88; compared to pollution
and witchcraft, 130–133, 145–146;
as competitive struggle, 72, 125;
and concern with group survival,
55–56, 100–102; court proceedings
regarding, 118–119, 199–200n7; as
covert coercion, 145–146; cures
for, 69–72; and defining of group
borders, 42; diseases attributed
to, 31–32, 56, 58, 60–64; and
disruption of kin hierarchy, 54; as
expression of grievance, 120; Fore
as reputed experts in, 28–30, 102,
140; as ideology of containment, 8;
as ideology of estrangement, 125;
increase in number of methods of,
74, 87; and intergroup relations,
58–59; and knowledge, 143; and level
of agricultural system, 126–127,
145; loss of power, 112–113; male
vs. female, 59, 121*t*; moralistic
discussion of, 127; paraphernalia
of, 126–127; patterns of dominance,
140, 142; preoccupation with, 71–72;
and protein, 136–137; and regional
districts, 138–139; sacred quality of,
98; as secret, 107–108, 123–124, 126,
131–132, 143, 145–146; and social
hierarchy, 135–137, 140, 142–143;
and status conflict, 55–56, 137;
symbolism of, 65–67; Wanitabe-Nabu
dispute about, 118–120; and wealth
redistribution, 126–127; and women,
68, 120, 121*fig*, 128
Sorcery Act of 1971, 184–185
South Fore: *See also* Fore; North Fore;
dialect groups among, 6; geographical
mobility of, 38–39, 43, 47; hamlets of,
5, 28, 43, 198–199n5; hunting among,
22, 24; marriages, 165; political
affiliations of, 117–120; and politics
of residence, 37–43; population of,
6, 37, 140; religions of, 172; social
hierarchy among, 86–88, 135–137,

145–146; sourthern areas feared by,
137–138
Spirits. *See* Ples Masalai spirits
SSPE (subacute sclerosing
panencephalitis), 27, 197n33
STDs (sexually transmitted diseases),
190–191
Steel tomahawks, 78
Strokes, 32, 60
Subacute sclerosing panencephalitis
(SSPE), 27, 197n33
Suicide, 58
Sweet potatoes, 34–35, 37, 115
Syphilis, 32

Tairora people, 6, 35–36
Tauwa, 191
Tetanus, 31, 60
Tetegina, 17. *See also* White people
Theft of local resources, 188–189
Tiena, 159–160
Tinea imbricata, 135–136
Tobacco, 88
Tobaku, 60, 74, 87, 119, 199–200n7
Tolai, 74
Toogood, Patrol Officer, 80
Trade, regional, 76–86, 140–143, 146
Trade partners as kin, 49–50
Transmissibility of kuru, 176, 183
Transumption, 208n21
Truth-telling, 187–189
Tuba gina, 44
Tuberculosis, 62, 67
Tugezajana, 59
Turner, Victor, 103–104

Ulcers, tropical, 32
Umasa, 19
Umasa-Ivaki-Intamatasa conflict,
settlement of, 154
Upper-respiratory infections, 31
Uvinda, Kassam, 168–170
Uwana as curer, 93–96, 98

Vaccinations, 150–151, 182
Variant Creutzfeldt-Jakob disease
(vCJD), 179
Venereal disease, 32
Viral infection, 60